Critical Approaches to Children's Literature

Series Editors: **Kerry Mallan** and **Clare Bradford**

Critical Approaches to Children's Literature is an innovative series concerned with the best contemporary scholarship and criticism on children's and young adult literature, film, and media texts. The series addresses new and developing areas of children's literature research as well as bringing contemporary perspectives to historical texts. The series has a distinctive take on scholarship, delivering quality works of criticism written in an accessible style for a range of readers, both academic and professional. The series is invaluable for undergraduate students in children's literature as well as advanced students and established scholars.

Titles include:

Cherie Allan
PLAYING WITH PICTURE BOOKS
Postmodern and the Postmodernesque

Clair Bradford
THE MIDDLE AGES IN CHILDREN'S LITERATURE

Clare Bradford, Kerry Mallan, John Stephens and Robyn McCallum
NEW WORLD ORDERS IN CONTEMPORARY CHILDREN'S LITERATURE

Alice Curry
ENVIRONMENTAL CRISIS IN YOUNG ADULT FICTION
A Poetics of Earth

Helen A. Fairlie
REVALUING BRITISH BOYS' STORY PAPERS, 1918–1939

Victoria Flanagan
TECHNOLOGY AND IDENTITY IN YOUNG ADULT FICTION
The Posthuman Subject

Margaret Mackey
NARRATIVE PLEASURES IN YOUNG ADULT NOVELS, FILMS AND VIDEO GAMES

Kerry Mallan
SECRETS, LIES AND CHILDREN'S FICTION

Andrew O'Malley
CHILDREN'S LITERATURE, POPULAR CULTURE AND *ROBINSON CRUSOE*

Christopher Parkes
CHILDREN'S LITERATURE AND CAPITALISM
Fictions of Social Mobility in Britain, 1850–1914

Amy Ratelle
ANIMALITY AND CHILDREN'S LITERATURE AND FILM

Mavis Reimer
SERIALITY AND TEXTS FOR YOUNG PEOPLE
The Compulsion to Repeat

Karen Sands-O'Connor and Marietta Frank
INTERNATIONALISM IN CHILDREN'S SERIES

Hazel Sheeky Bird
CLASS, LEISURE AND NATIONAL IDENTITY IN BRITISH CHILDREN'S LITER-
ATURE, 1918–1950

Michelle Smith
EMPIRE IN BRITISH GIRLS' LITERATURE AND CULTURE

Forthcoming titles:

Caterina Sinibaldi
TRANSLATING CHILDREN'S LITERATURE UNDER ITALIAN FASCISM

Critical Approaches to Children's Literature
Series Standing Order ISBN 978–0–230–22786–6 (hardback)
978–0–230–22787–3 (paperback)
(*outside North America only*)

You can receive future titles in this series as they are published by placing a standing order. Please contact your bookseller or, in case of difficulty, write to us at the address below with your name and address, the title of the series and the ISBN quoted above.

Customer Services Department, Macmillan Distribution Ltd, Houndmills, Basingstoke, Hampshire RG21 6XS, England

Technology and Identity in Young Adult Fiction

The Posthuman Subject

Victoria Flanagan

First published 2014 by
PALGRAVE MACMILLAN

Palgrave Macmillan in the UK is an imprint of Macmillan Publishers Limited,
registered in England, company number 785998, of Houndmills, Basingstoke,
Hampshire RG21 6XS.

Palgrave Macmillan in the US is a division of St Martin's Press LLC,
175 Fifth Avenue, New York, NY 10010.

Palgrave Macmillan is the global academic imprint of the above companies
and has companies and representatives throughout the world.

Palgrave® and Macmillan® are registered trademarks in the United States,
the United Kingdom, Europe and other countries.

ISBN 978-1-349-47252-9   ISBN 978-1-137-36206-3 (eBook)
DOI 10.1057/9781137362063

This book is printed on paper suitable for recycling and made from fully
managed and sustained forest sources. Logging, pulping and manufacturing
processes are expected to conform to the environmental regulations of the
country of origin.

A catalogue record for this book is available from the British Library.

Library of Congress Cataloging-in–Publication Data
Flanagan, Victoria, 1976–
    Technology and identity in young adult fiction : the posthuman subject /
Victoria Flanagan.
        pages   cm. — (Critical approaches to children's literature)
    Includes bibliographical references and index.
    ISBN 978-1-349-47252-9
    1. Young adult fiction—History and criticism.   2. Technology in literature.
3. Identity (Psychology) in literature.   4. Self in literature.   I. Title.
PN3443.F57 2014
809.3′00835—dc23   2014023270

To Sky,
whose unbridled enthusiasm for technology
inspired much of this book

Contents

Acknowledgements   viii

Introduction   1

1 Posthumanism in Young Adult Fiction   11

2 Narrating Posthuman Subjectivity   39

3 Digital Citizenship in the Posthuman Era   70

4 Reworking the Female Subject: Technology and the Body   100

5 Surveillance Societies: Privacy and Power in YA Fiction   128

6 Subjectivity in Cyberspace: Technorealism and the
   Merging of Virtual and Material Selves   155

Conclusion   186

Bibliography   192

Index   201

Acknowledgements

The preliminary research for this project was undertaken in 2009 when I was awarded a research fellowship at the International Youth Library in Munich, Germany. Apart from being an incredibly beautiful place, the library is filled with wonderful and passionate staff who each made my time in Munich – and the research process – immensely enjoyable. Claudia Soeffner and the indefatigable Petra Woersching deserve a special mention here, as they have both helped to turn my many experiences at the library into special memories.

I am also extremely grateful to Professor John Stephens, who provided sharp, insightful feedback on each chapter and prompted me to reassess some of my original ideas. Although he has officially retired from academia, his mind is as nimble as ever – and this book has benefited greatly from his editorial and conceptual guidance.

The Australian Research Council generously provided the funds for this research, for which I am very thankful. A big thank you must be extended to Dr Christine Boman and Peter McCarthy in this context, as they played an important role in helping me to identify the scope and aims of this project when I was at that initial planning stage of applying for research funding.

Last, but not least, I extend my heartfelt thanks to my boys, Riku and Sky. Both are technophiles (even three-year-old Sky) and remind me on a daily basis that children need to read books that celebrate, rather than demonise, technology.

Introduction

Posthumanism uses technoscience as the impetus for a radical revaluation of human subjectivity, exploring the many ways in which technological innovations such as virtual reality have changed our understanding of what it means to be human in the modern era. Yet the concept of the "posthuman" is often perceived as a threat to the humanities, those academic disciplines dedicated to the study of human nature and culture. If we consider how we arrived in the era of the posthuman, we might reflect on some of the questions that are posed by Geoffrey Harpham – "Did we do this to ourselves, or was it done to us?" (2012: 101) – and whether the posthuman refers to a new form of the human condition or, alternatively, resituates the boundaries of an existing category. There are two basic fears, according to Harpham, that underlie such lines of inquiry:

> first, that the human has been compromised even as it has been enhanced by technology, which has altered our social, intellectual, and even our physical lives; and second, that human beings are losing or have lost the attributes of individuality and autonomy as they become more tightly woven into distributed cognitive networks that include an indifferent mix of persons and computers.
>
> (2012: 101–2)

Prior to the mid-2000s, literature produced for children and adolescents that has thematically considered the effects of technology on human beings and society has been animated by these two fears about technology. The result has been the establishment of an anti-technology representational paradigm in children's literature, which has prevailed since the 1980s. Things are, however, slowly starting to change and a small but continually increasing number of children's authors are beginning to produce narratives about technology in much more life-affirming and positive ways. This paradigmatic shift, away from the dystopian rendering of techno-futuristic fictional worlds, corresponds with a rising scholarly interest in posthumanism and suggests that children's authors are engaged in a conscious effort to reflect in their work broader elements of social change. Such a shift also corresponds with children's real-life experiences of technology, which would seem to be overwhelmingly positive, given that computers, tablets and mobile phones are generally used by children and teens on a daily basis for the purposes of entertainment and pleasure.

The types of children's books that have started to appear since the mid-2000s thus redress a stark disjunction between the reality of children and teenagers' experiences with technology and the narrative representation of dystopian hyper-technical futures that has been common in children's books since the 1980s. Although dystopian elements are still evident in many of the young adult (YA) narratives discussed throughout this book, a noticeable change is apparent in the way that these fictions construct the relationship between human beings and technology – primarily because they represent technology as enabling, rather than disempowering, for child and adolescent subjects. *The Adoration of Jenna Fox* (2008) by Mary Pearson, "Anda's Game" (2004) and *Little Brother* (2008), both by Cory Doctorow, and *Skinned* (2008) by Robin Wasserman are examples of narratives published for YA readers that challenge the anti-technology themes prevalent for so long within the YA genre. Although each of these texts acknowledges that technology has the potential to render human subjects abject, they also highlight the ways in which young people might achieve agency through their interactions with technoscience. Instead of approaching with trepidation and/or hostility subjects such as biotechnology, virtual reality and artificial intelligence, these narratives engage imaginatively with the figure of the cyborg (attending to the dynamic interplay of humanity and machine in the construction of cyborgian subjectivity); they portray the friendly, supportive and collegial nature of various online communities and reveal the innovation and expertise required to hack into supposedly safe computer systems. Considered together, these contemporary YA fictions demonstrate that the posthuman need not be perceived as a threat to human individuality or agency. Rather, they use the category of the posthuman as the means for producing a new understanding of human selfhood and experience – one that emphasises the plurality and fragmentation of posthuman subjectivity, and conceives of agency in altruistic terms as collective and networked.

The aforementioned books – several of which were published in 2008 – are indicative of the process of ideological change that is evident within the genre of YA fiction with respect to the representation of technology. The reasons for this ideological shift are varied, yet because the process is still at an incipient stage it is difficult to articulate clearly what has been responsible for producing (or initiating) the transformation. However, it is possible to speculate about the causes. The most obvious reason for a move away from the negative technological paradigm identified by Noga Applebaum (2010) is the increasing ubiquity of technology in the everyday lives of children and adults all over the world. Recent studies of children and teenagers living in Australia, Britain and the United States suggest that rates of internet use are incredibly high amongst young people – with one US study from 2012 citing that 95 per cent of adolescents surveyed were online (Madden et al., 2013: 3). Children also tend to associate digital technology with pleasure and entertainment, as is evident from their use of computers and smartphones in their leisure time. That literature produced for children should also reflect their real-life positive engagement with technology does not seem especially surprising – but it is rather astounding that it has taken so long for a more affirming model of technological representation to become apparent within the genre.

A second explanation for the increase in pro-technology narratives for children since the mid-2000s can be attributed to the change in attitudes to digital technology that have arisen due to the tremendous growth in internet access over the past two decades. The internet first gained widespread popularity in the West during the early 1990s and has exerted a profound influence on almost all levels of life in the intervening years. It has affected social communication, business and even education (particularly in the tertiary sector) – and my contention is that the post-cyberspace generation, which includes those people born after 1990 but also individuals whose childhood and adolescence coincided with this decade, have been surrounded by technology from a young age and are much more likely to either celebrate or at least normalise its impact on human society. The authors considered here who might be regarded as part of the "post-cyberspace" generation include John M. Cusick, Susie Day, Rachel Gold, Marissa Meyer, Lauren Myracle, Jess C. Scott and Robin Wasserman – and, indeed, the pro-technology and posthuman themes evident in their work would indicate that their age is a relevant factor in their ideological depiction of technology. However, it is the work of Cory Doctorow and Ernest Cline that deserves a special mention in this context because both authors were born in the 1970s and were therefore in their early twenties (rather than children or adolescents) at the start of the 1990s. Nevertheless, their YA fictions offer particularly pronounced representations of cyberspace as an activist, collectivist and empowering space for young people – and as such mirror the ethos of information-sharing that characterised the internet in the early 1990s. Of course the label of "post-cyberspace generation" is a generalisation and is not wholly applicable to the authors considered within this book. Writers such as Mary E. Pearson, Bernard Beckett, Michael Spooner, Scott Westerfeld and Tanith Lee, whose novels form an important part of this study, cannot be classified as belonging to the "post-cyberspace" generation but have each produced narratives that offer fine examples of the way in which contemporary YA fiction has recently started to engage with posthuman themes and conceptualisations of identity. Yet it is worth noting that the majority of texts that I have included in my primary corpus have been produced by a younger generation of writers.

The increasing prevalence of technology in our everyday lives since the 1990s (and especially in the new millennium) has also led to an increased scholarly interest in posthumanism over the corresponding period. One of the goals associated with posthumanism is the philosophical exploration of the relationship(s) between human beings and technology in the modern era. Posthumanism first came to prominence at the end of the 1990s with the publication of N. Katherine Hayles' *How We Became Posthuman: Virtual Bodies in Cybernetics, Literature, and Informatics* (1999). It has since gone on to become a major ideological force in academic debates about the status of the human subject in an evolving world, interrogating many of the humanist principles that have underpinned Western thought since the time of the Renaissance. Although the deconstruction of the human subject is a project that commenced several decades earlier with the advent of postmodernism in the second part of the twentieth century, children's literature has been hesitant to adopt postmodern ideology wholeheartedly – because it amounts to such a radical reformulation of human subjectivity. The lack of agency that defines postmodern conceptualisations of subjectivity has proven to be particularly problematic within the context of children's literature – as such a vision of child subjectivity is anathema to literature that deliberately seeks to prescribe desirable models of child behaviour and development. Posthumanism, however, seems to be immediately more applicable to child subjects – not least because of the ubiquity of technology in young people's lives. Posthumanism's engagement with technology and its impact on the human condition also provides a material context for the deconstruction of individual subjectivity, enabling abstract ideas about the nature of human subjectivity to be investigated in a more concrete manner. For instance, the notion of subjectivity as fragmented and plural is much easier to explore using contrasts between the self that inhabits social reality and the self (or selves) that we construct and operate in virtual reality. And within this posthuman context, various possibilities for agency exist. Rather than suggesting that agency is only illusory, as postmodernism does, posthumanism posits a rethinking of agency. It suggests that agency needs to be reformulated – through redistribution, for example, so that it is conceptualised as collective and networked, instead of being based purely on individualism. Agency can also be achieved through embodiment, in that material bodies – particularly those belonging to female subjects – that have traditionally been "othered" in dominant social paradigms are, in posthuman narratives, resignified and become the means through which such individuals achieve empowerment.

What I have discovered over the course of this study is that writers of young adult fiction have become increasingly eager to discard the established model of dystopian representations of technofuturistic worlds. Instead, these contemporary authors suggest that technology plays a critical role in constructing subjectivity and the modern digital era. Literature can play an important role in helping readers come to terms with new social developments. It allows us to explore hypothetical situations; to imaginatively test a variety of scenarios and investigate how they might affect human society at both a micro (that is, pertaining to one individual) and macro level. Such a point is not lost on N. Katherine Hayles, the pre-eminent proponent of critical posthumanism, who writes:

> Literary texts are not, of course, merely passive conduits. They actively shape what the technologies mean and what the scientific theories signify in cultural contexts.

(1999: 21)

Hayles' words are particularly relevant to literature written for children, which actively seeks to intervene in children's perceptions of self and their relationship to the world around them. Books that provide fictional representations of a future that involves technological advancement play a unique role in introducing children to issues that are relevant to scientific and technological progress, as in the moral and ethical implications of such developments, the different ways in which they might affect human beings, and how such progress might either contribute to or diminish what I shall term a "good society". Children's literature actively attempts to socialise and enculturate child readers, advocates particular forms of subjectivity and identity formation (by granting subjective agency to select characters) and endorses specific forms of social organisation (through the effects of thematic significance and narrative closure). An important consideration in children's literature that offers representations of technology is therefore whether such technology acts to empower or disenfranchise child subjects. As already mentioned, prior to 2000 many such books offered a resoundingly negative depiction of what a technologically advanced future might look like. Although representations of technology can be found in literature for children of all ages (Applebaum (2010) provides a survey of picture books with technological themes), young adult fiction engages with the complexity of technology most closely. This is partly because most narratives that imaginatively explore the effects of technology on human society are works of science fiction, a genre that is usually aimed at a sophisticated reader who is capable of dealing with what Farrah Mendlesohn calls "cognitive dissonance" (2009: 10), a rupture in the world as we understand it. Mendlesohn also describes science fiction as a genre that tends to be more "outward looking" (2009: 17), thus distinguishing itself from other children's genres, which commonly centre on personal relationships. My use of posthumanism as a critical framework for analysing these YA narratives is also more suited to literature produced for the adolescent reader, as it involves a reconceptualisation of individual subjectivity and social relationships. The enthusiasm for such a major ideological project shown by the up-and-coming group of YA authors discussed within this book is not yet evident in books for younger readers. Thus my decision to concentrate on YA fiction is also a reflection of a trend in the literature itself. YA fiction has become increasingly interested in posthuman issues and themes, so that while it is unusual to find texts published prior to 2000 that represented technology as empowering for child and adolescent subjects, since that date there has been a surge in such titles released.

The following chapters examine the narrative representation of technology in a selection of English-language YA novels from Britain, the United States, Australia and New Zealand, focusing on the willingness of these fictions to portray technology as empowering for "othered" child or adolescent subjects. Chapter 1 begins by discussing the meaning of posthumanism (a term that has multiple definitions, some of these competing). It addresses the overlap between posthumanism and concepts such as "transhumanism" and "anti-humanism", outlining the relevance of such terms to children's literature. It then outlines how the terms "posthuman" and "posthumanism" have been deployed in children's literature criticism to date, arguing that the concept has only been addressed in a handful of publications (and in some of these it has actually been defined and used inappropriately).

Chapter 2 centres on the subject of posthuman consciousness, analysing how the representation of posthuman thought, perception and awareness might diverge from more conventional humanist models of narration and point of view. It uses two novels written by the acclaimed young adult sci-fi writer, Tanith Lee, as a case study to illustrate how attitudes to technology have been transformed – even in the work of a single author – over a period of two decades. *The Silver Metal Lover*, first published in 1981, and its long-awaited sequel, *Metallic Love* (2005), both deal with the relationship between a human girl and her robot lover, but their handling of this subject material is distinctively different. *The Silver Metal Lover* foreshadows posthuman ideology, even if its themes remain deeply committed to liberal humanism, but *Metallic Love* continues the story of the robot named Silver in a manner that completely transforms the significance of the first novel – not just in terms of plot, but also in relation to the way that narrative discourse is used to shape the story and its meaning. The utopian romance of *The Silver Metal Lover*, in which a robot is perfectly capable of reciprocating human love, is replaced in *Metallic Love* with a depiction of a society where binary distinctions between human and robot have been erased – to the extent that human elitism is rendered problematic because it is so obviously fallible.

Digital citizenship is the subject of Chapter 3, a concept that refers to the way in which internet technology can be used by individuals for the purpose of engaging with society or politics. This chapter proposes that cyberspace allows young people to exercise the type of citizenship rights that are typically denied to them in the real world until they reach the legally deemed age of adulthood. Orson Scott Card's classic YA sci-fi novel *Ender's Game* provides a starting point for my analysis. (Although originally published in1985, Card updated the text and it was re-published in 1991, and it is to this later version that I refer throughout this book.) The representation of cyberspace and the digital arena as disempowering (and indeed manipulative) for children in *Ender's Game* is contrasted with a number of novels published since the mid-2000s which construct virtual reality as responsible for enabling child protagonists to achieve social and political agency. Novels such as Cory Doctorow's *Little Brother* (2008) and its sequel, *Homeland* (2013) counteract Card's negative depiction of cyberspace by employing a specifically posthuman concept of subjectivity as networked and collective. These narratives represent cyberspace as an arena that encourages community-building and collaboration, and facilitates political activism

Chapter 4 concentrates on the ways in which futuristic fantasy fiction for adolescents explores the effects of technology on human subjectivity and society, with a particular focus on the female body and feminine subjectivity. A selection of novels that use various forms of technology to highlight the crucial role that the female body plays in relation to feminine subjectivity form the primary corpus of this chapter, including Scott Westerfeld's *Uglies* (2005) and

Mary E. Pearson's *The Adoration of Jenna Fox* (2008). My analysis of these fictions draws on Donna Haraway's emancipatory vision of the cyborg and investigates how such narratives construct the ideological relationship between technology and feminine subjectivity.

Rather than seeking to overthrow surveillance regimes, fiction for young adults typically seeks to educate its readers about surveillance and its varied purposes. Chapter 5 analyses a broad range of children's fiction to support this claim, arguing that such narratives suggest that individuals can choose to be agentic – not interpellated – surveillance subjects. Young adult fiction accordingly reshapes a concept that has conventionally been associated with disempowerment, resulting in the representation of surveillance as a necessary part of modern life that does not automatically co-opt human subjects into passive surveillance subjects.

The final chapter looks at the increasing role of virtual reality in children's lives today. Despite media hysteria about the detrimental effects of the internet on children, a rising number of children's authors are using fiction to explore the positive ways in which virtual reality can enrich young lives. This chapter focuses on the individual and social effects of cyberspace (as experienced through the use of social media), suggesting that virtual reality can be responsible for empowering and activating young people. Identifying an emerging trend in children's literature – blogging and chat-room narratives – this chapter explores the positive social effects of virtual reality in these contexts, particularly for young girls, where online communities offer support and encouragement. Chapter 6 also highlights the various narrative strategies used in virtual-reality narratives, attesting that this particular subgenre is responsible for significant textual innovation – including the use of fragmented narratives, polyfocalised narration, genre mixing and typographic/linguistic experimentation.

In examining how young adult fiction responds to the concept of technoscientific progress, this book employs posthumanism as a theoretical and analytical tool for understanding and explaining the impact of technology on the human subject. As its name suggests, posthumanism offers new ways of making sense of the dramatic changes – particularly to humanist concepts of selfhood – that have occurred in the modern world due to technological and scientific development. Within the context of children's literature research, which has only recently begun to engage with the fragmented and tenuous forms of identity associated with postmodernism, this radical reconceptualisation of identity is highly significant – particularly in the sense that there is a growing body of children's literature that deals extensively with topics such as robotics, cybernetics, digital surveillance and the effects of computer technology on human identity and social organisation.

1
Posthumanism in Young Adult Fiction

At its most basic level, posthumanism – "after" or "beyond" humanism – is a critical discourse that seeks to reformulate and revision the humanist subject in the modern digital era. This, of course, is a major project, which perhaps explains why posthumanism has so many different (and sometimes competing) tenets. Even arriving at a definition seems to be a problematic exercise, because although theorists can agree that posthumanism goes beyond humanism, what this might actually mean or involve in precise terms is up for debate. Cary Wolfe maintains that posthumanism "generates different and even irreconcilable definitions" (2010: xi), while Timothy D. Harfield argues that "polysemy is built into the term 'posthumanism' itself, and in such a way as to make agreement with respect to its definition all but impossible" (2013: 266). One of the reasons for this lack of consensus and plurality of meaning lies in relation to exactly how the prefix "post" should be interpreted when applied to the concept of "humanism". While it might be tempting to view "posthumanism" as a negation of "humanism", this is not the case – because, as Harfield suggests, the "outright rejection of humanism might serve to perpetuate the very problems that many posthumanists seek to address" (2013: 268). Harfield's point is an important one, and it is especially relevant to my analysis of young adult (YA) fiction here. Posthumanism should not be understood as an ideology that entails the end of the humanist subject. Instead, it should be viewed as a reconceptualisation and expansion of the human subject. It involves an ongoing critique of the human condition – and this critique uses the principles of reason (on which humanism is also based) to deconstruct the privileged status of the humanist concept of subjectivity. In this way, posthumanism offers new understandings of what it means to be human in the world today – and, within the context of literature produced for children and adolescents, this agenda aligns neatly with the ideology that underpins many recently published narratives, each of which uses technology as a motif for exploring new relationships between the mind and the body, or forms of subjective agency that are altruistic, networked and collective.

Humanism

Before progressing further, it is important to first consider what is meant by the term "humanism". A rather obvious comment to make at this point is that "humanism", like "posthumanism", can be defined in different and competing ways. At its most basic level, humanism is the philosophy or ideological discourse that places the rational, autonomous and cohesive human self at its centre, rejecting the notion that identity is culturally produced and therefore conditional. "Humanism" also refers to the Renaissance intellectual movement, spearheaded by figures such as Petrarch, Machiavelli and Thomas More, which championed the study of the great classical authors. It can be defined as an ideology that rejects notions of the divine or supernatural, and instead perceives the human being as central. J.A. Symonds, author of *The Renaissance in Italy: The Revival of Learning* (1897), was responsible for popularising humanist concepts and ideas within Britain in the nineteenth century (at which time the term "humanism" was first coined). His books clearly articulate the spirit of humanism and emphasise the role of rationality in humanist concepts of selfhood – which appealed at this juncture in history because they coincided with the religious scepticism that characterised Enlightenment thinking. Symonds distils humanist ideology in the following way:

> The essence of humanism consisted in a new and vital perception of the dignity of man as a rational being apart from theological determinations, and in the further perception that classic literature alone displayed human nature in the plenitude of intellectual and moral freedom. It was partly a reaction against ecclesiastical despotism, partly an attempt to find the point of unity for all that

had been thought and done by man, within the mind restored to consciousness of its own sovereign faculty.

(Symonds, 1898: 52)

The construction of man as a rational and sovereign being, argues Tony Davies, stood in clear contrast to the transcendent authority of God and the Church. The appeal of humanism in this context lay in its metanarrative about human subjectivity, which Davies terms a "particularly powerful and complex notion of the 'human' – a quality at once local and universal, historical and timeless... [which] continues to shape not just the identity and subjectivity but the practical existence of a large proportion of the people, and the peoples, of the world" (2008: 22). Davies here articulates the essentialism that he calls a "precondition if not a definition of humanism itself" (2008: 123). The notion of an essential and universal human nature, which transcends time and culture, is an immensely appealing and comforting idea – and Davies reminds us that it is an idea that has endured for over 200 years and still retains currency today.

Pramod Nayar's definition of "the human" as it relates to humanism emphasises rationality and self-determination, but also implies that such a construct hinges on exclusionary practices:

> The human is traditionally taken to be a subject (one who is conscious of his/her *self*) marked by rational thinking/intelligence, who is able to plot his/her own course of action depending on his/her needs, desires, wishes, and, as a result of his/her actions, produces history. The human has traditionally been treated as male and universal. It is always treated in the singular (*the* human) and as a set of features or conditions: rationality, authority, autonomy and agency.
>
> (2014: 5)

As Nayar's summation underlines, agency – the human subject's right to be self-defining and autonomous – is a central principle of humanism, as is human consciousness or self-awareness. Within Western children's literature and YA fiction, humanism is a dominant ideological force. As narratives for young readers generally pivot on the concepts of identity development and maturation, humanism has played an important role in the ideological conceptualisation of agency within these fictions. Underpinning much literature for children, especially narratives that engage with the heroic or quest paradigm, is a construction of agency based on the principles of individualism, action and autonomy. This is even more pronounced within the genre of YA fiction, where an individualistic construction of agency prevails in narratives that frequently revolve around the adolescent character's acquisition of independence and concomitant separation from the family unit.

Posthumanism: How to define it?

How, then, can posthumanism be defined *in relation* to humanism, rather than situating it *in opposition* to humanism? And in what sense might posthumanism be applicable to critical readings of contemporary adolescent literature? I would first like to make a distinction between the terms "posthuman" and "posthumanism", which are sometimes used interchangeably but should be taken as separate and distinct concepts – much like the terms "human" and "humanism". "Posthuman" refers to the technologically mediated human subject, whose existence has been transformed through technoscience – either chemically, surgically or mechanically. "Posthuman" can therefore also indicate the condition of existing in a world that has been irreversibly altered by technology.

"Posthumanism", in contrast, is the critical ideology that seeks to deprivilege the status of the humanist subject. It does so, according to Nayar, by providing "a new conceptualization of the human", which "addresses the question of the human in the age of technological modification, hybridized life forms, new discoveries of the sociality (and 'humanity') of animals and a new understanding of life itself" (2014: 3). It is this idea of posthumanism offering a "new understanding of life itself" that informs my own use of the concept throughout this book, as it is what I see reflected in my primary corpus' innovative and engaging narrative exploration of the relationship between youth subjectivity and technology. The model of posthumanism that I use here (and I would like to stress again that there are various – often competing – models of posthumanism currently in existence) is primarily influenced by the work of Nayar, Hayles and Donna Haraway. Cary Wolfe's emphasis on the role of animals in posthuman deconstructions of the humanist subject is something that I have not taken up here – however, I am very much in agreement with him when he contends that existence in the modern digital age requires "new theoretical paradigms" in order to make sense of the ways in which being and experience have been changed by technological development:

> posthumanism names a historical moment in which the decentering of the human by its imbrication in technical, medical, informatics, and economic networks is increasingly impossible to ignore, a historical development that points toward the necessity of new theoretical paradigms (but also thrusts them on us), a new mode of thought that comes after the cultural repressions and fantasies, the philosophical protocols and evasions, of humanism as a historically specific phenomenon.
>
> (2010: xv–xvi)

The overlap between posthumanism and other ideological movements such as poststructuralism, feminism and transhumanism points to the complexity of posthumanism as a critical philosophy. This complexity is something that children's literary criticism has, thus far, dealt with in a very limited way, which is not at all surprising given the pervasiveness of humanist ideological constructions of subjectivity in all genres of children's literature. My intention in this book is to redress this critical gap by considering a range of issues raised by posthumanism (such as the limitations of the human subject and the interrogation of the unified self in the modern digital age, the significance of embodiment, and the effects of virtual reality, advances in biotechnology and digital surveillance on human subjectivity) and exploring how such issues are represented in literary texts produced for adolescent readers.

The key issues raised by posthumanism include: the relationship between embodiment and cognition; the independent and unified humanist subject versus the fragmented, destabilised and collective posthuman subject; and the significance of the cyborg, a figure that plays a pivotal role in posthuman ideology because of the way in which it subverts binary distinctions between human/machine and real/artificial. Over time, this critical orientation has been complicated by the concurrent development of "transhumanism", a concept that intersects with posthumanism. Transhumanism focuses on the propensity for the human body to become radically transformed by technology (Bostrom, 2005). To the extent that this type of transformation affects our understanding of what constitutes the category of "human", there are parallels between posthumanism and transhumanism – both focus on the impact of technology on human subjectivity and social relationships. The technological modification of the human body is a recurring motif in sci-fi narratives for adolescents (as a result of genetic engineering or cybernetic intervention), and the dialogic interplay between the transhuman and the posthuman is one that has immediate relevance to a children's literary context. Young adult narratives that are set in technofuturistic worlds are typically concerned with exploring how technologically modified bodies might extend or challenge normative definitions of what it means to be a human being. They ask questions about the importance of human "authenticity" or originality (in the case of cloned characters), the role of memory in the production of human subjectivity (particularly since memories can be mechanically inserted or retained in genetically engineered bodies), and the relationship between embodiment and cognition. However, one of the defining characteristics of transhumanism as a critical philosophy is its ethical dimension. Transhumanism is thus an ideology that is underpinned by an ethical approach to technological human enhancement, as asserted by Nick Bostrom, whereby individuals should each have the right to choose whether or not to undergo such enhancement:

> Transhumanists argue that the best way to avoid a Brave New World [a reference to Aldous Huxley's novel] is by vigorously defending morphological and reproductive freedoms against any would-be world controllers. History has shown the dangers in letting governments curtail these freedoms... Because people are likely to differ profoundly in their attitudes towards human enhancement technologies, it is crucial that no one solution be imposed on everyone from above but that individuals get to consult their own consciences as to what is right for themselves and their families.
>
> (2005: 206)

Bostrom's comments here are useful in the sense that they clearly articulate a divide between transhumanism and the type of attitudes towards biotechnology that are evident in texts for children and adolescents. This is because the concept of free will or agency (which can be loosely defined as the ability of action to transcend its material context) is problematic when applied to children and adolescents, who are normally subject to the control of their parents or legal guardians and cannot experience or attain complete personal autonomy. This lack of agency is reflected in children's literature, which has traditionally sought to formulate in very specific ways the types of "agency" available to child characters. In a discussion of agency in children's literature, John Stephens writes that children's literature "has tended to reduce the degree and define the contexts in which the agency of young people is possible" (2010: 142).

The point to make here is that YA fiction that deals with the issue of technological body modification rarely depicts such modification as voluntary for child or adolescent subjects. In the context of body modification, child/adolescent characters are routinely depicted as disempowered or subordinated subjects. Decisions regarding these modifications are made by either parents, legal guardians or the state – and the role of the young protagonist is to come to terms with their body and the scientific engineering that has affected or produced it. In some cases, these protagonists have been born as a result of genetic engineering (and therefore played no role in the decision). Good examples of this type of narrative include: *Dusk* (2004) by Susan Gates, which focuses on a child character named Dusk who is a genetic mutation, her DNA a fusion of human and hawk genes; and *The House of the Scorpion* (2002) by Nancy Farmer, about a young boy who is actually a clone of an elderly drug lord, created for the purpose of providing replacement organs. In direct contrast to Bostrom's pronouncements about the need for transhumanists to defend "morphological and reproductive freedoms against any would-be world controllers", these novels depict dystopian visions of genetic engineering in fictive worlds that are ruled by totalitarian governments or individuals that use technology for unethical purposes. The child characters of these novels are the products of such regimes: they are victims of circumstance, rather than empowered advocates of technological progress.

Protagonists who were not born as a result of technoscientific intervention, but have experienced body modification as a result of surgical intervention after a serious accident, are similarly uninvolved in the decision-making process. *The Adoration of Jenna Fox* by Mary E. Pearson (2008), *Skinned* by Robin Wasserman (2008) and *Cinder* by Marissa Meyer (2012) each depict adolescent female characters who become cyborgs when inanimate (electronic, metallic or robotic) material is fused with their organic human body. These novels emphasise that such body modification does not constitute "morphological freedom", to use Bostrom's terminology, as it is made clear that without such medical intervention each character would have certainly died. Body modification is thus an alternative to death (instead of an opportunity to scale new heights of human intelligence and achievement), so is not constructed as an act of free will but rather as an act of desperation from parents willing to go to any lengths to save their children. That each young woman suffers significant social marginalisation as a result of her cyborg body further problematises Bostrom's utopian vision of ethical body transformation. For these reasons, my examination of various YA texts in this book only refers to posthumanism, as the ethical philosophy underpinning transhumanism is rarely evident in narratives produced for young readers. Posthumanism, which focuses more broadly on the end or transformation of the humanist subject as a result of modern technological developments, is much more suited to the type of ideological representation of technology and child subjectivity in this literature. This is because the emphasis on subjectivity in posthumanism, specifically in relation to the act of depriviliging the historical status of the human subject, complements YA fiction's thematic and ideological preoccupation with subject formation. Adolescence is often constructed in terms of its "otherness" or liminality within this genre, and thus parallels the alignment of the posthuman with "otherness" as a means through which to destabilise the exclusionary construction of the humanist subject.

A second ideology that is often associated with posthumanism is anti-humanism. Anti-humanism is a discourse or set of beliefs that is critical of humanism and its construction of humanity as the centre of all existence. Proponents of anti-humanism, such as Louis Althusser, Michel Foucault and Martin Heidegger, oppose the notion of "human exceptionalism" that has dominated Western thought and modes of being since the Enlightenment. Anti-humanists such as Nietzsche, according to Elizabeth Grosz, wished to interrogate the elevated construction of "the human" and did so by championing a "life conceived without man as its culmination or centre, life that unfolds through man rather than directs itself to man" (2004: 10). This critical attitude to the hierarchised positioning of human subjects above animals and the natural environment has played a crucial role in the development of posthumanism, which, as mentioned in the Introduction, is similarly committed to deconstructing the historically privileged status of the liberal humanist subject. However, the relatively minor differences in the two movements' nomenclature are offset by more substantial conceptual discrepancies in the methodological approach that each takes to the project of destabilising humanist ideology. Foucault provides an effective illustration of these differences through his work on the perception of human cognitive processes and behaviours. His writing famously provides an examination of the histories of disciplines in the social sciences in which the human subject was formed, focusing on how the concept of "human nature" has operated in particular cultures and time periods. His conclusion is that knowledge cannot be grounded in the human subject because knowledge, like the human subject, is socially constructed.

Posthumanism is indebted to the thinking of anti-humanists such as Foucault. However, it is epistemologically different from anti-humanism in terms of how it deploys the concept of a socially constructed human subject. Critiques of humanism, explains Nayar, such as Foucault's brand of poststructuralist anti-humanism, are based on the notion that:

> there are no *essential* features of the human subject because "human nature" is socially constructed and therefore knowledge cannot be grounded in the human subject and its cognitive processes because knowledge, like human nature is socially constructed. Posthumanism, especially the interdisciplinary tenet which is more properly referred to as "critical posthumanism", *begins* with this assumption of the constructed nature of the human – her/his body, functions, attitudes, behavior, relations, consciousness – in which the very process of construction of the human by the human is exclusionary.
>
> (2014: 30)

The phrase "critical posthumanism" was first used by Jill Didur in 2003 to describe "an interdisciplinary perspective informed by academic poststructuralism, postmodernism, feminist and postcolonial studies, and science and technology studies" (Simon, 2003: 2–3). In the decade that has passed since Didur identified "critical posthumanism" as an academic discourse, the term has simply been collapsed back into "posthumanism".

This focus on deconstructing normative understandings of subjectivity is especially evident in YA fiction that narratively interrogates humanist concepts of subjectivity through the depiction of non-human characters, such as robots and cyborgs. Often such narratives are focalised from the perspective of a non-human character, and it is the immediate "otherness" of this perspective that allows for the deconstruction of a coherent and autonomous sense of self. Posthumanism further differentiates itself from critical philosophies such as anti-humanism, as Nayar argues, because it intensifies the "concern with exclusion, difference and Otherness – racial, gendered, sexual, anatomical, species – and proposes that the human is constituted by difference" (2014: 30).

The central focus of posthumanism on difference in the constitution of subjectivity is, as I have indicated, very prevalent in young adult fiction. There are obvious parallels between the "otherness" of robot and cyborg characters and the liminality of adolescence as a category of identity, making narratives about the development of "othered" subjects appealing to young adult readers who see themselves as falling outside the constructs of either adulthood or childhood. Novels for adolescent readers also pursue this issue in less literal terms, however, frequently using virtual reality as a means for exploring the fragmented, tenuous and collective sense of self that arises out of regular experiences in cyberspace. Such narratives therefore explore the "otherness" of a subjectivity that does not conform to the humanist standard of a coherent and autonomous self.

Posthumanism and the possibility of agency

A common misconception about posthumanism is that it denies the possibility of subjective agency, a fundamental principle of humanist conceptualisations of selfhood. This is not necessarily the case, although it must be said that agency undergoes a reconfiguration within critical posthumanism. The prefix "post", meaning "beyond" or "after", is an insistent reminder that posthumanism is not predicated on the death of the liberal human subject. Hayles suggests that posthumanism rejects binary oppositions, stating: "the posthuman need not be recuperated back into liberal humanism, nor need it be construed as anti-human" (1999: 287). Nayar reiterates this position, specifying that "posthumanism is not a simple binary of the humanist/anti-humanist positions outlined above but a whole new conceptualisation of the human as a more inclusive, non-unitary entity whose boundaries with the world, with other life forms and species, are porous" (2014: 30). Because posthumanism has relaxed the boundaries that have traditionally been used to define categories such as "the human", the concept of agency can now be extended to non-human subjects such as animals or, in the case of many YA fictions, cyborg and robot characters. This broadening of the categories of subjectivity to which agency can be applied also involves an ideological reformulation, because humanism has always conceived of selfhood in highly individualistic terms. Posthumanism, on the other hand, views subjectivity as networked and collective. This is especially relevant to the construction of subjectivity in relation to intelligent machines such as computers. The impact of such technology on human subjectivity is a widespread theme in contemporary literature produced for adolescents, whether in the context of young people's experiences of cyberspace or of their increasing awareness of themselves as surveillance subjects. Hayles writes that human-machine interactions are reciprocal, asserting that:

> An essential component of coming to terms with the ethical implications of intelligent machines is recognizing the mutuality of our interactions with them, the complex dynamics through which they create us even as we create them ...
>
> (1999: 243)

In recognising that human subjectivity is necessarily transformed through interactions with technology, Hayles also implicitly suggests that the concept of agency will be similarly transformed in a technological context. This is an incipient but nevertheless significant thematic concern in very recent YA narratives, where innovative writers such as Cory Doctorow, Ernest Cline, Lauren Myracle and Jess C. Scott explore the development of adolescent identity in a virtual environment and construct subjective agency as a form of empowerment that is both embedded in the material body and defined by its collective nature. A collective sense of subjective agency is not common in either children's literature or YA fiction, as both genres have traditionally followed humanist ideology in their advocacy of individualistic forms of agency and empowerment. (The quest narrative, which remains an immensely popular motif in books for young readers, effectively illustrates this endorsement of individualism. The protagonist's literal journey typically acts as a metaphor for his or her maturation into a heroic figure. This model of heroism is one that places a humanist emphasis on the character's identity as special and unique.) In contemporary YA fiction, however, the aforementioned authors are responsible for producing narratives that subvert established humanist paradigms and advocate a collective and networked sense of agency. These narratives commonly represent youth experiences in cyberspace as potentially empowering, and construct virtual reality as a space that is defined by its collaborative and networked qualities. Individual protagonists are able to connect to virtual communities through cyberspace, and it is through their experiences with these communities that they attain a sense of their own worth. Cory Doctorow's short story, "Anda's Game" (2004), and novel *Little Brother* (2008) are excellent examples of this type of reformulation of humanist models of agency. ("Anda's Game" is discussed further in Chapters 3 and 4, while *Little Brother* is addressed in Chapters 3 and 5).

Posthumanism within children's literary criticism

The topic of the posthuman has been addressed in varying ways in children's literary criticism over the past decade – but perhaps owing to the theoretical developments in posthumanism itself over this time (which have led to an increased emphasis on embodiment and what has become known as "speciesism"), much of this critical engagement offers a limited view of how posthumanism might assist in the interpretation of children's fiction. A further problem relates to the availability of children's texts, because although the past decade has produced a plethora of narratives that have provided representations of the posthuman, it is not until recently that a recognisable group of emerging YA authors have produced fictions that actually demonstrate an ideological alignment with posthumanism. The term "posthuman" was first used in relation to children's literature by Elaine Ostry in 2004, in an article that explores representations of genetic engineering in young adult science-fiction writing. Ostry uses the work of Francis Fukuyama to frame her argument, asserting that: "we are entering a 'posthuman age', in which liberal humanist definitions of the human are challenged through scientific advances" (2004: 222). Her focus is on the technologically mediated human body, which she suggests is one that destabilises the binary distinctions between organic and inorganic, human and animal. Ostry surveys a large primary corpus (approximately 35 novels) and contends that such literature seeks to explore the issues surrounding controversial scientific phenomena such as cloning:

> Through literature, young adults can become aware of, and participate in, the debates surrounding biotechnology. What are the pros and cons of such advances as cloning? Of what value is the human versus the new, "improved" human? Literature confronts both the hopes and fears that biotechnology inspires.
>
> (2004: 223)

Although Ostry repeatedly uses the term "posthuman", she does not engage with posthumanism as an academic discourse of critical inquiry. Instead, her article relies solely on the work of Francis Fukuyama for its theoretical frame. Fukuyama may use the term "posthuman" in his writing, but he is actually deeply opposed to posthumanism and all that it stands for. Fukuyama's definition of "posthuman" is succinct – technoscientific advances in three main areas: neuropharmacology, the prolongation of life and genetic engineering – and it is on this definition that Ostry relies. However, Fukuyama's *Our Posthuman Future* (2002) is actually a cautionary warning about the dangers of technoscience – and an absolute defence of liberal humanism. In contrast to Fukuyama's definition of "posthuman" (and hypothesis about the detrimental effects of such advances in science and technology), "posthumanism" is a term with a much broader application. Critical posthumanism, as mentioned, draws on discourses such as postmodernism, feminism and postcolonial studies in its deconstruction of the humanist subject – but

Ostry's use of the term "posthumanism" for the purposes of her argument fails to recognise its intersection with these other discourses and, as such, constitutes a limited engagement with its ideological expansiveness.

What becomes increasingly evident throughout Ostry's discussion of YA science fiction is that she elides the distinction between "posthuman" and "posthumanism". Her investigation of how YA fiction represents the effects of technology and science concludes that these texts are involved in a process of extending the category of "human", so that it can incorporate technologically modified bodies – but only if these cyborgian or genetically engineered subjects can demonstrate their ability to perform humanity in conventional ways: "To be human [in these novels] is more than the sum of its parts, namely human DNA. It includes decision-making, free will, agency – all crucial concepts in young adult literature" (2004: 239). Although none of these concepts are incompatible with posthumanism, Ostry's use of them is implicitly linked to humanist paradigms of selfhood, rather than to their posthumanist reformulations. Ostry's position is considerably strengthened by repeated reference to Fukuyama, who emphasises the "essential nature" of humanity and then claims that this nature is under threat from new developments in biotechnology. One of the more obvious examples of Ostry's conflation of the terms "posthuman" and "posthumanism" is evident in relation to her contentions about the posthuman body. She comments that "the search for immortality is one of the components of posthumanism" (2004: 234), but this, in fact, contradicts posthumanism's focus on the material body, which necessitates an appreciation of the finite quality of human existence. The posthuman body does, however, symbolise a transgression of the boundaries that have traditionally defined human life, because it signals a merging of the organic body with technoscience – but this point is never really developed in Ostry's analysis. Admittedly, Ostry is primarily concerned with the posthuman body as a metaphor for adolescence and, as such, she only considers her primary corpus at the level of plot. Her analysis therefore does not consider the narrative strategies that are used to represent subjectivity textually – although this seems to be a missed opportunity given that posthumanism is focused so intensely on how technology is capable of challenging dominant conceptions of subjectivity. Ostry cites the YA novel *Turnabout* (2002), by Margaret Peterson Haddix, as an example of YA fiction that uses the motif of the technologically augmented body to challenge conventional understandings of human existence, stating: "Melly remembers one of the points when she realized that the turnabout had drastically altered her definition of what it was to live: she wonders if she can have a child, and realizes that it may not be possible as '[m]y body goes backward, not forward'" (2004: 234). This statement is never fully explicated, however, as Ostry does not extend it to a consideration of how narrative techniques such as focalisation and point of view might be used to align readers with non-human perspectives of the material body and its role in the production of identity. (The established link between posthumanism and feminism, which is especially pertinent in the context of the embodiment of female subjects, is also omitted from Ostry's commentary.)

Fukuyama's dire pronouncements about the effects of genetic engineering (that it will produce a "superclass" of elite human beings) are ideas that are entertained in YA fiction, according to Ostry, but then ameliorated by narrative and/or thematic closure that reinforces the perspective that although their bodies might be engineered, the essence of these "new and improved" humans is familiar and traditional. Although the narratives that Ostry examines may toy with the idea of technology producing new ways of being in the world, a humanist conceptualisation of human subjectivity remains dominant. The prevailing humanist vision of subjectivity in Ostry's corpus is therefore greatly at odds with posthumanism, a discourse that is actively engaged in deconstructing humanist ideologies of subjectivity.

Noga Applebaum's discussion of posthumanism in *Representations of Technology in Science Fiction for Young People* (2010), an important precursor for this book, is also limited – in that although she focuses on technology, she only engages with posthumanism in relation to the subject of cloning. The crux of Applebaum's argument is that most science fiction produced for children and adolescents is technophobic. In accordance with this contention, her discussion of how an ethically controversial issue such as cloning is represented in children's literature reproduces many of the claims made by Ostry. Cloned characters perform a very liberal humanist model of subjectivity, demonstrating that they have the propensity to be autonomous and highly individualised selves despite the conditions of their birth and existence:

> The clones latch on to various definitions as a means of separating themselves from their post-human state. What they define as "human" is ultimately what enables them to transcend their "clone-ness" and allows them to see themselves as unique, or as "normal".
>
> (Applebaum, 2010: 137)

While Applebaum discusses some of the central ideologies associated with posthumanism – such as the concept of subjectivity as hybridised and fluid, and Hayles' notion of the posthuman body as a prosthesis – she is unable to find any effective examples of children's texts that deal with these subjects. Instead, she proposes that the conservative representation of cloning in children's texts shares more in common with Jean Baudrillard's anti-posthumanist perspective, in that it is the special and unique qualities of these literary clones that allows them to join the category of "humanity": "many of the texts identify alterity as the essence of humanity in the vein of Baudrillard" (Applebaum, 2010: 137). Applebaum also mentions Donna Haraway's influential concept of the cyborg as a being that disrupts many of the binary concepts associated with liberal humanism (mind/body, self/other, culture/nature, male/female and so on), but her discussion curiously sidesteps a meditation on how various children's texts might entertain such an idea, by instead focusing on Haraway's claims about the cyborg's lack of origins. This leads into an examination of how "the family" is reconceptualised in clone narratives, which is obviously an important issue, but at the same time sets aside more fundamental questions about how a cyborgian figure challenges and disrupts preconceived notions about human subjectivity and consciousness.

To date, the seminal discussion of posthumanism and its relationship to children's literature is "The Struggle to be Human in a Posthuman World", the final chapter of *New World Orders in Contemporary Children's Literature: Utopian Transformations* (2008), by Clare Bradford, Kerry Mallan, John Stephens and Robyn McCallum. Opening with a comprehensive examination of posthuman ideology, with sustained reference to the work of Hayles, this chapter offers a sophisticated examination of numerous children's texts that cleverly use technology as a context for problematising humanist ideas about subjectivity. The strength of the discussion lies in its analysis of the textual strategies used to represent the subjectivity of cloned, computer-generated or robotic characters. As theorists of the posthuman such as Jill Didur and Hayles have emphasised, posthumanism shares much in common with discourses such as feminism, poststructuralism and postcolonialism, in that each is concerned with the deconstruction of the humanist subject. It is regrettable that other critical discussions of posthumanist themes in children's literature overlook this fact, preferring to concentrate on plot outcomes and characterisation. In contrast, "The Struggle to be Human in a Posthuman World" produces, as a result of its refined analysis of subjectivity, a highly innovative interpretation of the way in which children's literature and film embraces aspects of posthuman ideology. One area of focus is the representation of mechanoid characters, which "offer a hypothetical position of outsidedness and hence otherness from which to examine and revaluate the known and familiar world" (Bradford et al., 2008: 160). To demonstrate this assertion, Bradford et al. point to the Steven Spielberg film *A.I.* (*Artificial Intelligence*) (2001) and the Helen Fox novel *Eager* (2003) – acknowledging that: "in narratives about artificial intelligence, however, notions of cognition and consciousness are central to conceptions of 'the human' and, hence, of the possibilities for artificial intelligence and life. Being is always equated with consciousness and perception (both physical and emotional)" (2008: 161). Bradford et al. link these two texts through their use of point of view strategies, as both enable point of view to be located in mechanoid characters:

> Point of view strategies used in *Eager* and *A.I.*, whereby the narrative is significantly focalised by a mechanoid character, serve to highlight both ethical and philosophical issues... Strategies used to imply point of view in prose narrative highlight the extent to which Eager is a thinking, feeling, "real" being. The narrative presents him as if he were a human being and, as the distinction between the human and non-human begins to dissolve, what we imagine as "natural" feelings are attributed to the machine.
>
> (2008: 164)

In addition to addressing the textual representation of mechanoid subjectivity, Bradford et al. also consider the concept of virtual reality and the "ethical questions which the use of computer technologies in contemporary society raises" (2008: 172). Embodiment is a central concern in posthuman ideology and "The Struggle to be Human in a Posthuman World" uses virtual reality narratives to investigate how the relationship between cognition and embodiment is affected by computer technology. Again, one of the strengths of this particular investigation is its acknowledgement of the role that narrative strategies play in the construction of textual meaning:

> In *Noah and Saskia* [an Australian children's television series], the central characters communicate from opposite sides of the world through avatars in an internet chatroom. Both construct online personas for themselves, but representation of the real and virtual is further complicated by the multiplication of diegetic levels of narration and by their own constructions of each other; despite its playfulness, the series ultimately has a serious concern with ethical issues arising from the construction of virtual and real identities.
> (Bradford et al., 2008: 172)

Owing to the deeper engagement with posthuman ideology displayed here, which is coupled with astute textual analysis, the conclusions drawn by Bradford et al. are accordingly more complex than those offered by either Ostry or Applebaum. They recognise that a small subset of children's books is responding to posthumanism in a highly innovative manner. Rather than just using "the posthuman" as a technofuturistic setting within which to confirm humanist concepts of the subject (which Ostry and Applebaum maintain is a common response to posthumanism in children's books), Bradford et al. propose that the narratives which constitute their primary corpus are engaged in a more subtle process of redefining the category of "human" and redistributing difference, so that hierarchical notions of what is human and what is "not human" are actively redressed (2008: 181).

My own use of the term "posthumanism" and sense of how this critical discourse might be best employed in critical interpretations of children's fiction and film is greatly indebted to Bradford et al. My intention in this book is to develop and extend the ideas and concepts established in this chapter, which constituted an entirely new direction in children's literary scholarship when first published in 2008. At that time, the subject of posthumanism had only been cursorily raised in children's literary criticism – so the approach taken by Bradford et al. was to provide an overview of the issues associated with posthumanism and a synopsis of the varying ways in which children's texts have sought to engage with such issues. Since that publication very little criticism has focused on posthumanism and its implications for children's literature – despite an abundance of primary material that explores the impact of technology on human society. *Contemporary Dystopian Fiction for Young Adults: Brave New Teenagers* (2013), a collection of essays edited by Balaka Basu, Katherine R. Broad and Carrie Hintz, contains two chapters that deal with posthumanism, but each does so using a limited critical lens. Erin T. Newcombe provides a perceptive analysis of Nancy Farmer's *The House of the Scorpion* (2002), a YA novel that explores posthuman subjectivity from the perspective of a clone. Although she does not cite Bradford et al.'s earlier discussion of this novel, Newcombe's analysis offers another perspective by showing how the novel combines "the narratives of religion and biotechnology as opposed to seeing them as oppositional" (2013: 184). She argues that this combination illustrates the way in which recent YA fiction uses the "othered" perspective of posthuman subjects to destabilise humanist categories of being and experience, yet her restricted focus on just one novel makes her arguments difficult to apply to the posthuman condition as it is represented and explored more broadly in adolescent fiction.

Thomas J. Morrissey's contribution to the essay collection is more attuned with my own readings of technologically focused YA fiction, as he writes that while novels such as *Feed* (2002) by M.T. Anderson and *The Adoration of Jenna Fox* "capture the dystopian zeitgeist", they also "offer hope in hard times, and challenge young readers to understand that there are ways to make sense of our times and to salvage the future" (2013: 290). It is this notion of "making sense of our own times" to which I believe posthumanism is deeply committed. Because technology has exerted such a profound effect on human existence and experience, new theoretical paradigms are needed to explain what it means to be human in an era where the previously sacrosanct boundaries of the humanist subject are constantly being redrawn. Nevertheless, Morrissey's discussion of posthuman YA fiction is not principally concerned with the ideology of posthumanism per se, but rather in articulating how these novels represent "postmodern indeterminacy and posthuman selfhood" (2013: 199). He thus never explicitly considers the relationship between humanist and posthumanist assumptions about subjectivity (as is my intention in this book), preferring instead to deal with how each of his primary texts explores the fate of the human species in the posthuman era.

There are two noteworthy exceptions to the dearth of criticism that deals with critical posthumanism as it applies to children's literature: Kerry Mallan's "All That Matters: Technoscience, Critical Theory and Children's Fiction" (2011) and Richard Gooding's "*Clockwork*: Philip Pullman's Posthuman Fairy Tale" (2011). Mallan's essay charts familiar territory to Bradford et al. in "The Struggle to be Human in a Posthuman World" (which is not especially strange, given that she was a co-author). She provides readers with an enlightening history of the origins of posthumanism, identifying how differences between human beings and machines have become less distinct as a result of technological change. Like Bradford et al. and Newcombe, she considers the function of the cyborg in narratives produced for children – but extends the concept of the cyborg to encompass Deleuze and Guattari's notion of "becoming". This theorising of the body is an important element of my own arguments about the significance of posthumanism in children's literature, as one of my central areas of focus is the role of embodiment in the production of feminine subjectivity in a posthuman context. Although my own discussion of embodiment does not consider *affect* in the same way as Mallan does, I am similarly interested in how posthuman ideology can open up new ways of theorising the body and conceptualising its relation to the mind in the production of subjectivity. For the purposes of this book, this is particularly applicable to the construction of feminine subjectivity – because women have traditionally been excluded in humanist constructions of the subject, due to the way in which feminine identity has always been closely related to the physical body. (See Chapter 4 for further discussion of the role of embodiment as it relates to feminine subjectivity in the posthuman era.)

Gooding's analysis of Philip Pullman's fairy tale of sorts, *Clockwork, or All Wound Up*, is the perfect precursor to this book, as it examines how images of posthuman characters and worlds are narratively constructed. Although Gooding only examines one text, his comments about the representation of the posthuman condition through narrative discourse are an apt introduction to my own course of inquiry here:

> Another way [of] approaching posthumanism in writing for young readers is to consider how the posthuman condition affects narrative form, from patterns of figurative language, to the representation of narrative voice, to the construction of plot. Implicit in this approach is the position that, rather than simply defending liberal humanism, such writing accepts – for better or worse – that the posthuman condition is already upon us and therefore seeks ways of working within the new paradigm.
>
> (2011: 311)

While writing this book, my primary agenda was to uncover those newly emerged narratives that took a similar approach to posthumanity, and which correspondingly acknowledged that the new ideological models for human existence and experience that are suggested by posthumanism demanded new narrative forms. I am therefore extremely grateful to Gooding for initiating this project with his study of *Clockwork*.

The initial impetus for this book grew out of an increasing concern regarding the prevalence of negative thematic messages about technology and science in a wide variety of literature produced for children. Noga Applebaum describes this negativity as "technophobia". Her study of science fiction produced for young readers over the past three decades (she concentrates on books published after 1980) concludes that in the vast majority of these narratives "the relationship between technology and young people does not empower the next generation" (2010: 153). Applebaum surveys these narratives in terms of the oppositional construction of science and nature, the adult–child relationship (she suggests that adults feel threatened by the technological prowess of teenagers and children) and the negative representation of cloning. The most typical narrative representation of technology in sci-fi for children is, writes Applebaum, one "in which technology is demonised as the devastator of nature, the enemy of the Arts and Humanities, and a force capable of destabilising social order and undermining human identity" (2010: 153).

Applebaum attributes this negativity towards technology to the adult–child dichotomy, wherein adults have become progressively anxious about children's use of technology (and their highly proficient technological skills) because it threatens ingrained ideas about the nature of childhood:

> As I have argued throughout this book, adults' increasing anxiety regarding young people's use of technology, born of the Romantic perception of childhood as innocent combined with the fear of being left behind in the technological race, has shaped SF [science fiction] novels for young readers.
>
> (2010: 154)

Applebaum's concerns about the reactionary qualities of these children's fictions are echoed by Farah Mendlesohn in *The Inter-galactic Playground: A Critical Study of Children's and Teens' Science Fiction* (2009). Mendlesohn is primarily concerned with the issue of why children's science fiction is different from (and in Mendlesohn's mind, often inferior to) adult science fiction. Her study focuses on the specifics of sci-fi as a genre, relying on the definition devised by John Clute: "the essential structural elements of a science fiction book: dissonance, rupture, resolution and consequence" (Mendlesohn, 2009: 180). She proceeds to claim that contemporary sci-fi for young adults regularly fails to engage with these structural requirements, resulting in the production of what she perceives as second-rate literature. Her contention that most sci-fi writing for children is mediocre (or not "full" science fiction) is primarily related to the issues of theme and ideology. For Mendlesohn, the best science-fiction writing is literature that places an emphasis on the intellect, on the acquisition of knowledge related to science, technology, etc. This is something that she finds missing in such writing for children and young people, because of the conservatism and negativity that surround the ideological representation of technology in such narratives. Discussing the presence of themes such as cloning, genetic engineering and nuclear disaster in sci-fi for children, Mendlesohn argues that:

> there is no sense that *these* themes are chosen by children. What they are...is a direct imposition of the concerns of the wider world for "the condition of the child" and the child's response to

the world. Issues such as consumerism, fear of nuclear holocaust, and the various takes on the alien/immigration issue are extensions of adult concerns about the world and the orientation of the solutions are problematic: they are rarely "move into the future" solutions as one might find in the adult genre, but are couched instead as either warnings to refuse the future entire or an advocacy of utopian retrenchment. This helps to explain both why the choices offered to young protagonists are oddly absolute ... and why they frequently seem to deny the reality of lived experience.

(2009: 173)

I am not entirely in agreement with Mendlesohn's comments, as she seems to be arguing that a reason for denigrating the science-fiction writing produced for children is that it engages with topics that have been selected by adults, rather than child readers themselves. This is, of course, an argument made famous by Jacqueline Rose in *The Case of Peter Pan: The Impossibility of Children's Fiction* (1984), and which is also duly recognised by Applebaum, who states that: "the generational gap in terms of attitudes towards technology, and the acquisition of technological skills, highlighted in a number of studies and surveys certainly comes into play in literature" (2010: 2) because, as indicated by Rose, there is an acknowledged difference between the writer and the addressee in relation to books produced for children. My issue with this proposition is that it maintains a binary opposition between children and adults, which is distinctively problematic given how amorphous the categories of "adult" and "child" are (this is an argument to which I will return shortly, as it also constructs all adults as anti-technology, which is definitely not the case). Mendlesohn's gripe that children's science fiction grapples with concepts that would not necessarily be chosen by children themselves is, I believe, immaterial to a discussion about the represented relationship between children and technology – because it ignores the reality that this is also the case in every other genre of children's literature. Such a proposition also suggests that children's literature need not reflect or engage with broader social and political concerns. This is a peculiar claim, given that children's literature is a distinctive literary genre precisely because it acts as a tool of socialisation and, therefore, explicitly seeks to intervene in children's perceptions of themselves and the world in which they live. However, Mendlesohn's final point about children's science fiction providing hostile representations of technology that "deny the reality of lived experience" forms an apposite introduction to the corpus of YA novels in this book, if only because it is no longer applicable.

Applebaum and Mendlesohn provide a dire assessment of the representation of technology in fiction for children and teenagers, asserting that such narratives rarely construct utopic (or even positive) visions of a technologically advanced future. Instead, technology is something to be feared and tightly controlled. If not properly regulated, these children's narratives insinuate that technology poses a direct threat to human subjectivity and social relations. However, it is not my intention to produce the type of literary histories and plot surveys performed by Applebaum and Mendlesohn. Rather, my interest lies in deconstructing those children's narratives that offer the most innovative textual representations of technology, for the purpose of assessing the kinds of strategies that can be used by authors to explore the effects (many of them positive and socially beneficial) of technology on human identity and society. Like Mendlesohn, my frustration with much of the YA sci-fi published since the 1990s is that its cautionary depiction of technology does not accord with children's real-life experiences. My own observations of children interacting with technology tell me that they associate technology with pleasure, play and learning, rather than something that has the potential to destroy human society. The technophobia that is present in so much contemporary sci-fi for children is, as Applebaum frequently attests, an aspect of generational difference. Many of the children's books that both Applebaum and Mendlesohn identify as conservative in their handling of imagined technofuturistic scenarios were produced by a generation of authors born at a time when the Cold War and the threat of nuclear disaster pervaded the social consciousness. This generation has also witnessed extreme technological and scientific development during its life thus far, and it is not wholly unexpected that such rapid change might be greeted with at least a certain degree of scepticism or anxiety (particularly in the context of younger people's obvious technical proficiency, which may prove destabilising and unsettling to an older generation struggling to keep up with technological momentum). Both Applebaum and Mendlesohn survey non-contemporary children's literature (Applebaum's primary corpus dates back to 1980, while Mendlesohn's is more extensive, covering the period 1950–2010), and are completely correct in asserting that negative representations of technology have become the norm in both children's literature and YA fiction. Recently, however, this situation has started to change – and it is the ideological shift regarding representations of technology for young readers that this book takes as its focus.

Despite the prevalence of anti-technology messages in YA fiction since the 1990s, novels have emerged in the new millennium that directly challenge such a representational paradigm by offering affirmative narrative depictions of technology and its social impact. A combination of factors are arguably responsible for this phenomenon, including the emergence of a small but increasing group of writers who have grown up in a post-cyberspace era and are less anxious about the negative social consequences of technology than their forebears and the increasing prevalence of digital technology within our everyday lives. The YA fictions considered in this book suggest that a seachange has occurred with respect to the representation of technology since the start of the twenty-first century, as an increasing number of narratives have abandoned the negative technological paradigm that was established in the 1970s, 80s and 90s in favour of more positive constructions. Posthumanism opens up new ways of understanding the subject in a world where technology is becoming increasingly significant – and for this reason it offers an ideal theoretical frame for deconstructing children's narratives that seek to explore the interactions between humans and technology. Elaine Graham sums up the ability of technology to challenge established ideas pertaining to individual identity and social organisation:

> new technologies have done more than simply introduce new patterns of work, leisure and social interaction; they have called into question the immutability of boundaries between humans, animals and machines, artificial and natural, "born" and "made". In challenging the fixity of "human nature" in this way, the digital and biotechnological age engenders renewed scrutiny of the basic assumptions on which matters such as personal identity, the constitution of community, the grounds of human uniqueness and the relationship between body and mind are founded.
>
> (2002: 1–2)

Graham's comments here perfectly capture the varied form and function of technological representation in the YA fictions. From more radical science-fiction scenarios, such as the construction of an artificial human body (*The Adoration of Jenna Fox* (2008), *Skinned* (2008)) or the development of mechanoid consciousness and agency (*Metallic Love* (2005), *Genesis* (2006)), to narratives that explore what it is like to live in a surveillance society (*The Hunger Games* (2008), *Little Brother* (2008)) and more realist narratives that depict young people's daily interactions with computers (*serafina67 * urgently requires life** (2008), *Being Emily* (2012), *Entr@pment: A Highschool Comedy in Chat* (2009)), the novels that are discussed in this book scrutinise how technology constructs subjectivity in the modern digital age. Technology allows us to transform the human body, to connect with other humans in ways that have never occurred before, and to create intelligent machines that can replicate many of the actions (such as high-level thinking) previously considered to define human beings as separate and distinct from all other species. Each of the narratives that constitute my primary corpus demonstrate an awareness of the transformative potential of technology, and suggests that young people can benefit from technology in varying ways.

Although this book is not a feminist reading of technology in children's narratives per se, feminist discourses have played an essential role in my interpretation of how technology might be viewed as an enabling force in the endowment of agency to marginalised subjects (be these subjects children, females, or both). There is a significant conceptual overlap in the way that both posthumanism and feminism seek to interrogate humanist assumptions about subjectivity. Both ideologies take as their focus the power structures that have been used to reify the white, male subject of humanism, embracing Bart Simon's declaration that "the emancipatory impulse of liberal humanism has come to be understood as being unwittingly complicit in colonialist, patriarchal, and capitalist structures" (2003: 4). Posthumanism, like feminism, offers new ways in which to destabilise hierarchised concepts that pertain to ideologies of subjectivity – although it can also be perceived as extending the prerogatives of feminism, as the focus of its inquiry lies in the binary construction of nature/culture and human/machine, as well as man/woman.

The specific focus of this book will be the represented relationship between technology and the human subject in fictions produced for adolescents, identifying the strategies used by YA narratives to validate particular forms of identity and social structures. Such strategies include focalisation and point of view, and the creation of ideologically coded subject positions for readers. Applebaum and Mendlesohn's research about technology and children's literature focuses mainly on story content and theme, rather than providing an analysis of the discourse used to encode ideological significance in their chosen texts. Although Applebaum (2010: Ch. 3) provides an excellent analysis of how narrative discourse is used to represent technology in novels such as M.T. Anderson's *Feed* (2002), this attention to discourse is not a cohesive methodology applied throughout the book's entirety. Her arguments in the chapter on Anderson are addressed in my discussion of the experimental narrative techniques used in YA fiction to depict young people's experiences in cyberspace, the subject of Chapter 6.

A further area of significance will be the analysis of two central issues, citizenship and surveillance, and their represented relationship with technology in children's narratives. Citizenship (within the context of a technologically advanced and globalised world) and surveillance (as a result of technological development) are recurring themes in futuristic fantasy fiction produced for child/adolescent audiences and often have a profound effect on the way that human identity and social relations are conceived in these narratives. The representation of these issues in children's literature and film raises important questions about the role that technology can play in enabling or eroding personal autonomy and human interrelationships.

One of the most appealing aspects of posthumanism as a theoretical discourse is its ability to subvert and destabilise dominant ideological paradigms of human subjectivity and existence. Kim Toffoletti describes this effect in the following manner:

> A tension between the human and the technological is indicative of the posthuman. And it is this tension that disrupts traditional understandings of selfhood, identity, the body and reality. It is for this reason that posthuman images can be appealing. It is because they are contradictory and unstable, not because they transcend the body or offer a better version of human existence.
>
> (2007: 4)

This type of tension is patently evident in adolescent fiction that deals with the subject of technoscience. Posthuman YA narratives offer young readers and viewers a site from which to explore and question the various ways in which technology and science can affect human beings and the societies they live in. Rather than reinstating or abandoning the humanist subject, a small but ever-increasing group of narratives are choosing to use technology as the means for both expanding and critiquing the category of "human" in the modern digital age. This book will explain how these texts reflect social attitudes towards technology, ethics and adolescence itself, the extent to which they engage with posthumanism as a critical discourse, and the strategic ways in which they seek to intervene in young adults' perceptions of themselves and the world by legitimising particular forms of identity and social relations.

2
Narrating Posthuman Subjectivity

The focus of this chapter is the narrative representation of posthuman consciousness and subjectivity – which seems a fitting place to begin a discussion about children's literature and technology, as each of the following chapters will also touch upon the extent to which the portrayal of technologically mediated identity differs from more conventional (that is, humanist nuanced) ideological paradigms. One of the most apparent similarities between the novels discussed throughout this book lies in the conceptual link that many of them create between femininity and posthumanism. These narratives offer representations of feminine identity that subvert or challenge humanist assumptions about subjectivity, particularly in the sense that these novels present individual identity as embodied, pluralistic and fragmented – for example, *The Adoration of Jenna Fox*, "Anda's Game", *Uglies* and *The Hunger Games* (all of which are discussed in more detail in Chapter 4, which examines the intersection of gender and posthuman ideology in its discussion of the feminine posthuman subject). My purpose here, however, is to concentrate more broadly on the subject of posthuman consciousness: to analyse how the representation of posthuman thought, perception and awareness might diverge from more conventional humanist models of narration and point of view. This will be a core component of my argument throughout this book, as what I seek to explore in the proceeding chapters is the various and diverse ways in which technology has been responsible for enacting a profound change in the conceptualisation of subjectivity and social relationships in the modern era. I therefore hope to offer in this chapter a wide-ranging consideration of posthuman subjectivity as it is represented in contemporary books written for children, investigating both the thematic and narrative implications of this conceptual transformation.

One of the points that I made in Chapter 1, and reiterate here, is that posthumanism is a critical discourse that offers a new and expanded understanding of what it means to be human in the modern technological era. Such a reformulation of human subjectivity does not spell the end of humanity, nor does it negate the possibility of subjective agency, pointing instead to more fluid definitions of these categories and concepts. As Elaine Graham points out:

> The "end of the human" need not necessarily entail a choice between "impersonal deterministic technologized posthumanism" and "organic unmediated autonomous 'natural' subjectivity," but may involve modes of post/humanity in which tools and environments are vehicles of, rather than impediments to, the formation of embodied identity.
>
> (2002: 199)

Graham's argument is especially germane to the nuanced manner in which literature for children engages with posthuman themes and subject matter, in that such writing typically explores the issue of technologically mediated subjectivity in highly nuanced ways, considering issues such as how artificial intelligence might differ from (or be similar to) human consciousness; how technology can transform the human body and the consequent role of embodiment in the production of identity; and the contribution of virtual reality to new understandings of subjectivity. The notion that posthumanism encompasses multiple modes is a principle that also underscores Bradford et al.'s (2008) examination of posthuman children's literature. Their discussion forms a suitable epigraph for my own claims about posthuman subjectivity in recent children's fiction, in that they use a posthuman critical framework to argue that contemporary children's narratives and films offer representations of subjectivity that successfully disturb the binary classifications on which humanism is based, providing their readers with an optimistic vision of technologically mediated subjectivity. Accordingly, Bradford et al. suggest that novels such as *Ferren and the Angel* (Harland, 2000) and *Eager* (Fox, 2003) involve a "reconceptualisation of what being human means... leading to visions of a transformed human world" (2008: 180), especially in the context of the relationship between cognition and the body. Such a position is an appropriate introduction for the subject matter and primary texts that I intend to discuss here, because as I will argue throughout this book, the tendency for children's authors to view a posthuman future (and, accordingly, posthuman subjectivity) as dystopian is a representational paradigm that is slowly being superseded in the new millennium. It must also be pointed out, however, that Bradford et al.'s primary corpus is comprised of books, films and television programmes that were produced over a decade ago (between 1994 and 2004), and is thus not entirely representative of some of the more substantive ideological shifts that have occurred in recent years. A case in point is their brief reference to cyborg figures, which they largely dismiss: "On the whole, such hybrid forms of being [as cyborgs] are treated in YA fiction and film negatively, usually as aberrations, and social commentary tends to be much fiercer and more satirical in tone" (2008: 165).

In what has proved to be an interesting development, many of the claims that Bradford et al. make in relation to robot figures are now equally applicable to the representation of cyborgs, which have become increasingly prevalent in literature for adolescents. Bradford et al. emphasise the important ideological role of narrative strategies such as focalisation within fictions that explore issues relating to robotics, asserting that "robot figures, especially when they function as focalising characters within a narrative, destabilize boundaries between self, other and world, and hence raise questions about 'humanness' and human subjectivity" (2008: 163). The function of techniques such as focalisation and narration in the ideological representation of posthuman subjectivity is the focus of my enquiry in this chapter.

A common element in many of the novels discussed throughout this book is the decision to allow non-human characters to narrate or focalise their own experiences. This allows for the "otherness" of robot or cyborg subjects to be textually mediated (through the act of reader alignment, for example) and critiques the processes of exclusion that is inevitably invoked in the production of (white, male) humanist subjectivity. *Metallic Love* (2005) by Tanith Lee (the long-awaited sequel to the acclaimed *The Silver Metal Lover* (1981)) uses first-person narration to represent cyborg subjectivity, while *Cinder*

(2012), the first book in Marissa Meyer's ongoing *Lunar Chronicles* series, uses closely focalised third-person narration to present to readers an updated cyborg version of the classic Cinderella fairy tale. *Girl Parts* (2010) by John M. Cusick begins with alternating third-person focalisation from two human boys, but as the narrative gradually turns to the robot character, Rose, she is increasingly permitted to focalise her own experiences. *Genesis* (2006) by Bernard Beckett is the most experimental of these novels, as it is actually structured as Socratic dialogue (interspersed with instances of closely focalised third-person narration). Its most striking narrative feature is that it is told purely from a non-human android perspective, although this fact is initially concealed from readers. The revelation of this trick at the novel's end prompts a complete revaluation of humanist ideology, as the carefully constructed boundaries between the categories of human/machine or natural/artificial are skilfully destabilised. In using these types of narrative strategies to tell the stories of cyborg and robot characters, each of these novels indicates a willingness to explore posthuman subjectivity from a centralised, as opposed to marginalised, position. By aligning readers with posthuman characters, such novels raise genuine questions about the nature and status of humanity in technologically advanced, futuristic worlds.

The Silver Metal Lover and *Metallic Love*: Posthuman motifs in the work of Tanith Lee

To begin this discussion of posthuman subjectivity I first briefly consider *The Silver Metal Lover* (a story of a human girl who falls in love with a robot) and its sequel, written 24 years later, *Metallic Love*. These two novels showcase the ideological changes that have occurred in attitudes to technology since the 1980s and provide an instructive example of how posthumanism has gained momentum as a critical discourse – even within the confines of just one particular author's work. *The Silver Metal Lover* foreshadows posthuman ideology, even if its themes and outcomes remain deeply committed to humanism. Strangely, given that it offers a utopian view of technological advancement that was greatly at odds with the dystopian "disaster fiction" that emerged for young adults in the 1980s (see Bradford et al. (2008) for further discussion of this phenomenon), it is a novel that has garnered only minimal critical attention, mentioned in the final chapter of Bradford at al. as one of two novels that acted as "significant precursors" (2008: 155) to posthuman children's fiction, but not discussed in any detail. In light of its importance as a forerunner for posthuman ideology, I would therefore like to remedy this situation and analyse it in more detail here, especially in relation to its sequel, *Metallic Love*.

Published almost three decades after *The Silver Metal Lover*, it is not unexpected that *Metallic Love* would differ from its predecessor. However, the extent to which this sequel transforms the form and content of *The Silver Metal Lover* is what makes a comparison of the two works such an invaluable contribution to critical discussions about the emergence of posthuman ideology in children's literature. While *Metallic Love* continues the story of the robot named Silver (and is also a romance of sorts), it displays substantive differences – not just in terms of the plot and its thematic outcome but also, more importantly, in the narrative discourse used to shape the story, in the subject positions constructed for readers and in terms of the ideological representation of social interactions within a posthuman world.

First-person narration is a defining feature of *The Silver Metal Lover* – and Lee's decision to use a human narrator (16-year-old Jane) is partly responsible for the novel's humanist orientation, despite its utopian construction of robotic subjectivity. Access to Silver's subjectivity is only permitted through his dialogue, and thus always remains limited. He is represented only through the mediating lens of Jane's human perspective. This is problematic, because Jane quickly reveals herself to be an anxious, under-confident and almost neurotic narrator. This anxiety is caused by a number of factors, such as the lack of emotional warmth that characterise her social relations (including her relationship with her mother), and the dystopian physical setting of the novel. The city in which Jane lives is plagued with earthquakes and hence literally unstable. These earthquakes are the legacy of an asteroid that was mechanically "trapped" before it was able to destroy the planet (1999: 7). The asteroid now looms ominously in view on the horizon, a constant reminder of the devastation that was narrowly escaped. Its presence simultaneously serves as a warning, because if the asteroid manages to break free, the future of the planet will once again be in jeopardy.

Jane's limitations as a narrator arise from her profound discontent. Although a member of the privileged wealthy elite, her life is defined by a dearth of genuinely intersubjective relationships. Her narration opens with an account of her conception and birth, which function as a metonym for the emotional disconnectedness that exemplifies her technologically advanced society:

> She decided to have a child rather late, but the Rejuvinex made that perfectly all right. She selected me, and had herself artificially inseminated with me, and bore me five months later by means of the Precipta method, which only takes three or four hours.
>
> (1999: 4)

Jane's factual description of her own birth is devoid of any of the emotive or intimate language typically associated with the arrival of a new baby. Despite the repeated use of the pronoun "me" throughout this passage, it is only included as an object of the technological processes described. The wonders of technology (Rejuvinex, artificial insemination, Precipta method) are the focus of the narration, at the expense of the new life – Jane herself – that has been created and brought into the world. The final clause of the second sentence operates in an almost comic mode, as the most incredible element of the whole conception-to-birth process undertaken by Jane's mother is not the arrival of a baby daughter, but that the Precipta method is capable of reducing labour to only "three or four hours". Jane's disconnection from her mother is echoed in her relationships with her friends. Although she explains that she has six friends in total, she quickly adds: "I don't really like my other five friends" (1999: 6). Surrounded by people she dislikes, and whose behaviour suggests that the feeling is mutual, Jane's subjectivity is defined by feelings of inadequacy and detachment. Her strong emotional response to Silver is therefore produced in the context of this social dysfunction.

Silver (an acronym for silver ionised locomotive verisimulated electronic robot) is the perfect antidote to Jane's emotionally anaesthetised world. He has been manufactured primarily as a sexual companion for humans, and is thus programmed to please his human partners (an oddity for Jane, as she seems to derive so little pleasure from anything). Yet as the narrative progresses, this quality (or "purpose") is ideologically transformed as it becomes clear that the desire to please others is actually a basic component of intersubjective human relations – and precisely what is missing from Jane's narcissistic and shallow society. As Silver tells Jane:

> "I can adapt to whomever I'm with."
> "In order to please them?"
> "Yes."
> "It gives you pleasure to please."
> "Yes."
> "You're pre-programmed to be pleased that way."
> "So are humans, actually, to a certain extent."
>
> (1999: 93)

Jane's use of the term "pre-programmed" here is designed to elicit an inherent distinction between human subjects and robots (or machines), and it is a distinction based on the presumption that a robot cannot attain subjective agency in the same way as a human subject. Intrinsic to this idea is the notion that human consciousness is superior to any kind of manufactured digital cognition achieved through computer programming, as such cognition necessarily lacks free will. Silver's retort, however, ingeniously subverts Jane's intended meaning, as it broadens the notion of "pre-programmed" to encompass human subjects as well, suggesting that certain human behaviours and bodily processes might also be designated as predetermined and involuntary (examples of this include, for example, immune system responses or the brain's "reward system", a complex neurochemical process activated during the experience of pleasurable activities). Silver's response thus undermines Jane's humanist conception of human subjectivity, which is premised on Cartesian mind/body dualism. One of the more important developments associated with posthumanism is its endorsement of embodied subjectivity, which is exactly what Silver's answer to Jane advocates. At the same time, however, Silver's protestation that his programming mimics the reality of human behaviour is undermined by the novel's continued representation of him in human terms. His "otherness" as a non-human subject is systematically downplayed, both by his behaviour (he is the perfect lover because his primary concern is Jane's welfare) and also because it is only through Jane's adoring eyes that he is perceived.

When Lee returned to the story of Silver almost 25 years later, she did more than simply continue her narrative about a handsome robot capable of love. *Metallic Love* is an entirely different novel to its predecessor: the straightforward first-person narration of the first novel is replaced by narration that is decidedly more complex because of its use of intertextuality. Loren, the narrator of *Metallic Love*, does not know Jane personally but is familiar with her story, as the diary Jane kept of her relationship with Silver has been published and Loren has read it (and returns to its pages regularly throughout *Metallic Love*). Loren's narration makes constant intertextual reference to *The Silver Metal Lover*, quoting whole passages as Loren persistently compares her experiences with Silver to those of Jane. Further, Loren frequently addresses the reader as someone also familiar with Jane's memoir – which, given the prolonged period of time that elapsed between the publication of the two novels, is an interesting tactic. The interpretive position constructed for the reader is therefore a critical one, demanding direct comparisons between this novel and its predecessor. Unlike many sequels that can be read independently from the original text, *Metallic Love* strives for a constant connection with *The Silver Metal Lover*. Because of this overt intertextuality, the two stories must necessarily be compared – an effect that draws attention to their construction, to their narrators and to their very different handling of what might, superficially, appear to be similar subject material. John Stephens and Sylvie Geerts identify a similar trend in recent children's and YA fiction, where they argue that readers are encouraged to leave the text they are reading and look things up. The children's books that Stephens and Geerts point to by way of example are primarily adaptations of traditional stories and motifs – which *Metallic Love* is not – but their explanation of the effects of this strategy happily coincide with a posthumanist view of existence and experience:

> in the "online era", a time of rapid growth of information and textual forms, young people are active consumers of images, signs and commodities through which such life-worlds are modelled, and they require texts of a kind which adapt the cultures of the past to engage with the diffuse nature of contemporary textuality and information flows.
>
> (2014: 211)

This account of the type of texts and meaning-making processes that are most suited to modern readers in the digital age accurately reflects *Metallic Love*'s creation of an intertextual relationship with *The Silver Metal Lover*. The past is not rejected in *Metallic Love*, but the older narrative about Jane is adapted and repurposed for a posthuman world.

Intertextuality is not absent from *The Silver Metal Lover*, but is used for a quite different ideological purpose. *The Silver Metal Lover* draws on two established pretexts, the fairy tale of Tam Lin and the classical story of Orpheus. Tam Lin is the tale of a charming young man who is ensnared by the Queen of the Fairies and then rescued by an assertive young woman, while the story of Orpheus is about a charming and beautiful musician's unsuccessful attempt to rescue his wife from the underworld. Both pretexts deal with the transgression of sexual mores, but this theme is explored to radically different effect. Tam Lin is a story that closes with the successful rescue of Tam Lin – and modern retellings, according to John Stephens and Robyn McCallum, typically "illustrate female resourcefulness and courage" (1998: 221). Orpheus, on the other hand, is a tragedy. Eurydice, his wife, is doomed to an eternity in the underworld because Orpheus breaks the interdiction specifying that he must not look back as he guides her home. The narrative's significance therefore hinges on the dangers of overzealous passion. Elements of both pretexts are evident in *The Silver Metal Lover*, which seizes on the notion of female agency produced through the transgression of dominant sexual codes (which occurs as Jane commits herself to Silver and thus distances herself from the permissive yet superficial sexual codes of her society) but simultaneously warns of the tragic social consequences that may accompany such rebellious behaviour (at the novel's close, Silver is repossessed by the corporation that owns him). The novel's preliminary affinity with the posthuman is problematised by these intertextual allusions (amongst other things), as they operate to construct a sense of cultural continuity through the alignment of this futuristic sci-fi narrative with not one, but two traditional stories of human love. The symbolic configuration of Jane and Silver's relationship as linked to existing stories about human relationships and sexual desire also serves to erase Silver's "otherness", suggesting an essentialist conception of subjectivity that elides difference through the instantiation of commonality and cohesion. The intertextuality of *Metallic Love* abandons this link with familiar stories, however, in favour of a more unconventional use of intertextuality. This novel uses the concept of intertextuality not to reinforce thematic links with older or more traditional texts, but rather to complicate the process of textual reception and the production of meaning. Loren's constant intertextual references to Jane's story initially suggest that the experiences of the two women are exactly the same, subverting the concept of narrative originality in what appears to be a rehash of the previous novel (and also a nod to posthuman models of subjectivity as plural, rather than individualistic). Yet, ultimately, this intertextual relationship serves to reinscribe difference as a valid category of identity and experience. Loren's relationship with the male robot in *Metallic Love* is not represented as transformative or intersubjective, as it is for Jane. Instead, Loren eventually comes to fear her possessive robotic lover and the power he holds over her. Although her story shares some commonality with Jane's, the two characters' experiences with Silver/Verlis are a study in contrasts.

Whereas *The Silver Metal Lover* offers a utopian and romantic vision of robot subjectivity, *Metallic Love* conceives its robots in apocalyptic terms: they violently assert their superiority over humans and mount an offensive to escape human control and take over a planet of their own. In representing this posthuman future as dystopian, this novel outwardly conforms to the previously dominant paradigm of technological representation in children's literature. The robots are "out of control": violent, murderous and manipulative in their desire for domination over the human species. The novel is ostensibly technophobic in its warning of the dire consequences that can occur if technology is not "handled" appropriately. An interpretation of this kind is complicated, however, by the sophisticated manner in which the story is narrated and structured, and through the textual strategies used to position readers critically with regard to the narrative's subject matter. The methods used to tell and shape the narrative in *Metallic Love* prompt readers to rethink long-standing assumptions about the nature of humanity, the concomitant nature of agency, and the role of the material body in the production of identity.

The nature of posthuman subjectivity, as identified by Hayles, is that it is "an amalgam, a collection of heterogeneous components, a material-informational entity whose boundaries undergo continuous construction and reconstruction" (1999: 3). This conception of subjectivity as fragmented, pluralistic and always in a state of becoming is exemplified in *Metallic Love*'s use of narration and focalisation, its intertextual relationship to *The Silver Metal Lover*, and in the resulting critical subject position that it constructs for readers. *Metallic Love* thus plays with the notion of textuality, as the distinction between social reality and textual construction becomes blurred within Loren's narration. Loren compares her feelings for Silver to Jane's narration about her own experiences with the robot lover, examining passages from Jane's books and reproducing them in her narration – to the extent that *Metallic Love* takes on metafictive qualities in its constant references to another written text. This effect also has repercussions on the novel's ideological construction of subjectivity. While Jane's romantic desire for Silver in *The Silver Metal Lover* is represented as unique, Loren's desire for him in *Metallic Love* is a repeat occurrence, a continuation. The humanist concept of a unique self is thereby problematised, as Loren functions as a doppelganger of Jane; her story as another version of Jane's story (despite its very different resolution). Loren herself is reflexive about this similarity, as is evident in her narration when she is introduced to Silver (now called "Verlis" – the two syllables of "silver" rearranged) for the first time: "I was speaking, so nearly, Jane's dialogue. Some figment of me said, 'Don't you remember?' " (2005: 65). The structure of Loren's speech closely corresponds with Jane's in *The Silver Metal Lover*, although the adverb "nearly" qualifies that it is not identical – and therefore accords with a definition of posthuman subjectivity as fluctuating and variable. This particular example also shows the powerful effect of Jane's words/narration on Loren. Loren's subjectivity is explicitly constructed in relation to Jane's, to the extent that she repeats Jane's sentences, compares her own behaviour to Jane's, and questions Verlis about his memories of the love affair with Jane. This pluralistic representation of subjectivity is mirrored in the character of Verlis, who repeatedly tells Loren that he is different from the robot that loved Jane:

> When I read her Book, as I told you, Jane's hero wasn't me. I clearly recollect all of what happened when I was with her, but my perspective isn't the same.
>
> (2005: 110)

The doubling of characters and stories is also reflected in the shifting subject positions created for readers. *Metallic Love's* unconventional construction of interpretive positions is explicitly foregrounded in the novel's opening, as the narrative commences with this metafictive epigraph:

> What do you do about a story that has a beginning, a middle, and an end – and one day you find that the ending has altered – into a second beginning?

> (2005: 3)

Following Hayles' observation that the boundaries of the posthuman undergo "continuous construction and reconstruction" (1999: 3), this epigraph suggests that the process of storytelling might also serve as an effective analogy for posthuman subjectivity. It constructs storytelling as a process of renewal and reconstruction, where certain components – such as endings – are reformulated into different components – beginnings – and therefore generate new narratives. (The use of the adjective "second" to describe a new beginning is important here, as it accentuates the cyclical process of story construction.) Perhaps the most intriguing element of the epigraph is that it is structured as a rhetorical question, intended to remain open-ended, unfinished and unanswered, just as posthuman subjectivity renders humanist notions of identity – that is, the essential, fixed and autonomous self – problematic and inadequate.

The type of interpretive position that *Metallic Love* constructs for its readers is one that is constantly shifting. These shifts encompass changing attitudes to the story's narrator, Loren, and the robot Verlis, expectations about how the story will end and, ultimately, how to evaluate the narrative itself. In a discussion of humanist-oriented life-writing practices, Leigh Gilmore attests that such narratives insert an "I" into the story that is "capable of mastering the chaos of experience in self-narration" (2012: 84). The effect of this powerful form of narration is to "narrow the human to powerful men who tell a coherent story of life with themselves at its center" (2012: 84). Gilmore's comments provide an insightful critique of the ways in which humanist ideology can underpin narrative form, influencing the process of narration, narrative structure and thematic closure.

Metallic Love actively repudiates this humanist tradition. It achieves this most overtly through the revelation, at the novel's close, that the story's narrator is not human, but a cyborg. The assumption that Loren is a human is important within the context of her relationship with Verlis, because she immediately positions him as robot, and therefore "other" to her own status as a human subject. However, the narrative uses multiple strategies to distance readers from Loren. Her first-person narration is both abrasive and intrusive, frequently including direct address to the reader, which serves to disrupt the story's spatio-temporal boundaries in its references to another book, another character and another narrative:

> You're not going to like me. I apologise for that.
> It was Jane; she was the one you liked.
>
> (2005: 3)

Loren's narration is similarly unsettling because it withholds certain information from the reader (such as the names of people with whom she lived as a child) without initially providing any reason for doing so. This act of withholding information overtly reminds readers that the narrative they have in front of them is only partial, and this in turn acts as an analogy for the process of interpreting and understanding what is being described and explained. When Verlis explains himself to Loren, his language hinges on the possibility of existence and subjectivity being predicated upon plurality:

> I'm telling you that those things belong in another life. And that, just possibly, what Jane innocently wrote in her book wasn't entirely either what anyone else supposed had happened, or what in fact *did* happen. The one she thought she knew as Silver – isn't necessarily who I am.
>
> (2005: 74)

Here, Verlis does not discredit Jane's version of events but instead insists that they belong "in another life". The use of the term "another life" is ambiguous, as Verlis does not specify if this "other life" refers to Jane or himself, or simply the prospect that individual subjectivities inhabit different realities and, accordingly, produce different perspectives. The use of the adverb "possibly" supports this interpretation, as Verlis never directly refutes Jane's claims about her experiences with Silver. The ambiguity of Verlis' statement is further emphasised by the insertion of the adverb "necessarily" into the final clause of the last sentence, which again functions to efface a direct answer about his relationship to Silver. Verlis' response to Loren's questions about his past, and his relationship with Jane, is distinctively posthuman in its conceptualisation of subjectivity as tangential, disconnected and pluralistic. His comments also elicit distinctions between textuality and reality (in terms of what Jane "innocently wrote in her book"), further problematising the act of interpretation for the reader.

The most overt strategy used in *Metallic Love* to subvert traditional humanist modes of interpretation is the revelation that the story's narrator, Loren, is actually a cyborg. This information is not disclosed until the novel's end, but it necessarily prompts a re-evaluation of Loren's entire narration and, in particular, her relationship with Verlis. Loren consistently constructs Verlis as "other" because he is a robot, and therefore not human. She becomes increasingly horrified by his actions, yet remains inextricably drawn to him. The ending of *Metallic Love* poses a number of challenging questions – most notably because the novel resists humanist patterns of narrative closure, but similarly fails to embrace alternative posthuman possibilities. The subversion of standard (within children's literature) humanist modes of closure is evident in the manner that Loren's narration professes to have come to an end, but then refuses to do so, adding yet another element (a new beginning, even) to the narrative that has just been completed:

> So I finished the story. And that was where the story ends, back there when we leave the mountains and go off on our own unclassified journey... Aside from that, I must tell you nothing at all. I won't risk it. Except –
>
> There was an airport.
>
> (2005: 296)

The ending that Loren "finishes" (here she is referring to the act of writing down her experiences, yet another way in which her story mirrors the narrative of *The Silver Metal Lover*) may have offered the type of cohesive and complete closure typical of humanist children's narratives: in that Verlis and Loren are free, and she has been able to remain on Earth. Yet such an interpretation would be overly simplistic, ignoring Loren's status as a subordinated feminine subject. (A very disturbing aspect of the novel is that Verlis maintains sexual power over Loren. The ecstasy that she feels during their lovemaking ensures that she remains bonded to him, an outcome that is inherently misogynistic.) However, Loren is too reflexive as a narrator not to be aware of this – and this self-reflexivity is clearly demonstrated in her narration in the extract above, where she states: "Aside from that, I must tell you nothing at all". The effect of the modal auxiliary verb "must" in this sentence, which expresses personal obligation, is then quickly overridden by the preposition "except", as Loren breaks her own promise to the addressee in a manner that parallels the various shifts and attitude reversals that underpin this narrative. These narrative fluctuations are an effective realisation of the ideological transformations heralded by posthumanism in relation to subjectivity and experience.

Metallic Love closes properly with reference to the soul, proposing that it is possible for a soul to emanate from a mechanoid body. Loren's narration describes meeting a human child, a boy who recognises Verlis. The child's guardian says to Verlis that "he tells his mother he was a robot once" (2005: 299), and Loren immediately concludes that the child is a reincarnation of Silver. While it is possible to view this scenario as undermining the novel's posthuman representation of subjectivity – as "the soul" has been associated in classical thought with an essential view of selfhood that is capable of transcending the material body – the act of reincarnation closely relates to the posthumanist concept of subjectivity as fragmented and plural. In a review of *Digital Soul: Intelligent Machines and Human Values* (2003) by Thomas M. Georges, Wendy Robinson writes: "the topic of [the] synthetic soul is of eternal interest, ranging from classical myth to science fiction and contemporary research into computers, prosthetics, genomes, networking, and digital code" (2008: 97). Lee's decision to end her novel about a posthuman simulacrum with an indication that this being possesses a soul can therefore be interpreted as a distinctly posthuman gesture, as it redistributes what has traditionally been conceived as purely human – a soul and free will – to a non-human subject.

A comparison of Tanith Lee's *The Silver Metal Lover* with its sequel, *Metallic Love*, provides an instructive case study of the ways in which, over the past three decades, the posthuman has affected contemporary thinking about the impact of technology on human existence. Despite dealing with similar subject matter, the two novels display profound differences in their ideological conceptualisation of subjectivity, the strategies used to position readers and the thematic treatment of technological advancement. The utopian dream of a robot that is capable of reciprocating love, as features in *The Silver Metal Lover*, is replaced in *Metallic Love* by an image of a futuristic society where binary distinctions between human and robot have been erased, replaced by a more fluid view of intersections between humanity and machines because, as Loren explains at the beginning of her story, "plenty of people are partly *robot*" (2005: 54). This concept of subjectivity as hybridised, multiple and resistant to traditional binary classifications is complemented by the use of narrative discourse that positions readers to interpret the story in a critical fashion – through the use of an intrusive and unreliable narrator and a constant metafictive comparison of this text with its prequel. However, a significant issue that *Metallic Love* overlooks is how to conceptualise agency within a posthuman context. Verlis' interiority is denied to readers because he never focalises any of the narrative, so references to his programming are only in relation to what Loren perceives, or because he has raised the subject himself through dialogue with her. Loren's own identity as a cyborg is similarly diminished within her narration because it is something that she herself is unaware of, thereby negating a sustained exploration of posthuman agency.

The question of agency

The question of agency within a posthuman context is problematic, according to Hayles, because:

> the distributed cognition of the posthuman complicates individual agency. If "human essence is freedom from the wills of others," the posthuman is "post" not because it is necessarily unfree but because there is no a priori way to identify a self-will that can be clearly distinguished from an other-will.
>
> (Hayles, 1999: 4)

Hayles' use of the term "distributed cognition" refers particularly to the cybernetic posthuman – that is, the posthuman subject who is a manifestation of information and code – and the concomitant notion of posthuman subjectivity as collective, rather than individualistic. Although *Metallic Love* holds the potential for a representation of this nature (the robots are portrayed as telepathic, and are always conscious of themselves as a collective), it is never properly fulfilled. In contrast, a YA novel that does specifically seek to address the issue of agency in a posthuman context is *Genesis*, first published in 2006, an award-winning and highly innovative narrative from New Zealand author Bernard Beckett. The novel is set in a futuristic New Zealand, which has been named "The Republic" by its revolutionary governor, Plato. Isolated from the rest of the world, which has been destroyed by war and disease, the Republic is fortified by fences and closely guarded. Refugees seeking shelter are shot on approach. Like *Metallic Love*, one of *Genesis'* most conspicuous features is its narrative experimentation and consequent positioning of readers in critical interpretive positions. Told primarily in the form of Socratic dialogue, the unfolding narrative (it is set in the year 2075) is the story of a young girl named Anaximander who is participating in an oral exam that will determine her entry into the Academy, the most elite and prestigious institution in her society. Anaximander has chosen the historical figure of Adam Forde as the topic of her examination, and the narrative is comprised of dialogue between herself and the Academy members on the selection panel, brief passages of focalised narration as Anaximander is provided with short breaks from the examination room, and holograms, digital presentations of scenes from Adam Forde's life – some of which have been constructed by Anaximander herself, in support of her theories about him, and others that function as official, historical recordings (and are the property of the Academy).

Central to the narrative is the nature of artificial intelligence, a theme that is developed because of the historical significance of Adam Forde (Anaximander's hero), a figure who gained notoriety because of his interactions with an android named Art. In Anaximander's interpretation of the relationship between Adam and Art, she takes the nature of humanity and also of free will as her prime areas of focus. The narrative's exploration of the central ideas underlying the concept of the posthuman is cleverly designed to position readers in alignment with humanist ideas about subjectivity, agency and the development of human civilisation. This is achieved most overtly through the use of intertextuality. The novel's title, for instance, is taken from the first book of the Bible, which details the creation of human beings. It is also part of the title of the first section of Plato's *The Republic* ("Genesis and Order of the Polis"), the most well-known of his philosophical writings. The subsequent discussion of Anaximander's society and its origins heavily references Plato's text, which is generally considered to be the foundation of modern Western ideas about the development of human civilisation. The early historical period of Anaximander's society is referred to throughout the novel as "Plato's Republic" (or simply "the Republic"), despite being set in the future. Unlike *Metallic Love*, which draws attention to textuality and reality as separate and distinctive constructs, the intertextual references to *The Republic* in *Genesis* act to erase distinctions between textuality and what is constructed in the narrative as social reality, suggesting that the two have inherent correspondences. *Genesis* also creates parallels between a known past (the period of classical Greece) and an imagined future, clearly referencing the humanist idea that history is a consistent and cohesive continuum, and that human nature is essentially fixed.

The alignment of readers within a humanist interpretive frame is continued by way of Anaximander's discussion of, and holographic re-creation of, Adam Forde and his relationship with Art. Simulating the Socratic form of the primary narrative, Anaximander's holograms also depict Adam and Art discussing the nature of consciousness and free will. Within these discussions, Art's assertions that he is a conscious being with free will are rarely countered in an effective way by Adam, who generally seems unable to articulate how or why his own powers of cognition are superior to Art's:

> "I think I'm conscious. What more do you need?"
> "It's just the way they programmed you."
> "I'm not denying that. So how do you know you're
>   conscious?"
> "You wouldn't have to ask that if you had real thoughts.
>   If you had consciousness, you'd know."
> "I think I do have it," Art told him. "I think I do know."
>
> (Beckett, 2008: 67)

Art's statements here act to minimise the differences between Adam and himself. They also make a mockery of humanist attempts to situate consciousness at the centre of definitions of what it means to be human. Adam's only way of defining consciousness is to assert that it is innate: that conscious beings simply "know" they possess consciousness, a variation on Descartes' pervasive "I think therefore I am" dictum. This Cartesian doctrine is directly invoked in Art's response because of the repetition of the verb "think": "I think I do have it... I think I do know." His assertion that he can do the very thing that Adam suggests is what defines human subjects – that is, be aware of his own consciousness – serves to diminish Adam's position, because it is a position that Art is able to emulate with seeming ease. He rejects each of Adam's feeble definitions of consciousness as unique to humans, asserting that his own form of mechanised cognition is one and the same: "You think the thing you call consciousness is some mysterious gift from the heavens, but in the end, consciousness is nothing but the context in which your thinking occurs. Consciousness is the feel of accessing memory" (Beckett, 2008: 104).

Like *Metallic Love*'s association of a soul with a posthuman mechanoid body, which implicitly invokes nineteenth-century debates about the nature of the human soul, *Genesis* similarly taps into this history – although it does so in a much more explicit manner, aided by its Socratic structure. Art's perspective of consciousness is closely aligned with nineteenth-century discussions that "drew upon and often contested controversial aspects of Cartesian theory" (Stiles, 2006: 144). In particular, Art's ideas about consciousness being a mechanical process closely reference the materialist thinking of late-Victorian neurologists such as Thomas Huxley, who declared that "the human body, like all living bodies, is a machine, all the operations of which will, sooner or later, be explained on physical principles. I believe that we shall, sooner or later, arrive at a mechanical equivalent of consciousness" (1870: 191). These ideas underlie posthumanism, which rejects the idea that consciousness is at the heart of human subjectivity. In a discussion about the development of posthuman ideology, Nayar argues that: "first-order cybernetic theory... took the radical step of declaring consciousness, cognition and perception (integral components of human subjectivity) to be constructed: cognition as the effect of an information flow from the environment, and contingent upon the feedback mechanism, upon a process rather than material or structural elements". Consequently, "human beings, in this view, were no different from any intelligent machines, because they were simply information-processing entities" (2014: 36). Art is similarly certain that the differences between himself and Adam are negligible. The narrative representation of Art initially appears to confirm his status as equal to Adam, at least verbally. His presence in the narrative is confined to two confrontational verbal exchanges with Adam (the scenes that Anaximander has selected to re-create as holograms), each of which demonstrates that his questions and statements are able to probe and push Adam into examining the nature of his own human identity and status. Adam's rejoinders to Art, on the other hand, repeatedly indicate that he cannot logically justify his own superiority over the android.

In Anaximander's re-creation of the scenes between Adam and Art, the novel discloses that she has included many additions of her own: attitudinal markers that reveal her personal bias and position readers to interpret the relationship between Adam and Art in particular ways. Significantly, the man and the android are always portrayed as combatants, with Adam fighting to maintain the "integrity" of the human subject, which Art is similarly intent on violating. Anaximander makes Adam more handsome than the records indicate, but the licence she shows in the physical re-creation of Adam is not extended to Art, whose metal body is topped with "the face of an orang-utan, wide-eyed and droopy-mouthed; his stare restless, his toothy grin always mocking" (Beckett, 2008: 60). These indicators of an ideological bias towards Adam imply that Anaximander's sympathies lie with a humanist conceptualisation of subjectivity – and the reader necessarily assumes that this is because Anaximander herself is a human being, whose alignment with a human subject (as opposed to a machine) in a debate about human subjectivity is a natural outcome. Until the concluding pages of *Genesis*, the subject position constructed for readers concurs with a traditional (and also conservative) humanist view of human subjectivity, which places human beings in a hierarchical relationship with non-human beings and things. As is the case with *Metallic Love*, however, the close of the narrative reveals that this subject position has been constructed on false assumptions. Anaximander, it is disclosed, is an android herself, as are all the other members of her society. These androids are descendants (or, more correctly, versions) of Art, each taking the material form of an orang-utan.

The androids' physical appearance is noteworthy, as it engages with a broader definition of posthumanism as a discourse that seeks to dismantle the hierarchical relationship between humans, machines, plants and animals. Anaximander and Art are androids with the physical features of animals, and as such are doubly "othered" according to humanist categories of existence. In this context, it is Anaximander's sympathy for the human Adam Forde that is ultimately responsible for her demise. Her "examination" before the Academy members is simply a pretence, designed to locate "problem androids" with wayward loyalties to human subjects. This ending is problematic when considered within a posthuman ideological framework, as it is a vision of a technologically advanced future that remains intrinsically dystopian. It is also largely in keeping with dominant paradigms of technofuturistic representation in fiction for young adults – where technology is often portrayed as "out of control", resulting in ethically bankrupt social organisations. The effect of aligning readers with Anaximander's android subject position is therefore immediately undone, as the murderous actions of the Academy clearly demonstrate that such a position is corrupt.

The posthuman subject: Focalisation and reader alignment

Genesis and *Metallic Love* both employ a technique in which the closure of the narrative contains a major revelation: that the non-human identity of the main focalising character has been carefully concealed from readers. In realising that the focalisers of these novels are not human, readers must then re-evaluate the preceding narrative from this non-human perspective. A limitation of this approach, however, is that readers are generally prevented from accessing the interiority of these posthuman characters in a manner that might comprehensively explore key issues associated with posthumanism. Issues such as how posthuman processes of cognition might differ from humanist conceptualisations of consciousness, how to define agency in a posthuman context, or how an embodied subjectivity might produce new forms of posthuman selfhood are omitted from novels such as *Genesis* and *Metallic Love*, because they act to obscure from their readers the posthuman subjectivity of their focalising characters. The final part of this chapter will therefore focus on representations of posthuman subjectivity that are focalised from a posthuman perspective. This enables posthuman subjectivity and experience to be centralised within the narrative and endowed with thematic significance, a process that results in the gradual destabilisation of humanist concepts of self and identity.

Fictional depictions of the posthuman subject, states Nayar, are generally confronting not because this subject is portrayed as an "alien other", but precisely because of its familiar, human shape: "it is not in its radical difference from the human body or form that horror lies but in its *similarity* to the human, being taken for and passing as human" (2014: 55). This is an important element of posthuman representation in the YA novels *Cinder* (2012) by Marissa Meyer, and *Girl Parts* (2010) by John M. Cusick, each of which features either a robot or cyborg protagonist, where the "otherness" of posthuman subjectivity is not always immediately obvious as a physical manifestation. The posthuman body therefore plays an important role in these fictions, as its capacity for both social integration and exclusion are explored in the production of posthuman subjectivity. One of the more notable achievements of *Cinder* and *Girl Parts* is the way in which their consideration of the "othered" posthuman body advocates a variety of ethical social transformations. As Sherryl Vint comments, the body "functions as both a tool for articulating self and as a conduit through which cultural meanings shape the body/subject" (2007: 27). New understandings of the body, therefore, "are able to create a new version of the social, a more ethical social world which does not insist upon forming self through repudiation of the Other" (Vint, 2007: 27).

As I have argued throughout this chapter, the thematic engagement of contemporary YA fiction with posthuman ideology is frequently accompanied by experimental narrative forms, so that the construction of posthuman subjectivity as multiple and fluid is correspondingly reflected in the construction of the text itself. *Cinder* and *Girl Parts* illustrate this trend, as both novels are adaptations of traditional stories: *Cinder* is a radical reworking of the fairy tale *Cinderella*, while *Girl Parts* is a variation of the *Pinocchio* tale, which also incorporates elements of the Pygmalion myth and E.T.A Hoffman's short story "The Sandman" (1816). (*Cinder*, as mentioned previously, is

Book 1 of Marissa Meyer's ongoing *Lunar Chronicles*, a series that offers radical retellings of classic fairy tales. The series also includes *Scarlet* (2013), a reworking of *Little Red Riding Hood* and *Cress* (2014), which adapts elements of *Rapunzel*.)

Within the context of cyberspace, intertextuality is a basic element of virtual experience. The internet operates by virtue of its intertextual links, creating multiple pathways and connections between individual pages that result in a reading process that is fragmented, random and non-linear. Although intertextuality works in a less overt fashion in a printed book, it nevertheless functions to construct multiple voices in a particular text, as thematic significance is produced only by considering the interrelationship between the narrative and its pretext. This is certainly true of *Cinder* and *Girl Parts*, where each novel uses the motif of technology to ascribe radically new meanings to familiar narratives, creating a dialogic relationship between humanist ideologies of the past and the transformative potential of posthumanism. In contrast, a novel such as *The Silver Metal Lover* uses intertextuality within a humanist ideological framework, so that its two pretexts create cohesive thematic links between the futuristic narrative and more traditional stories. In *Cinder*, the focalising character is a cyborg who is financially exploited by her human stepmother. Combining sci-fi futurism with parody, the narrative's familiar trajectory – that is, a romance between Cinder and Prince Kai – is transported into more complex social territory, as Cinder's status as an outsider hinges not only on her cyborg origins, but also her racial hybridity and her gender identity.

Girl Parts is the story of a female "intimacy-robot" named Rose, who is purchased as a companion for David. She is designed to cure his dissociative disorder by enabling him to "intimately connect" with others again, but as soon as David discovers that she is missing correct female genitalia, he is horrified and abandons her. The novel constructs technology within a patriarchal paradigm, where the "connectedness" of modern life (violent video games, webcams that enable men to secretly record and objectify women for their own prurient pleasure) is responsible for the subordination of women. While this may appear to be at odds with posthumanism, Rose's quest for a legitimate identity that extends beyond "sex object" is aligned with many of posthumanism's core principles. Drawing upon the critical discourse of transgender rights, *Girl Parts* represents a surgical procedure that gives Rose functioning female genitals as an agentic right of passage. This surgery is a technological procedure, performed by a female doctor and, by depicting it as a pivotal step in Rose's development, *Girl Parts* highlights both the physical impact of biotechnology on the body, as well as the significance of embodiment in the production of posthuman subjectivity.

The posthuman body

Debates about the "natural" body as opposed to the culturally produced body are central in both *Cinder* and *Girl Parts*. Cinder and Rose possess bodies that have been culturally constituted as the "alien other" within their communities. Beginning with a description that seems to have come straight from a horror film, *Cinder* presents the cyborg body in monstrous, decaying terms:

> The screw through Cinder's ankle had rusted, the engraved cross marks worn to a mangled circle. Her knuckles ached from forcing the screwdriver into the joint as she struggled to loosen the screw, one gritting twist after another...
>
> ...Having loathed the too-small foot for four years, she swore never to put the piece of junk back on again. She just hoped Iko would be back soon with its replacement.
>
> (Meyer, 2012: 3)

This opening subverts one of the more typical schemas associated with technology – that is, the supposed connection between technology, social status and wealth. Her prosthetic foot is Frankenstein-like, a grotesque construction that is badly made and falling apart. The pejorative adjectives used in reference to Cinder's body, such as "rusted" and "mangled", initially seem to indicate that her identity be constructed by the reader in similarly deprecatory terms. However, such an interpretation is countered by the parodic and intertextual pun that follows: this girl is sawing off the very foot that was responsible for her marriage to the prince in conventional versions of the fairy tale. The act of cutting off her "too-small" foot is immediately transformed into a feminist act, the significance of which is strengthened by the setting of the novel in New Beijing, a futuristic city of China. Female foot-binding (which involved each toe being broken before they were tightly wrapped in bandages and forced into small shoes) was a cultural practice in China for centuries, as small feet were a symbol of female beauty. The practice literally limited female movement, and in this context, Cinder's violent act in freeing herself from a patriarchal symbol of feminine subordination is a powerful symbol about the construction of cyborg subjectivity in this novel. Her reference to Iko procuring a new foot also maintains an ideological connection with posthuman models of subjectivity, where the boundaries of the body are subject to constant change and modification.

The culturally produced female body is similarly prominent in *Girl Parts*, a novel whose very name appears to reduce women to their sexual organs. Its opening foregrounds female objectification, as "Chapter 0" (an epigraph of sorts) is a description of a young girl committing suicide in front of a webcam. It is narrated in the third person by an omniscient focaliser, who remains curiously detached from the events he or she is describing, ending the description of the girl's death with the lines: "The show was over. It had been her best attended video blog to date" (Chapter 0, no page number in original). Female bodies are constructed in this opening as a spectacle for male viewers. They are the objects of a male gaze that perceives them only as sexual playthings. As a woman, Rose is already marginalised in this world. But as a robot, this marginalisation is increased to the extent that it renders her abject. The misogynist David finds her "unbelievably, *unspeakably* hot" (Cusick, 2010: 33), but when he discovers that she lacks a vagina, this visual appreciation turns to denigration: "You're incomplete, Rose. You're a Barbie Doll" (2010: 100). Even the gentle and more intersubjective Charlie can only conceive of Rose in terms of lack:

> Her skin felt real, soft and pliant. Even the rigid structures beneath felt like real bones. And yet there was something wrong. He felt hard bumps at regular intervals, and knots of what seemed to be wiring at her joints. Where her ears connected to her skull there was a tiny seam, and even her hair itself grew from her scalp in a grid.
>
> (2010: 121)

Like David, Charlie's focalised description of Rose focuses on her ambiguous physical presentation. Although her skin feels "real" to him, it is also "wrong". This "wrongness" is compounded by her doll-like characteristics ("there was a tiny seam"; her hair that grew from a "grid"). These repeated references to Rose's body as "doll-like" position her as an interpellated subject, one that is the plaything of men.

The posthuman body is initially represented in *Cinder* and *Girl Parts* as marginalised and even abject, calling to mind "the way in which discourses representing women and non-whites as more closely bound to the body have been used to deny such 'embodied' subjects access to political and social power" (Vint, 2007: 93). Each novel thus embarks on a quest to restore this subordinated body. Central to both narratives is an awareness that "the body is part of the subject" and "always-already cultural" (Vint, 2007: 94). The body is accordingly critical to how individuals experience the world, but its significance is always socially constructed. The narrative representation of characters such as Cinder and Rose is ever mindful of this, which is why the act of transforming the physical body that occurs in each novel produces such significant personal and social effects. Cinder's body has already been radically altered by the surgery that turned her into a cyborg, but for the duration of the narrative this cyborg body is a deformed and disabled one, as it is lacking a foot. Cinder's foot is replaced in the final scene of the narrative, indicative of the posthuman body's propensity for renewal and rejuvenation. Rose gains functioning female genitals, which don't exactly make her human – "the ovaries don't work, obviously, and the womb is, well... a little simplified" (Cusick, 2010: 193) – but the installation of these parts thwarts the design agenda of the company that produced her, as it enables Rose to sexually pleasure herself. The novel also hints that May Poling – the outlawed technician/designer who illegally alters Rose's robotic body – is a lesbian, which constructs Rose's female-assisted physical transition as even more transgressive within the patriarchal status quo of the novel's setting. (For further discussion of embodiment as it relates to feminine subjects in a posthuman context, see Chapter 4.)

One of the more central prescriptions of humanism is its emphasis on the freedom and autonomy of the individual. This has been an enduring theme in children's literature, where the pervasive influence of humanism has led to the prizing of individuality at the expense of more community-oriented achievements. In contrast, proponents of posthumanism such as Sherryl Vint suggest that it is a discourse that favours a far more collective approach to identity and social relations:

> the only viable posthumanism is one that goes back to the liberal humanist subject and starts anew, moving beyond the exclusions of the false universality of the humanist self and beyond the moral vacuity of the excessive individualism of the liberal self.
>
> (Vint, 2007: 13)

Within this model of the posthuman, individuals are viewed as embodied subjects whose identities are reconfigurable and plural, and also as interconnected parts of a co-operative community. *Cinder* and *Girl Parts* both rewrite the humanist endings of their pretexts, providing readers with a form of narrative closure that defies the liberal humanist traditions that have become conventional within the genre of children's literature. The Charles Perrault version of *Cinderella*, which has become the most well-known version of the tale, concludes with the prince identifying Cinderella as the owner of the glass slipper, and then promptly marrying her. In contrast, although Meyer's novel accedes to the convention of a romance between the upper-class Prince Kai and the lower-class (because she is a cyborg) Cinder, their union does not close the narrative. The romantic ending of the fairy tale is substituted with a violent parody, where Cinder deflects an attempt on her life by the murderous alien Queen Levana and escapes – leaving not her shoe behind, but her whole metallic foot. Circumventing the relationship between Cinder and the prince, the novel closes with Cinder being rescued from jail by Dr Erland, and embarking on a trip to Africa so that she can assist in finding a cure for the disease that has taken hold of the planet. Individual desires are supplanted by the needs of the community in this unconventional ending: Cinder's romantic interest in Kai is sidelined for the sake of pursuing a goal that will benefit not just the two of them, but the whole of the population. This closure is only partial, however, as Cinder and Kai's story is continued in the next volumes of the series – but even so, the emphasis on collective rather than individual goals has important implications for the ideological representation of posthuman subjectivity. Cinder's constant association with the plague – cyborgs are compulsorily drafted as test subjects for plague-related research and, when her identity is ultimately revealed to be Lunar (a type of alien), she is then suspected of being a carrier of the disease – is typical of the way in which racist discourse constructs racial or cultural "otherness" as both dirty and diseased (see Joel Kovel's 1970 study, *White Racism*, for further discussion of this phenomenon). Cinder's hybridised identity – as a cyborg, as a foreign "alien", as a woman – renders her an "othered" subject on multiple counts and demonstrates how posthumanism uses a critique of "otherness" to deconstruct the hegemony of the humanist subject.

Girl Parts likewise eschews a thematic and ideological closure that endorses the humanist value of individual autonomy. This is partly the result of its narrative structure, which takes the form of alternating passages of character-focalised narration. David and Charlie act as the primary focalising characters and their points of view are a study in masculine contrasts: the wealthy, popular and narcissistic David versus the sensitive yet alienated Charlie. As the narrative progresses, however, it ceases to be purely about these boy narrators and morphs into a story about Rose and her quest for an identity that is separate from David, the boy for whom she was created. This change is accompanied by an increase in narration that is focalised from Rose's point of view, as well as from other minor female characters, such as Rebecca. A progression of this kind would seem to suggest that *Girl Parts* was headed for what has now become a thematic cliché – a dramatic ending that celebrates girl power – but the novel ingeniously frustrates such an expectation by having Rose "disappear" soon after her surgical procedure. The narrative then returns to its David/Charlie focus, and as such emphasises both the circular nature of storytelling, and its collective context. If agency, in a literary context, is perceived to be the mastery of individual experience and the processes of narration, then Rose would remain an alienated and abject subject as she vanishes from the narrative before she can demonstrate the acquisition of either. Yet, her departure is not constructed as tragic in any sense, thus signalling a reformulation of subjective agency so that it is linked to collective goals. Rose's absence is simply one aspect of a whole range of interconnected events that link the characters of the novel – and it is this exploration of "connectedness" that gives *Girl Parts* its most overt association with posthumanism.

The idea of "connectedness" lies at the core of posthuman ideology. To become posthuman, Hayles asserts that we must become part of a "cybernetic circuit that splices [one's] will, desire, and perception into a distributed cognitive system in which represented bodies are joined with enacted bodies through mutating and flexible machine interfaces" (1999: 193). This rather specific definition of posthuman subjectivity has been widened by subsequent theorists such as Vint, who use more general terminology to propose that "the self is seen as something that emerges from community rather than as something threatened in its autonomy by others" (2007: 13). "Connectedness" is an acute issue for Rose, as her programming is controlled by the Sakura Corporation. It is this programming that is responsible for her interpellation as a subject, as the Sakura Corporation have designated her role as David's subservient companion. But while Rose is portrayed as desperately wanting to escape her cybernetic connectivity with Sakura, the novel concomitantly endorses other forms of social connectivity. It does so in a manner that is characteristic of its subtle interrogation of the humanist subject, reflecting metonymically on the concept of "connection" in relation to each of the primary male characters. Just before Rose disappears, she and Charlie sleep together. Their union, as focalised by Charlie, is conceived in explicitly posthuman terms:

> Their bodies connected, a complete circuit. An arc of blue-white electricity jumped from Charlie to Rose and back again, like a ribbon of light... They were joined, linked up, bound together.
>
> (Cusick, 2010: 205)

In many ways this passage mimics Hayles' description of the conditions that are necessary to become posthuman. The act of sexual intercourse is defined using the metaphor of an electrical circuit, and it becomes an intersubjective experience for both robot and human subjects as their bodies interface. It is, of course, also possible to view this description as simply cliché, but the novel's closing page suggests that this image of connection is linked more deeply to theme. *Girl Parts* ends by returning, in circular fashion, to the character of David. He is in his bedroom, chatting to his latest female conquest online, but surrounded by two other computer monitors that continually flash up images of "famous blondes like Marilyn" or "pages on dating advice" (Cusick, 2010: 218). The implication is that his attention is never fixed for more than a second, and that the virtual world he inhabits is one that embraces male domination, solipsism and misogyny. This critical presentation of virtual reality would seem to indicate an anti-posthuman stance, but it would be a mistake to ignore the novel's complex and empathetic consideration of feminine posthuman subjectivity. David's connectivity in the virtual world is portrayed throughout the narrative as superficial and illusory. His behaviour forsakes the possibility of meaningful, intersubjective relationships with others, rejecting Vint's call for a posthuman self that emerges out of, and in relation to, a community. The novel's final sentence consequently functions as a metonym for David's solipsism:

> With all the lights on and the monitors going and his music on the speakers and Willow's bright smile, David felt better, and forgot about everything unconnected.
>
> (Cusick, 2010: 218)

"Unconnected" here acts as a signifier with multiple meanings. On a literal level it refers to any experience outside the virtual reality produced within David's "three-monitored" bedroom. Yet the sentence must also be interpreted in metaphorical terms, especially since it occurs just 15 pages after the scene detailing Charlie and Rose's lovemaking, with its special attention to the feelings of connectivity that their union produces. The two scenes must therefore be compared, and David's individualistic detachment can only be appreciated in the context of Charlie's feelings of a euphoric and heightened connectivity. David's perceptions of "connectivity" are limited, as indicated by the reference to his forgetfulness, and this sentence must be interpreted in the context of the narrative's systematic deprivileging of David's point of view. This closure therefore further cements his status as an unreliable and deluded narrator.

The novels that I have discussed in this chapter demonstrate that literature produced for adolescents has become increasingly critical of humanist conceptions of selfhood over recent years. These fictions, all of which were published in the new millennium, explore the different ways that traditional definitions of human identity and human experience can be destabilised by technological developments. They focus on the potential for robot and cyborg subjects to render problematic concepts such as consciousness and agency in the context of humanist ideological frames. Novels such as *Metallic Love, Genesis, Girl Parts* and *Cinder* openly contest established humanist paradigms of selfhood and identity, using non-human protagonists and narrators to interrogate ideas about subject formation from a position of "otherness". What is most notable about these contemporary narratives is that their critique of humanist ideology is accompanied by the use of experimental narrative forms. Implicit within each of these fictions is an understanding that humanist forms of selfhood – which view subjectivity as coherent, unified and autonomous – cannot be deconstructed effectively without a concurrent focus on the form and style of linguistic expression used to represent subjectivity textually. As a result, these novels use unreliable narrators, withhold vital information from readers, create clever and parodic intertextual relationships with traditional texts and generally act to position their readers in critical interpretive roles. Importantly, these fictions do not present a technologically sophisticated future in idealised, utopian terms. They recognise that technology has its drawbacks, but are also aware that it has the potential to enrich human life and experience in innumerable ways.

3
Digital Citizenship in the Posthuman Era

The creation of the internet has had a profound effect on human communication, transforming the daily lives of millions of people around the world. One of the most obvious benefits offered by cyberspace is the ability to participate in a wide variety of social transactions – often from the comfort and safety of home. This has also, however, been the cause of much anxiety and paranoia with respect to children and their use of the internet, as the globalised nature of cyberspace and the ease with which individuals can assume multiple identities while online raise questions about the extent to which children's developing media literacy skills can protect them from predatory adults. Much public debate about children/teenagers and the internet has thus focused on how to minimise harm, rather than on the ways in which the internet and other digital technologies might actually foster and enable a range of productive behaviours in young people. Kathryn Montgomery and Barbara Gottlieb-Robles write that "youth are more than just consumers of digital content; they are also active participants and creators of this new media culture" (2006: 132). Don Tapscott takes this argument a step further, suggesting: "for the first time in history, children are more comfortable, knowledgeable and literate than their parents about an innovation central to society...Boomers stand back. Already these kids are learning, playing, communicating, working and creating communities very differently than their parents. They are a force for social transformation" (1998: 1–2).

The productive relationship that Tapscott articulates here between children, virtual reality, community building and social transformation will be the focus of this chapter. As more and more of life's daily activities are transferred to the online arena, the nature of concepts such as nationhood, government, governance and political activism are being gradually transformed. This chapter centres on the concept of digital citizenship as it applies to children and teenagers, proposing that cyberspace allows young people to exercise the type of citizenship rights that are typically denied to them in the real world until they reach the legally deemed age of adulthood. Contrary to media hype about the negative effects of virtual reality on children and adolescents – in terms of video games that promote violence or the notion that spending large amounts of time online can lead to antisocial and other dysfunctional behaviour – recent literature published for adolescents seeks to represent cyberspace as an arena in which children can directly partake in the building of virtual communities and the political activism that such communities facilitate. This emergent group of texts draws on the posthuman concept of subjectivity as networked and collective and, in constructing digital citizenship as an intrinsic benefit of internet culture, suggests that virtual reality functions as an empowering and enabling space for children and teenagers.

Jacqueline Bhabha, in an examination of children's legal rights in the context of territorial belonging, writes that "little consideration has been given to what it means for a child to be a citizen" (2004: 91). While this may be true in a legal context, it is certainly not the case in children's literature, where the relationship between child and state, and the nature of citizenship as it applies to child subjects, are recurring themes in contemporary sci-fi or speculative fiction produced for adolescent readers. Since the new millennium, such narratives have begun to consider the impact of digital culture on child citizenship, using cyberspace as a means for exploring the rights of the child in a globalised, digitally connected world. The world as we currently recognise it has been altered in these narrative fictions, creating an environment where the concept of what it means to be a productive member of society is inherently complex and uncertain. Owing to the dystopian flavour of such literature, these texts also prompt readers to consider the question of how individuals can be "good citizens" in corrupt, destructive worlds. They ask questions about the future of human beings and the societies in which they live, speculating about the consequences of current human behaviours, investigating the imagined effects of technological advancements and advocating social transformation.

The novels discussed in this chapter examine important philosophical issues in relation to child citizenship, including the rights of a child within the broader framework of a nation state, whether children should be allowed to exercise such rights themselves (or if they should be protected by adult guardians), as well as more basic questions about what constitutes a "good citizen". These thematic concerns indicate the readiness of these novels to contemplate the concept of "childhood" within a broad social context: frequently on a global scale, and therefore removed from the more familiar domestic setting that tends to be associated with children's identity development in both literature and the real world. The novels selected for this chapter's primary corpus construct the collective and collaborative nature of cyberspace as the perfect arena for playing out such concerns, and in doing so signal a deliberate shift away from humanist ideology, which is so often fixated on the needs and desires of the individual. The internet has become increasingly commercialised in the twenty-first century, but this was not always the case. Initially, it was a "publicly funded network centred among universities, research institutions and governments" (Kidd, 2003: 55). First and foremost it was created as a way to share information freely, as a network that could operate "without centralised control centers" (Kidd, 2003: 55). This decentralised and egalitarian ethos was most prevalent in the early years of the internet's popularity (roughly the early 1990s), a time when "hundreds of individuals and groups, loosely collected in the open-source movement, were distributing information for free, sharing new software and hardware, and challenging the operating protocols of intellectual property through regulatory and entrepreneurial means" (Kidd, 2003: 57). Writers such as Cory Doctorow and Ernest Cline were in their early twenties during this period (Doctorow was born in 1971 and Cline in 1972) and it is thus possible to surmise that their initial use of the internet was informed by this collective spirit. Both writers present a vision of cyberspace in their work that is anti-establishment and anti-corporate – and also particularly attractive to adolescents because it enables organised rebellion and protest. Situated on the borderline between childhood and adulthood, adolescence can be a period of great emotional and physical turmoil as teenage subjects come to terms with their changing identity in the real world. In this context, the fiction of authors such as Doctorow and Cline offers adolescent readers an appealing and engaging virtual world: one that is firmly within their grasp (in that it simply involves accessing a computer and going online) and that offers tantalising opportunities for empowerment through the membership of collaborative and co-operative communities committed to achieving political and social change.

The novels examined in this chapter each explicitly address the issues of citizenship and nationhood in a posthuman future. As I have outlined above, cyberspace plays a critical role in the construction of children as agentic digital citizens in literature published since 2000. This has not, however, always been the case. In order to illustrate the significant paradigmatic and ideological transformation that has occurred in the recent past, the primary corpus that I have assembled for this chapter includes three works by Cory Doctorow (two novels and one short story, published between 2004 and 2013), one by Ernest Cline (published 2011), and a novel that is now considered to be a classic example of YA sci-fi, *Ender's Game* (1991), by Orson Scott Card. (The revised version of the novel published in 1991 was updated to reflect historical phenomena such as the end of the Cold War.) *Ender's Game* has been included primarily for the purpose of comparison, because it deals explicitly with issues pertaining to child citizenship but constructs virtual reality as responsible for the disempowerment of its child protagonist. Card's novel, which won the Nebula Award for best novel in 1985 and the Hugo Award for best novel in 1986, tells the story of Andrew "Ender" Wiggin, who is taken from his parents at the age of six to attend Battle School, a virtual training ground for the world's brightest children. There, they are instructed in the skills of warfare, in the hope that they will one day defeat Earth's enemy, an undisclosed alien race known only as "the Buggers". Card's text pivots on questions about the responsibilities that citizens have to their nations or states, and also on the reciprocal duties of such nations to their citizens. Ender's very birth has been overseen by officials, and these same officials monitor his every breath and movement. They also manipulate various situations in Ender's life, engineering events purely for the purpose of encouraging Ender to learn certain skills or experience certain emotions that they feel will make him a better military commander. The novel suggests that the covenant between nation and citizen has been enforced too emphatically in Ender's case, rendering him an abject subject.

Ender's Game is a cautionary tale about the dangers of blurring the distinction between what is "real" and what is not (particularly in terms of the violence that is encouraged within the game of battle), and therefore exemplifies the paradigm of conservative technological depiction that has dominated literature for teenagers over the past three decades. A further reason for including Card's classic novel in my primary corpus is that Cory Doctorow, an author who has produced two YA novels, *Little Brother* (2008) and *Homeland* (2013), which offer representations of technology as empowering for adolescent subjects, has also written a short story – "Anda's Game" (2004) – which explicitly redresses the negativity and gender bias of *Ender's Game*. Doctorow specifically wanted to challenge Card's dystopian representation of virtual reality in this novel as a site or experience that encouraged violence in young children, stating in the "Author's Note" that his story "is meant to tackle some of the themes in Orson Scott Card's *Ender's Game*, a wildly popular novel that talks a lot about how gaming can numb kids to violence ... " (2008a: 205).

Virtual reality has the potential to be dystopian in "Anda's Game", but the narrative simultaneously displays utopian possibilities: young female gamers from around the world are united while playing, and the game acts as a site of co-operation, camaraderie and, ultimately, social transformation. Ernest Cline's *Ready Player One* (2011) also offers a depiction of online gaming as an enabling activity for teenagers, similarly taking the issue of gaming and politicising it as a form of anti-corporate protest. Citizenship is an implicit thematic concept in both narratives, as the story in each revolves around the notion of belonging to a virtual community – and the reciprocal rights and responsibilities of these members.

Doctorow's *Little Brother* (2008) and its sequel, *Homeland* (2013), further develop many of the themes about online communities evident in "Anda's Game", although both novels are much more explicitly political pieces of work. (As a testament to Doctorow's faith in online communities the novels were released as a free download from his website. This has not hurt book sales as, amongst other awards, *Little Brother* picked up the 2008 Indienet Award for bestselling young adult novel in America's top 1000 independent bookstores.) The two novels are closely linked to real-world social and political events: *Little Brother* centres around a terrorist attack in San Francisco, which enables the narrative to investigate how the civil rights landscape in the US has changed in the wake of legislation that was enacted after the September 11 attacks, while *Homeland* takes the global financial crisis (GFC) of 2007–2008 as setting and inspiration, using a Wikileaks-type handover of confidential information to expose the ruthless corporations who seek to benefit (with government sanction) from vulnerable individuals during such a period.

Little Brother provocatively draws on the multiple cases reported in the international media, which involved individuals who were imprisoned at places such as the Guantanamo Bay detention camp following the terrorist attacks of 2001. The evidence on which such people were arrested was often flimsy, but the then president, George W. Bush, signed an executive order that gave the US military the power to detain indefinitely any non-citizens if these people were suspected of international terrorism. *Little Brother* draws on this historical background, but imaginatively subverts historical facts by placing its protagonist, Marcus, an innocent minor and a legitimate US citizen, in the same situation as the "non-citizens" who were detained at Guantanamo Bay. By telling the story from the perspective of this child, Doctorow clearly exposes the brutality and injustice of such imprisonment and interrogation practices, and makes a compelling case for the argument that once such powers have been exercised in relation to non-citizens, it may not be long before they are also exercised upon actual citizens. *Homeland*, which takes place a few years after the events depicted in *Little Brother*, returns to Marcus' life just as the American economy has collapsed: he has been forced to drop out of college and his parents are both unemployed. While attending the renowned Burning Man event (a globally recognised community-arts festival), itself a potent symbol of anti-corporate and collective values, he is handed a USB stick filled with scandalous evidence of political and corporate behaviour that is highly incriminating. Following in *Little Brother's* footsteps, this data frequently involves young people being victimised by authorities. For example, Marcus finds evidence of student loans sold off by governments to private firms that charge ridiculously high "missed payment" fees if individuals default on their loans. The original loan amount then triples or quadruples and the private firm is allowed to garnish the students' welfare payments, making a tidy profit. He also discovers a software installation designed to allow the user to undertake covert surveillance of individuals by taking over the cameras in their laptops. The program is being used by school officials to spy on their students, often in the privacy of their own bedrooms. The dilemma that propels the narrative is that Marcus is uncertain about how to go public with these documents. He is fearful of the government's response – for good reason: his memories of being tortured in *Little Brother* are all too fresh – but he has an additional reason for being cautious: after coming into possession of the flash drive he scores an enviable job with a Californian senate candidate. He is therefore concerned that he will lose this position if he does anything illegal. In many ways, Doctorow's two YA novels constitute a complex examination of adolescent subjectivity. While *Little Brother* actively encourages teenagers to become politically aware of their own rights as citizens, loudly advocating for adolescents and young people to fight for these rights in spite of oppressive government regimes, *Homeland* tempers such idealist political activism with a more adult-oriented awareness of how social realities (such as the need to maintain an income, or the fear of recrimination) can impinge on principled motivations.

Both novels are overtly anti-government in sentiment, critical of the repressive powers now wielded by supposedly democratic governments in the post 9/11 era. *Homeland*, however, redresses the more overt negativity of *Little Brother* through its depiction of Joe Noss, the senatorial candidate who employs Marcus. Noss is himself highly critical of the major parties and chooses to run as an independent. He is also routinely presented as sympathetic to Marcus' perspective about the importance of digital activism, and the narrative thus uses his character to suggest that governmental power can be recuperated as democratic process.

Cyberspace as an arena for political activism

In the face of government oppression and corporate greed, *Little Brother* and *Homeland* depict cyberspace first and foremost as an arena for political activism – an interesting departure from popular notions of virtual reality as primarily facilitating either entertainment or social communication (as is the case in gaming narratives such as "Anda's Game" and *Ready Player One)*. In doing so they cast the internet as a new and emerging political domain: one that is defined by the speed with which actions and directives can be broadcast to a huge audience, and also by the community ethos that drives online political initiatives. It is this community ethos, in particular, which links Doctorow's work to the larger online resistance movement that has arisen in response to the commercialisation of the internet. (Doctorow is a self-described "technology activist" in the "bio" section of his website, www.craphound.com.) This protest movement, often associated with the practice of hacking, challenges the hegemony of multinational companies (especially global media giants that seek to control news and information) in cyberspace and advocates a return to the open and collective philosophy that initially typified online practices. Doctorow's attitudes to the internet are, to some extent, generational. Born in 1971, he came of age at roughly the same time in which internet use grew rapidly in the West. His advocacy of cyberspace as a medium that is non-hierarchical in structure, open to all and committed to the free sharing of information is therefore typical of the attitudes that were prevalent in relation to internet programming during the 1990s, prior to the commercialisation of cyberspace. The thematic and ideological purpose of Doctorow's YA novels is thus to open up this egalitarian and community-minded world to young readers. In effect, his fictions share information about how to use technology more effectively and powerfully. They contain helpful tips about the latest open-source software as well as instructions about how to protect oneself from unwanted digital surveillance. In short, *Little Brother* and *Homeland* act as a sort of beginner's guide to digital citizenship, informing young people about their political rights and how to protect these rights using a wealth of free, collectively developed software.

Citizenship and child subjects

Children's citizenship is necessarily perceived within the larger social concept and context of citizenship in general. Broadly defined, "citizenship" refers to a person who is a member of a political community, who is loyal or adheres to a particular government and, in return, is entitled to certain rights and protections. In *The Stanford Encyclopedia of Philosophy*, Dominique Leydet (2006) suggests that there are three main elements or dimensions of citizenship:

> The first is citizenship as legal status, defined by civil, political and social rights. Here, the citizen is the legal person free to act according to the law and having the right to claim the law's protection. It need not mean that the citizen takes part in the law's formulation, nor does it require that rights be uniform between citizens. The second considers citizens specifically as political agents, actively participating in a society's political institutions. The third refers to citizenship as membership in a political community that furnishes a distinct source of identity.
>
> http://plato.stanford.edu/entries/citizenship

It is particularly difficult to apply the first two of Leydet's definitions of citizenship to child subjects, argues Jacqueline Bhabha, because "many of the cardinal attributes of citizenship – including the right to vote, to serve on a jury, and to stand for public office – are denied children. No other group of citizens has such partial access to the benefits of membership" (2004: 93). Children thus represent a marginalised group in the context of modern concepts of citizenship – something that each of the examples of YA fiction selected for this discussion explicitly recognises. *Ender's Game*, *Little Brother* and *Homeland* call attention to the way in which children's rights can be eroded by nation states in extreme situations and therefore highlight the vulnerability of child subjects. "Anda's Game" and *Ready Player One*, in contrast, use the virtual world of an online game to advocate on behalf of child subjects, constructing an alternate reality in which adolescents belong to a political community, use their membership as a form of identity and act as "political agents" (to use Leydet's phrase) within this community.

Globalisation and child citizenship

In addition to the problem of applying traditional definitions of citizenship to child subjects, the concept of citizenship has itself become exceedingly complex since the mid-twentieth century. This is because established models of citizenship have been destabilised by two major factors in the modern era: the increasingly diverse cultural make-up of Western democracies and the "pressures wrought by globalisation on the territorial, sovereign state" (Leydet, 2006). The concept of globalisation plays an important role in the texts discussed here and, as Leydet claims, the increasing emphasis on global communities has a direct influence on the resulting representation of citizenship. There is an obvious discrepancy between the negative treatment of globalisation in *Ender's Game* and the much more positive representation that is evident in the more recent YA novels of Doctorow and Cline. *Ender's Game* provides a hostile depiction of globalisation that clearly associates it with the loss of cultural identity. There is a general tendency to associate globalisation with Western culture, in particular the culture of the United States. This association results in the perception of "deterritorialisation", according to Gutierrez, who argues that it produces a weakened connection "between socio-cultural processes and place" (Gutierrez, 2009: 160). Thus globalisation, at least within the social consciousness or popular imagination, is often regarded negatively and associated with cultural imperialism. It frequently provokes anxieties that the "global" is abolishing, subsuming or subverting the "local", the national or the regional. This is the case in *Ender's Game*, which depicts a world that is hyper-globalised, and where the dominant political powers have deliberately tried to erase cultural difference. Card's novel never provides readers with detailed background information about its futuristic setting – and since the novel is closely focalised by Ender, who is six years old at the commencement of the story, this is perhaps a reflection of Ender's lack of political and social awareness. The pupils at Battle School are of various nationalities, but it is clear that these countries have now formed a common political alliance. The two examples provided below reveal much about the development of Ender's subjectivity and his attitudes to state-imposed ideology. In the first, Ender's point of view is closely aligned with this national ideology as it applies to cultural difference:

His name, Ender quickly learned, was Bernard. He spoke his own name with a French accent, since the French, with their arrogant Separatism, insisted that the teaching of Standard not begin until the age of four, when the French language patterns were already set.

(Card, 2008: 49)

The second sentence in this extract is ambiguous in terms of whether it reflects Ender's attitudes or those of the narrator. (Either way, the point of view expressed positions readers against Bernard because of his nationality.) This sentence is also interesting because of the alignment between "arrogance" (a popular cultural stereotype of the French) and the political ideology of separatism (which is turned into a proper noun, giving the term emphasis and gravity). "Separatism" is a cause for derision and suspicion in the novel's world, and it functions in opposition to "Standard", which is similarly presented as a proper noun and is the name of the official language that people speak. Language is generally a key indicator of cultural difference, so the policy of standardising verbal and written communication is one of the means used to create a monocultural and homogeneous society in *Ender's Game*. ("Standard" is an exaggerated form of English in the novel.) However, within the culturally uniform and sterile environment of Battle School, language also functions very specifically as a measure of otherness. As the children are constantly monitored, and must communicate in the same language despite their different backgrounds – in a way that parallels the historical disappearance of indigenous languages in Australia and the Americas – language that signifies cultural difference can be used in powerful ways. As the novel progresses, Ender begins to question the processes of globalisation that define his world. The extract below is evidence of his implicit opposition to the state ideology of globalisation:

> Alai suddenly kissed Ender on the cheek and whispered in his ear, "Salaam." Then, red-faced, he turned away and walked to his own bed at the back of the barracks. Ender guessed that the kiss and the word were somehow forbidden. A suppressed religion, perhaps. Or maybe the word had some private and powerful meaning for Alai alone. Whatever it meant to Alai, Ender knew that it was sacred; that he had uncovered himself for Ender ...
>
> (Card, 2008: 70–71)

Alai's use of the unfamiliar and presumably forbidden word "salaam" operates as a signal of intersubjectivity between the two boys. Despite Ender's lack of knowledge as to the word's real meaning, he recognises that Alai has used it as a demonstration of friendship and intimacy. Perhaps more significantly, Ender is aware of the word's power – and that by using it Alai has dared to reveal a special, private part of himself (his cultural identity), despite the widespread prohibition of such behaviour. This conversation between Ender and Alai also suggests that such rigidly enforced globalisation is detrimental to individual subjectivity. The prohibition on languages and expressions of cultural ethnicity is equated with a stifling of individuality – although as Ender's reaction demonstrates, such signs of cultural difference are risky and dangerous, but also carry a profound emotional weight.

Little Brother, Homeland, "Anda's Game" and *Ready Player One* differ from *Ender's Game* in that each offers readers a more optimistic perspective of globalisation and its impact on cultural identity. They do so through their representation of the internet as a globalised space that is capable of promoting community-building and citizenship activities, particularly for children and young people. *Little Brother* and *Homeland* are narratives that are centrally preoccupied with civil liberties – or, more precisely, the erosion of individual rights in the post 9/11 era. Doctorow's work is regularly classified as "cyberpunk", although it is actually a hybridised version of realism, sci-fi and cyberpunk. Applying the term "cyberpunk" to his novels is problematic, however, as posthuman theorists such as Pramod Nayar are sceptical of cyberpunk's engagement with posthuman discourse because of the way in which this genre repeatedly articulates fantasies of disembodiment (2014: 8). Vint links this "fear of the body" in cyberpunk to Cartesian mind/body dualism, explaining that the "cultural context of cyberpunk's emergence, the 1980s, includes the threat of human obsolescence in an increasingly automated workplace, the increased globalization of capitalism, and an increasing gap between rich and poor. This context offers an explanation as to why escape from the body might appeal" (2007: 23). *Little Brother* and *Homeland* offer no such escape from the material world, in effect emphasising their protagonist's physicality through the brutal torture that he suffers in each novel at the hands of the police and also (in *Homeland*) corporate mercenaries. While the inclusion of torture scenes might seem to indicate a desire to escape the body, as does the dystopian urban setting of each narrative, Doctorow's YA novels (and also "Anda's Game") insist on a dialogic relationship between social reality and cyberspace. In response to the increasing governmental and corporate surveillance of civilians, and the physical brutalising of such individuals for the purpose of extracting information, *Little Brother* and *Homeland* construct cyberspace as the most effective way of mobilising community resistance. Thus cyberspace becomes the means through which corrupt institutional practices in the real world can be resisted and derailed, ultimately resulting in social and political change.

Cyberspace and the production of networked, collective subjectivity

An integral element of *Little Brother* and *Homeland* is the posthuman construction of subjectivity as networked: adolescent identity is depicted in each narrative as, in Nayar's formulation, an "instantiation of a network of connections and exchanges" (2014: 35). Although both novels are narrated in the first person by the teenaged Marcus Yallow, giving a seemingly singular perspective, the key to Marcus' subjectivity is the ideology of collectivity that informs all of his thoughts and behaviour. This collectivity distinguishes itself from the social homogeneity that characterises *Ender's Game* because it is genuinely de-hierarchised, meaning that within the cyber community there are no designated "leaders". This egalitarian structure is designed to encourage individuals to collaborate with each other and resolve problems or issues collectively – and thus agency can be attained through the establishment of intersubjective relationships. This collectivity is not simply an aspect of plot, however, in that an important feature of Doctorow's prose is the way in which he positions his readers as potential members of Marcus' politically conscious and informed online community. This occurs because Marcus' focalisation includes detailed information and instructions about how to use various open-source software and applications in order to protect one's rights, whether these be in relation to freedom of speech and the dissemination of information, or the protection of individual privacy. Kristi McDuffie criticises Doctorow's writing for being "heavy-handed in educating young adults about technology" (2013: 154), but fails to provide any textual analysis in support of what she means by "heavy-handed". I agree that Doctorow's YA novels have a definite pro-technology agenda – this is not in dispute – but I disagree that readers might find the expression of this agenda overbearing. Such a reaction seems more probable in an adult reader who has no intention of ever partaking in the techno-activities described, and thus finds reading about them tedious. My own interpretation contradicts McDuffie's, as I would argue that the appeal of regular references to real-world digital technologies in *Little Brother* and *Homeland* is that Doctorow has a gift for explaining complex processes in simple and engaging language, as this extract from *Homeland* demonstrates:

> If you haven't been paying close attention, you might just think BitTorrent = "pirate movie download," but there's plenty of cleverness in the way it works. Files are broken up into thousands of little pieces, and you can request any of the pieces you're missing from anyone who's got it. As you get more and more pieces of the file, you start to get requests from others, too – the whole thing is called a "swarm" and as you can see, the more people who are downloading, the faster the download gets. That's pretty cool, since in the physical world, the more people there are trying to get something, the harder all of them have to try to get at it. Imagine if food was like BitTorrent: every time you ate a meal, there'd be more left over for everyone else to eat.
>
> (Doctorow, 2013: 81)

This passage is exemplary of both novels' stylistic and ideological representation of digital technology. It employs regular direct address to the reader in an easy, conversational style that is anything but patronising to those of us who may have been ignorant about the exact way in which file-sharing systems like BitTorrent operate. (Notice that Marcus doesn't construct the reader as unaware or ill-informed, but uses the softer and less-confrontational category of people who "haven't been paying close attention".) He also positions the reader as the subject in his sentences, involving the reader in the process he is describing: "As you get more and more pieces of the file...". His enthusiasm for technology is similarly evident, revealed in attitudinal comments that refer to BitTorrent as both "clever" and "cool". Cementing the novel's commitment to the dynamic relationship between real-world politics and cyberspace, which parallels the commitment of posthuman discourses to subjectivity as embedded in a material world, the passage closes with a real-world analogy that likens BitTorrent to food distribution. Although this analogy draws attention to the distinctive properties of cyberspace as opposed to physical reality (in that they operate according to reverse logic), it simultaneously constructs a relationship between these two ways of being and reminds readers that they do not exist in isolation from each other.

Little Brother and *Homeland* are distinctly dystopian in their conceptualisation of post 9/11 America, thereby confirming the arguments of Applebaum (2010), Bradford et al. (2008) and Basu et al. (2013) regarding the prevalence of dystopian settings in contemporary YA fiction. However, Doctorow's novels differ from paradigmatic models of dystopia within this genre because of their advocacy of collective, rather than individual, action as a response to oppressive social conditions. Basu et al. contend that an enduring theme in YA dystopias is "the valiant attempt to retain individuality in a totalitarian world" (2013: 4), an ideological standpoint that emphasises the endorsement by these narratives of humanist concepts of the self that prioritise individuality over collectivity. The dystopian premises of *Little Brother* and *Homeland* are suitably countered by Marcus' sophisticated and clever use of internet technologies in each novel: mobilising the adolescent community in *Little Brother* and publicly disseminating highly sensitive information in *Homeland*. In Basu et al.'s discussion of dystopian fiction and its functions, they contend that a dystopia "generally differs from the utopia in that its prescription is negative, rather than positive: it tells us not how to build a better world, but how to perhaps avoid continuing to mess up the one we've got" (2013: 2–3). This is most certainly not the case in *Little Brother* or *Homeland*, each of which uses a dystopian political setting to make a compelling case about what young people can do to campaign for political and social change. Aware of this phenomenon in YA fiction, Basu et al. distinguish recent dystopian writing for adolescent audiences by virtue of its utopian potential, writing that such literature is "expressly concerned with how to...create new possibilities for utopian hope within the space of the text" (2013: 3). An obvious distinction between many of the dystopian YA fictions discussed in Basu et al. (2013) and Doctorow's writing is the orientation of such literature to social reality. While the primary corpus of Basu et al. is largely constituted of works that could be classified as futuristic, fantasy or sci-fi (such as *The Hunger Games*, the *Chaos*

Walking series or *Uglies*), *Little Brother* and *Homeland* deliberately blur the distinction between fantasy and reality. This is because although each narrative draws on recent world events, these are reimagined in certain ways (such as the depiction of terrorist attacks in San Francisco, or the secret handing over of a huge amount of scandalous, Wikileaks-type data to a 19-year-old boy). The technological environment of the novels is similarly a conglomeration of real and imagined applications, but even the futuristic depiction of intense surveillance tactics used at Marcus' school, for example, only gently exaggerates real-world phenomena. As a result, *Little Brother* and *Homeland* can be read as realist examinations of the American political and social landscape in the aftermath of 9/11. Their thematic call for adolescents to become educated about their civil rights, and active campaigners in the fight to protect these rights, is therefore presented within a mostly familiar realist context. The technological "call to arms" of the two novels is also based firmly in reality (to the extent that the websites, programs and software applications referred to generally have an actual existence), showing young readers exactly how they can become active and committed digital citizens.

Digital activism

This positive and activist representation of the internet is also emphasised in "Anda's Game" and *Ready Player One*, where the virtual world of online gaming is transformed from mere entertainment into meaningful civic engagement. An important issue that I have only dealt with implicitly thus far is *why* the internet is represented as facilitating political activism in these YA fictions. Indeed, the argument that cyberspace lends itself to civic engagement, particularly in relation to young people, runs counter to the mass media's routine emphasis on the negative impact of virtual reality on children and young people. Such a position is advanced by commentators such as Robert Putnam, who contends that digital technology such as the internet promotes social isolation and results in decreasing levels of civic participation (2000). There is also, however, research that supports the much more celebratory and collective representation of cyberspace found in the YA narratives discussed here. Mossberger et al. contest Putnam's pronouncement that the internet produces dysfunctional or flawed social interaction, and rather propose that:

> The Internet's interactivity, diversity, flexibility, speed, convenience, low cost, and information capacity potentially allow the public to become more knowledgeable about politics and government...
>
> (2008: 52)

They elaborate this argument a step further, suggesting that one of the specific benefits of virtual communication (as opposed to social interaction in the real world) is that the anonymity of cyberspace enables "online discussions [that] are more frank and egalitarian than face-to-face meetings" (2008: 52). It is the egalitarian nature of cyberspace that is especially relevant to fictions such as "Anda's Game" and *Ready Player One*, because both texts confirm Mossberger et al.'s proposition that cyberspace acts to elide or minimise the gender, racial and age-related forms of discrimination that are often the hallmarks of real-world social interactions (2008: 52). Anda and Wade, the protagonists of "Anda's Game" and *Ready Player One* respectively, are not initially constructed at the commencement of these narratives as politically aware or politically active subjects (unlike the character of Marcus in *Little Brother* and *Homeland*). Anda is female and overweight (see Chapter 4 for a more detailed consideration of embodiment as it relates to posthuman subjectivity in "Anda's Game"), and alienated from most of her peer group in the real world; and Wade is poor. They are teenagers who are disempowered and marginalised in social reality, and each consequently views online gaming as a welcome respite from a world that is not particularly inviting. Their awakening as political subjects over the course of the narrative is gradual, as is their realisation that cyberspace offers – to young people in particular – multiple opportunities for political mobilisation and empowerment.

A common element of both "Anda's Game" and *Ready Player One* is an emphasis on cyberspace as a global arena. Globalisation is not always presented as a positive phenomenon, however. In "Anda's Game", Anda initiates a project that enables female teenage players from the First World to assist young women in developing countries from being economically exploited by multinational companies.

In this context, globalisation is simultaneously responsible for diminishing and developing traditional concepts of citizenship. Although it is globalisation that has allowed these girls from poverty-stricken regions to be oppressed by greedy companies anxious to employ them because of cheap labour rates, it is also the worldwide reach of the internet that makes it possible for Anda and some of her fellow teammates to join together and take a stand against such practices. The story's closure affirms this optimistic construction of virtual reality, as Anda's behaviour causes Clan Fahrenheit (the political community, with its own governance practices, to which she belongs in "the game") to alter its democratic rules and institute new ones. While she may have little agency in the real world, and is denied any of the attributes of adult citizenship listed by Bhaba (such as the right to vote or to serve on a jury), Anda is able to redress this disempowerment when she is gaming. Her membership of Clan Fahrenheit is crucial in this respect, especially since the membership ties of the group are eventually strengthened because of the assistance they offer (at Anda's instigation) to girls living in poverty in the Third World. Anda acquires subjective agency because of her involvement with both the project and with Clan Fahrenheit, but it is important to emphasise that this agency is constructed as a collective rather than individual form of empowerment. The story's representation of adolescent subjectivity as networked and collective is therefore significant, because it deviates from humanism's ideological emphasis on individuality. Doctorow's shaping of agency within cyberspace as collective also confirms the potential for virtual reality to facilitate civic engagement. While children and teenagers are prevented from accessing many basic citizen rights, "Anda's Game" clearly illustrates that the internet can offer what Leydet refers to as the third category of citizenship: membership of a political community that provides individuals with a distinctive sense of identity.

A similarly complex representation of globalisation is evident in *Ready Player One*, a quest novel set in 2045 where the Oasis, "a globally-networked virtual reality most of humanity now used on a daily basis" (Cline, 2011: 1), takes precedence over what the reader would consider to be consensus reality. Like "Anda's Game", Cline's novel emphasises the internet's potential for "community-building", especially amongst the young, but these utopian possibilities are accompanied by an acknowledgement of the problems and pitfalls associated with globalism, specifically those related to an increase in corporate power. The great attraction for Wade of the Oasis is that it offers an escape from an environmentally degraded and socially dysfunctional "real world".

A recurring technique throughout *Ready Player One* (and one that is common to the genre of fantasy) is the defamiliarisation of established concepts, and the most obvious of these relates to the representation of Wade as a socio-economically marginalised character. The digital divide, which refers to systemic inequalities in access to home computers, is not an issue that is raised very frequently in YA fiction, where the implied reader is usually middle-class. Given that the novels discussed in this chapter all explore child citizenship as a theme, it is not unexpected that they would consider the implications of the digital divide in relation to the capacity of cyberspace to promote civic engagement. However, most do so from an unabashedly middle-class perspective. In "Anda's Game" the digital divide is an obvious theme, but the narrative is focalised totally from the perspective of middle-class Anda. *Homeland* also raises issues of class, since the novel opens with both Marcus and his parents unemployed. As is the case with *Little Brother*, Doctorow incorporates real-world events into the narrative. Here, it is the global financial crisis that began in 2008 which is responsible for the situation of Marcus and his family. Yet this lack of income seems to have little effect on Marcus' ability to access digital technology. While parental job loss is "associated with a lesser likelihood of children obtaining any postsecondary education" (Kalil and Wightman, 2011: 58), and is therefore directly linked to downward class mobility, this outcome is quickly ameliorated in *Homeland* through Marcus' successful acquisition of a prestigious job. He is employed as a digital technology expert and these white-collar IT skills also confirm his middle-class status. The representation of Wade in *Ready Player One* as a character who is not just poor but impoverished thus marks a point of real departure from the other narratives discussed here. Wade lives in a trailer park with his aunt (his mother died from a drug overdose), in a three-bedroom trailer that houses 15 people. He is often hungry, cold and traumatised from the sounds of gunfire that reverberate around his neighbourhood, and in this context the virtual reality of the Oasis is a welcome respite from a life that is bereft of happiness or pleasure.

Despite Wade's awareness of his own poverty, the language used in the novel's opening, which is focalised in the first person by the 18-year-old Wade, constantly constructs identity and experience in global terms. As he explains the history of the Oasis to readers, describing how it was created by a genius called James Halliday whose death sparks a massive virtual-reality treasure hunt (the winner of which will be declared Halliday's heir), Wade's narration persistently uses global rather than local terms. His language avoids the kinds of local, cultural, ethnic/racial and geographical boundaries that are commonly used to construct boundaries between "self" and "other", instead depicting humanity in this futuristic context as a collective mass. He describes himself as one of "the people of Planet Earth" (Cline, 2011: 1), who vividly remembers hearing the news about Halliday's treasure hunt – news that had "everyone from Toronto to Tokyo crapping in their cornflakes" (2011: 2) – because it was information that was to change the course of his entire generation's life: "My entire generation would come to know every second of Halliday's message by heart" (2011: 2). Interestingly, as indicated in this quotation, age socially defines and categorises individuals in the fictional world of the novel. The narrative's construction of cyberspace and online gaming therefore accords with the real-world phenomenon of children and teenagers possessing more technological skills and competencies than many adults. *Ready Player One's* approach to the concept of "generational identity" is exceptionally playful, because in addition to representing Wade's generational peers as members of a collaborative community linked by their desire to locate Halliday's "Easter eggs" (various items of "treasure" embedded in the virtual-reality world of the Oasis), the Oasis itself is a re-creation of Halliday's childhood in America in the 1980s. The novel's futuristic, technologically sophisticated world is therefore a nostalgic re-creation of 1980s popular culture: the movies, music, video games and fashion that defined the decade often referred to as "the one that taste forgot". Cline accordingly subverts reader expectations of what constitutes a futuristic, sci-fi narrative, as the novel's world is actually a historical rendering of a decade that ended over 20 years previously. (The 1980s was also the decade that defined the early childhood of people who grew up or came of age in the post-cyberspace era of the 1990s, consequently creating another link between this particular demographic and the activist, utopian construction of cyberspace that is evident in many of the YA fictions considered within this chapter.)

The construction of the Oasis as a homage to the 1980s does nonetheless problematically underscore the narrative's attempts to create a technologically advanced and truly globalised form of virtual reality. This is because the Oasis, like the internet in the real world, is so utterly "Americanised". Although the Oasis allows socio-economically marginalised individuals like Wade to participate in global online culture, this culture is not "global" in any real sense – because of its slavish devotion to Americana. Joanne Lebert comments on the cultural homogeneity of cyberspace in today's world, writing that much criticism of the internet derives from its overt propagation of American values: "Many parts of the world view the Web as representing consumerism, lax morality, and the unrelenting drive of American culture" (2003: 224). The "unrelenting drive of American culture" is plainly evident in *Ready Player One*'s nostalgic re-creation of the 1980s, which it achieves through constant references to the decade's music, films and video games (all of which are consumer products), but the novel does mount a critique of consumerism through its portrayal of Nolan Sorrento and his company's repeated efforts to control the Oasis and monetise it. The tension that is produced within a narrative that overtly critiques consumerism, but is simultaneously constructed as an elaborate tribute to the consumer items that defined a particular decade, is therefore never adequately resolved within *Ready Player One* (the novel's video game-like structure is partly to blame for this, as it operates on a seek-and-reward system that allows Wade to progress in the hunt for Halliday's Easter eggs whenever he correctly remembers 80s trivia). Nonetheless, the novel does use the collaborative relationship between Wade (aka Parzival), Aech and Art3mis to convey the potential for virtual reality to function as space that enables co-operation, collectivity and open-ness. An obvious manifestation of the communality fostered by cyberspace within *Ready Player One* is that it renders invisible and irrelevant the class and gender differences between Wade and his fellow "gunters" (Easter egg hunters).

Digital citizenship and the nation state

In seeking to define the "good society" (often by virtue of its absence), narratives such as *Ender's Game*, "Anda's Game", *Little Brother*, *Homeland* and *Ready Player One* necessarily address the concomitant issue of what makes a good citizen. The similarities between these particular stories lie in that they are all set in a world that differs from consensus reality (even if only slightly) because of the presence of technological and scientific innovations. The presence of these "fantasy" technologies thus means that conventional definitions of citizenship are examined in terms of how they might be affected – beneficially or adversely – by technology.

Traditionally, most discussions of citizenship have revolved around the idea that "the necessary framework for citizenship is the sovereign, territorial state" (Leydet, 2006). A citizen is therefore a member of a political community that resides within specific territorial boundaries, "within which citizens enjoy rights and exercise their political agency" (Leydet, 2006). *Ender's Game*, "Anda's Game", *Little Brother* and *Homeland* are narratives that directly set out to problematise and interrogate a definition of this nature. *Ender's Game* does so by portraying a world where multiple countries have joined to form a political and cultural alliance, forcibly erasing any visible signs of cultural difference. The territorial boundaries between nation states have been collapsed in a bid to create a united front against the Buggers. Hence, Ender is a citizen of an unclearly defined political union (the implication is that this union is led by North America) – although as a citizen of this "nation state", he is expected to devote his life to serving its needs. "Anda's Game", *Little Brother* and *Homeland* provide a very different perspective of child citizenship in the posthuman era, as they both consider citizenship within a virtual environment – considering how children and young adults might exercise their civic rights and responsibilities as members of online communities.

The concept of citizenship is particularly pertinent to the construction of identity, an issue of primary significance not simply in these texts but also within the genre of YA fiction as a whole. Dobrowolsky and Jenson propose that "a citizenship regime encodes within it a paradigmatic representation of identities, of the national as well as the model citizen, the second-class citizen, and the non-citizen" (2004: 156). This is especially relevant to discussions that revolve around children. Ender and Marcus may be classified as legal citizens, but both are effectively treated as non-citizens (this is emphasised more forcefully in *Little Brother* than in *Homeland*) – in that their civil rights are vehemently denied by government officials and agencies and they are expected to be "good citizens" by silently accepting such treatment because it is for the benefit of their country. Anda, in contrast, becomes a "model citizen" by exercising her right to ignore mission directives and agitating for positive political change.

"Citizenship" refers to the relationship between a person and a nation state. As described by Bhabha, it is:

> the legal correlate of territorial belonging. It signifies official recognition of a particularly close relationship between person and country, typically characterized as a bundle of reciprocal rights and duties, a set of entitlements owed to the citizen by the country, and of duties owed to the country by the citizen.
>
> (2004: 93)

Ender's Game takes this concept of citizenship to extreme lengths, because Ender has been created solely to serve his country. He is a "Third", referring to the fact that he is the third child born to his parents in a society that carefully regulates the number of children born to each family. Three children are not permitted, but Ender's family has received special dispensation: "It was not his fault he was a Third. It was the government's idea, they were the ones who authorised it – how else could a Third like Ender have got into school?" (Card, 1991: 5). Ender's birth was permitted because his older brother and sister had both shown promise as potential recruits for Battle School, but had ultimately been rejected (Violet because of her compassionate nature; Peter because of his propensity for violence). Ender's status as a Third would usually deny him his civic rights (education is not permitted for Thirds, who are clearly classified as "non-citizens"), but his is a special case. The relationship between Ender and his country is therefore exceptionally close, but instead of producing "a bundle of reciprocal rights and duties", to use Bhaba's expression, the relationship serves to diminish Ender's status. He becomes not so much a "non-citizen" (a term generally applied to foreigners or aliens) but a slave or a prisoner: a subject whose rights have been forfeited.

Ender's lack of agency, which eventually becomes so debilitating that it results in abjection, can be directly attributed both to his status (or lack of status) as a child and also as an individual who does not possess full citizenship rights. (Although the other students at Battle School are treated in a similarly manipulative fashion, none are treated as harshly as Ender, because they are not being primed for leadership positions. Further, these students are all older than Ender, who is six years old when he first begins at Battle School.) The powerlessness that Ender feels in all aspects of his life is accentuated by the novel's mode of narration, specifically in relation to the way that Ender's third-person focalisation is regularly interrupted by conversational exchanges between nameless people (although Graff, one of the Battle School instructors who is responsible for recruiting Ender is often one of those involved) who monitor his every move. Ender is unaware of the extent to which the life situations he faces have been carefully orchestrated in a bid to isolate him from his peers and produce certain reactions and characteristics that will make him a better and more efficient battle commander:

'That's where you're mistaken. He's even sweeter than he looks. But don't worry. We'll purge *that* in a hurry.'
'Sometimes I think you enjoy breaking these little geniuses.'
'There *is* an art to it, and I'm very, very good at it. But enjoy? Well, maybe. When they put back the pieces afterward, and it makes them better.'
'You're a monster.'
'Thanks. Does this mean I get a raise?'

(Card, 2008: 27–28)

These interludes are unsettling because readers are never provided with details about the speakers (aside from Graff). Their cavalier attitude to Ender, who is only a child, is chilling. The regularity of these exchanges (which usually occur at the beginning of each chapter) also conveys the extent to which Ender's behaviour is scrutinised. His seeming lack of awareness of this surveillance can also be viewed as a violation of his privacy, constituting yet another aspect of Ender's existence where he is denied the rights that typically constitute citizenship in the modern day. Ender's subjectivity eventually becomes so abject that he even begins to behave like long-term prisoners, on one occasion mutilating his own body in his sleep (2008: 287).

Little Brother is comparable to *Ender's Game* in that its central character is deprived of his civil rights when imprisoned without cause following a terrorist attack. Nevertheless, while *Ender's Game* is concerned with the disastrous affect that the denial of civil liberties (such as the right to freedom of movement and the right to privacy) can occasion, *Little Brother* uses Marcus' imprisonment as the impetus for his increasing political awareness about the importance of civic rights. The central element of citizenship as represented in *Little Brother* is the way in which it is used to prescribe governance practices. Dobrowolsky and Jenson state that this aspect of citizenship involves the formulation of "democratic rules, including the institutional mechanisms giving access to the state, the modes of participation in civic life and public debate, and the legitimacy of specific types of claims making" (2004: 157). In *Little Brother*, the normal rules of democracy have ceased to operate, as evidenced from the multiple arrests made without proper legal cause. Public debate is not permitted; criticism of government policy is unacceptable; and protests are violently disbanded. But Marcus refuses to be interpellated by the dominant social discourses that demand acquiescence in the face of these political events. Instead, he uses the American Declaration of Independence to support his fury at being silenced and to agitate for political reform:

> Because it seems to me that the founders of this country said that governments should only last for so long as we believe that they're working for us, and if we stop believing in them, we should overthrow them. That's what it says, right?
>
> (Doctorow, 2008b: 73)

Marcus' construction as an agentic subject is assisted by the novel's use of first-person narration, so that readers are intimately aligned with Marcus' subversive point of view. Jolu, one of his friends, dejectedly tells Marcus that it is impossible to fight back against the government (2008b: 31), but Marcus refuses to listen and immediately starts using his programming skills to destabilise the government computer systems designed to spy on citizens. A central idea in Marcus' conceptualisation of government is its democratic obligation to the people, articulated through his belief that the government should be "working for us". Kerry Mallan persuasively argues that the novel's repeated references to the Bill of Rights is "intended to abruptly awaken readers from any self-deceptive dreams of self-mastery or an ideal existence in a democratic society" (2013: 106), but Marcus' expression of his beliefs about government function on more than just the story level. His use of the phrase "working for us" in relation to the government is thematically significant because it connects with an earlier statement made by Marcus in relation to technology, thus linguistically and ideologically linking the concepts of technology and governance (or, more properly, citizenship). The narrative portrays Marcus as a sensitive, bright and articulate young man, but as much as his personal characteristics might help him in his anti-government quest, technology is also awarded a primary role in bringing about the downfall of the security regime that temporarily grips San Francisco. Marcus' computer knowledge is a key facilitator of his subjective agency, and it is here that readers can identify a recurrence (with only a slight grammatical discrepancy) of the "working for us" sentiment:

> The best part of all this is how it made me feel: in control. My technology was working for me, serving me, protecting me. It wasn't spying on me. This is why I loved technology: if you used it right, it could give you power and privacy.
>
> (Doctorow, 2008b: 37)

Marcus may feel some sense of ownership over the computer technology he uses throughout the novel ("my technology"), but Doctorow also endows this technology with human characteristics ("was working for me"). Marcus' relationship with technology is positive and enabling, and it is his ability to work with computers in new and innovative ways (effectively sabotaging government attempts to monitor adolescent behaviour, online and off, and politicising adolescent internet users so that they unite against such government practices) that ultimately helps to save the day.

The interrelationship between technology, subjective agency and civil rights in Doctorow's novel make it a smart counterpoint to the examples of futuristic YA fiction (such as *Ender's Game*) that view hyper-technological environments as potentially damaging for human subjectivity. Technology allows adolescents to participate in civic life in the novel's posthuman world – even if this "participation" is partially constituted out of civic disobedience. As its title suggests, *Little Brother* inverts the technological Big-Brother situation of George Orwell's classic dystopian novel, *Nineteen Eighty-Four* (1949), and the popular TV series named after the dictator in Orwell's novel. The pervasive technological surveillance responsible for disempowering human subjects in *Nineteen Eighty-Four* is, in *Little Brother*, undermined by an ingenious teenage hacker who then uses the same technology to mobilise his peers for protest demonstrations. In short, this "little brother" turns government surveillance on its head. Although Marcus has little power in real life, his technological skills allow him to assert his right to free speech and freedom of movement, and to participate (or intervene) in the processes of governance.

Whereas *Little Brother* harkens back to the Declaration of Independence for its formulation of citizenship as the right to participate in the democratic processes of governance, "Anda's Game" sets out to establish new concepts of citizenship appropriate for online communities. One of the more important strategies it uses to construct an inclusive and egalitarian online environment is its centralisation of feminine subjectivity and experience. The masculine bias traditionally associated with the genre of science fiction (and with technology itself) is evident in both *Ender's Game* and *Little Brother*, where female characters perform only peripheral narrative functions. In "Anda's Game", however, femininity takes centre stage in a narrative that focuses on the adolescent Anda and her experiences with Clan Fahrenheit, a group of online female gamers. "Anda's Game" does not suggest that there are inherent differences between the games that male and female gamers like to play, or in their skill levels. Anda's game of choice is fairly typical of modern video games in that it involves capturing enemies and killing them, but the narrative does intimate that the patriarchal codes and conventions of online gaming might be positively transformed by a collective feminine influence. (I will examine the gender ideology in "Anda's Game" in more detail in Chapter 4.)

"Anda's Game" also contradicts the presumption that virtual reality is a globalised space without national boundaries. Anda and her Fahrenheit teammates may hail from different countries across the globe, but the story specifies that these are all First World countries. Anda herself is British, Lucy (her sergeant) is from the US and Liza, the leader of the Fahrenheits, is Australian. Their virtual world soon reveals its similarities to planet Earth when Anda is confronted by a generic avatar (which is suitably different to her own, fully customised avatar) that plaintively sends her this text: "no porfa necesito mi plata" (Doctorow, 2008a: 182), which translates as "no, please, I need my money". Anda has been ordered to kill the avatar (a mission directive from her sergeant), which she does, but afterwards her curiosity about this strange statement is piqued. She then discovers that her virtual world has become a microcosm of the world that she inhabits physically: the First World has begun to exploit the Third World:

> The bosses used to use bots, but the game has countermeasures against them. Hiring children to click the mouse is cheaper than hiring programmers to circumvent the rules. I've been trying to unionize them because they've got a very high rate of injury.
>
> (2008a: 190)

Anda's initial reaction reflects her lack of power and agency in the physical world, where as a child, she can do little to prevent such capitalist exploitation of Third World workers: "im just a kid, theres nothing I can do about it" (2008a: 190).

The dystopian element of the posthuman setting in "Anda's Game" is the epidemic of childhood obesity sweeping First World nations (although Doctorow has made only minor fictional alterations to a health problem very much evident in modern society). Anda's virtual life of aggressive action thus stands in sharp disjunction to her physical body, which is obese, and her sedentary lifestyle (she sits passively in a chair while playing online). But once Anda regains autonomy over her body, through diet, exercise and medication, she also begins to exercise this subjective agency in the game world. Instead of feeling apathetic about the situation of the players in Mexico, Anda begins to wonder how she might be able to help them. The text accordingly suggests that Anda needs to reconcile the two divergent parts of her life, creating a greater balance and unity between her virtual and "real" subjectivities.

At the heart of "Anda's Game" is the question of what it means to be a global citizen. Doctorow's short story uses virtual reality to explore the moral and ethical responsibilities of individuals and communities in a global context, suggesting that although children may be divested of many citizenship rights in reality, online they can play a significant role in reducing social and economic inequity. Anda achieves such an outcome by alerting her fellow Fahrenheit members to the situation with the Mexican avatars and eventually using her virtual fighting skills to act as a bodyguard for the girls' union leader.

In the period of time that has elapsed between the publication of Card's *Ender's Game* (first published in 1985 and then revised in 1991) and the YA fictions of Doctorow and Cline (published between 2004 and 2013), extensive and far-reaching developments have occurred in digital technology. Computers, in particular, have become an essential part of everyday existence – although the computer revolution has only just begun, according to James Martin, who claims that developments in computer intelligence throughout the twenty-first century will result in "spectacular changes in civilization" (2007: 208). Just what these changes will involve is a matter of speculation, but the six works of YA fiction discussed in this chapter each address the possible social and political transformations that might result from technological developments. In doing so, these fictions necessarily engage with the concept of citizenship, investigating how the rights and duties associated with being a member of a political community might be challenged, eroded or redefined in worlds altered by technological advancement. *Ender's Game* offers a bleak view of child citizenship, suggesting that increases in governmental power, combined with the forces of globalisation, will operate to weaken individual citizenship rights and diminish human subjectivity. Ender's abjection functions as a cruel reminder that children, whose access to citizenship rights is often only partial, will be the most harshly affected by these changes. This dystopian vision of the future is not uncommon in children's literature, which frequently uses hyper-technological, futuristic settings to caution readers about the negative (or even disastrous) impact that an over-reliance on or misuse of technology can have on both societies and individuals. However, while such thematic trends have become established in literature published over the past 20 years, a very recent shift in attitudes to technology is beginning to occur. *Little Brother, Homeland*, "Anda's Game" and *Ready Player One* exemplify this ideological change, in that although each narrative contains dystopian elements, they also construct virtual reality as a communal and empowering space for children and adolescents. More importantly, these narratives engage with the posthumanist concept of subjectivity as networked and de-hierarchised, using their child protagonists' experiences in cyberspace to explore the ways in which virtual reality can offer young people a site from which to explore and exercise the citizenship rights denied to them in the real world.

4
Reworking the Female Subject: Technology and the Body

The legacy of Cartesian mind/body dualism on Western concepts of subjectivity has been an enduring perception of the self as abstract. Identity is thus situated in the brain (or the soul, according to religious discourse) and is separate from the material body. Within this ideological framework, the human body is situated as an object, something to be controlled and dominated but which is not intrinsic to the formation or development of subjectivity. Developments in cognitive science, psychology and continental philosophy in the twentieth century have sought to redress this relegation of the body to a position of inferiority. In particular, the interdisciplinary concept of "embodied cognition" holds that all aspects of cognition are shaped by the processes of the body. The material body has often provided the basis for the exclusionary practices used to construct the unitary humanist subject – and for this reason embodiment is crucial to models of posthumanism that seek to redress such concepts of selfhood. Using the ways in which the body can be transformed and extended by technology as an ideological starting point, Nayar views embodiment as "essential to the construction of the environment (the world is what we perceive through our senses) in which any organic system (the human body is such a system) exists" (2014: 9). A similar vision of embodied posthuman subjectivity is endorsed by Hayles (1999), who argues against the tendency of early articulations of posthumanism to privilege informational pattern over embodiment. She contends instead that the posthuman is a condition that "recognizes and celebrates finitude as a condition of human being, and that understands human life is embedded in a material world of great complexity, one on which we depend for our continued survival" (1999: 5). These representations of the posthuman both place an emphasis on embodiment, contending that the material world and how we experience it is of vital significance – in that it "forces us to recall our own limitations and retain an awareness of our connections to the rest of the world and other beings in it" (Vint, 2007: 183).

The emphasis that critical posthumanism places on embodiment is of particular consequence for female subjects. Women have traditionally been excluded by humanist constructions of the subject, precisely because feminine subjectivity is so closely linked to the physical body and its cultural signification. Elizabeth Grosz's work deals extensively with the marginalising effects of Cartesian mind/body dualism on female subjectivity. While men, conventionally associated with the mind and the value of rationality, remain uninhibited by their bodies, women have historically been associated with their material bodies in a pejorative fashion: "Female sexuality and women's powers of reproduction are the defining (cultural) characteristics of women, and, at the same time, these very functions render women vulnerable, in need of protection or special treatment, as variously prescribed by patriarchy" (Grosz, 1994: 13–14).

Narrative fictions that address adolescent female readers and depict female characters progressing from childhood to adulthood are typically concerned with relations between physical appearance, subjectivity and interpersonal relationships. The role that the female body plays in the production of feminine identity is significant in the context of patriarchal discourses of femininity that seek to prescribe only certain body shapes, physical features and behaviours as desirable. Coming to terms with a body that may not fit within these perimeters is often a vital aspect of maturation within representations of adolescent femininity in YA fiction. This chapter examines the ways in which futuristic fantasy fiction explores the effects of technology on human subjectivity and society, with a particular focus on the female body and feminine subjectivity.

Posthumanism and embodiment

It is important to note at this juncture that early incarnations of posthumanism have not embraced embodiment so readily: in actual fact, cybernetics theory (from which posthumanism originated) actively resists embodiment and continues the humanist tradition of an abstract concept of self. The most famous proponent of this type of cybernetics theory is Hans Moravec, who proposes in *Mind Children: The Future of Robot and Human Intelligence* (1988) that it will eventually be possible for the human mind to be downloaded into a computer. Such a prospect confirms the inferiority of material existence within this framework, suggesting that the body is little more than an "inconvenience":

> The most exemplary advocate of radical disembodiment, Moravec envisioned a postbiological age where the increasing power and sophistication of computer technologies eventually facilitate the downloading of consciousness into computer memory that would survive the mortal physical body. For Moravec, the subject is located and constituted within the pattern of information in the brain, and as such the body is only ever a mechanical conveyance and often an inconvenience.
>
> (Currier, 2002: 522)

Moravec's ideas about mind/body separation have been extremely influential on the genre of cyberpunk, which constructs cyberspace as information-based and therefore inaccessible to the human body. Mind/body dualism likewise underpins transhumanism, which views technology as a means for transcending the limitations of the material human body. Although transhumanism is related to posthumanism in that both discourses are concerned with the impact of technology on human subjectivity, transhumanism does not make any attempt to deconstruct or deprivilege the humanist subject. Cary Wolfe likens transhumanism to the "intensification of humanism" (2010: xv), while Nayar argues that transhumanism "relies on human rationality as a key marker of 'personhood' and individual identity, and sees the body as limiting the scope of the mind" (2014: 6–7). Both Wolfe and Nayar, in the company of other prominent posthuman scholars such as Hayles, Haraway, Vint and Toffoletti, are active campaigners for a form of posthumanism that embraces embodiment, recognising that an emphasis on the material body, as embedded in a material world, is a crucial means through which the destabilisation of the historically privileged humanist subject can occur.

Nayar sums up the importance of embodiment to contemporary posthuman discourse in the following way:

> Critical posthumanism calls attention to the ways in which the machine and the organic body and the human and other life forms are now more or less seamlessly articulated, mutually dependent and co-evolving. It critiques the humanist and transhumanist centrality of reason and rationality (with its fantasies, sustainedly articulated in cyberpunk fiction and cinema, of disembodiment), and offers a more inclusive and therefore ethical understanding of life.
>
> (2014: 8)

Nayar's assessment of embodiment as central to posthuman ideology is something that has generally been overlooked in children's literary criticism. Bradford et al.'s handling of the concept is a case in point, as it elides the significance of the material body and presumes that the posthuman subject is simply represented as "disembodied consciousness" (2008: 168). Beginning with a quote from Hayles, Bradford et al.'s discussion of posthumanism in children's literature identifies one of posthumanism's core assumptions as the principle that "informational pattern is viewed as more significant than material instantiation" (2008: 156). They then proceed to suggest, quoting from Hayles again, that "embodiment has been systematically downplayed or erased within the cybernetic construction of the posthuman in ways that have not occurred in other critiques of the liberal humanist subject" (2008: 158). These cited extracts from Hayles are indeed correct, and Bradford et al. use them to assert that embodiment is subordinated within posthuman ideological frameworks. Such a position ignores, however, the argument that Hayles subsequently develops throughout *How We Became Posthuman* (1999), as well as overlooking the central role that embodiment has come to play in contemporary posthuman discourse. The issue of embodiment is sidelined within their discussion, relevant only to their analysis of *Ferren and the Angel* (2000), a YA novel by Richard Harland. The book tells the story of a fallen angel and her relationship with a "Residual", the name given to the primitive human beings who inhabit the earth. Bradford et al. explain: "As disembodied consciousness, Miriael, the fallen angel, parallels the posthuman subject as it is figured by the cyborg, that is, as consciousness transferred to, or re-embodied within, a machine" (2008: 168). This interpretation of the posthuman subject is limited as it fails to effectively critique the Cartesian concept of mind/body separation (a disembodied consciousness simply reinforces the mind/body split). Bradford et al.'s proceeding analysis does implicitly address the posthuman reconfiguration of an abstract sense of self (in their description of Miriael's gradual taking on of material form), but the relationship between embodiment and posthuman ideology is never clearly explicated.

A more successful investigation of embodiment in the context of posthuman discourse is provided by Kerry Mallan (2011). She draws attention to Donna Haraway's theorising of the cyborg as an organic/mechanic hybrid, which informs my own argument here about representations of femininity in posthuman YA fiction, but also points to what she sees as a deficit in literature that represents cyborgs characters: "despite the liberating cyborg figure that Haraway imagines, more often than not cyborg fictions fail to evade cultural stereotyping, and texts often fall back into clichéd iconography that reproduces conventional gender representations" (Mallan, 2011: 151). This argument builds on Mallan's earlier discussion of gender, embodiment and posthumanism (2009), where she surveys a range of textual representations of cyberspace within which she concludes that "the underlying fantasy is transcendence of the body" (2009: 124). Although the narratives she looks at "raise issues of moral decisions and ontological status with respect to technology and posthumanism" (2009: 124), they remain committed to the principles of liberal humanism in their ideological construction of subjectivity. Contrary to Mallan's contentions about cyborg representations frequently leading to clichéd constructions of gender, and the concomitant reticence of children's texts to engage meaningfully with posthuman models of embodiment, the position that I take here is that novels such as Scott Westerfeld's *Uglies* (2005), Mary E. Pearson's *The Adoration of Jenna Fox* (2008) Cory Doctorow's "Anda's Game" (2004) and Robin Wasserman's *Skinned* (2008) each use various forms of technology to highlight the crucial role that the female body plays in relation to feminine subjectivity. My analysis of these YA fictions draws on Donna Haraway's emancipatory vision of the cyborg in investigating how cyborgian figures destabilise the boundaries between categories such as human/

machine and natural/artificial, and interrogation of the relationship between subjectivity and the body. The novels selected for consideration in this chapter are significant not simply because they endorse posthuman ideology, but because of their reticence to abandon humanism completely. The resulting construction of feminine subjectivity is a hybridised form of humanist and posthuman ideology, and as such these fictions problematise the act of feminine subject formation, questioning what it means to be female (and, indeed, even human) in worlds that have undergone major social transformations as a result of technological change.

In response to scientific discourses that view human consciousness as a disembodied informational pattern – and which thus confirm the Cartesian privileging of the mind over the body – posthuman theorists such as Hayles (1999) and Balsamo (1996) emphasise the centrality of the body in the construction of subjectivity, while they reject postmodern contentions that the body is no more than a linguistic and discursive construct. By looking at how the human body can be technologically transformed – either through biological interventions such as genetic engineering and cloning, cybernetic or surgical modifications, or simply by being interfaced with a machine such as a computer – posthumanism interrogates established ways of understanding and conceptualising the body. Myra J. Seaman suggests that: "posthumanism rejects the assumed universalism and exceptional *being* of Enlightenment humanism and in its place substitutes mutation, variation, and *becoming*" (2007: 247; emphasis in original). Here, then, is a position that might be understood to be at variance with the dominant conceptualisation of selfhood in literature for children and adolescents as liberal humanist.

Haraway uses the figure of the cyborg, a hybrid between machine and organism, to subvert and challenge the essentialism associated with radical feminist politics in the 1980s. She describes the binary relationship between organism and machine as "a border war" (1991: 150), and argues that women, by aligning themselves with the figure of the cyborg, can take "*pleasure* in the confusion of boundaries" and "*responsibility* in their construction" (1991: 150; emphasis in original). For Haraway, the cyborg "has no origin" and "is a creature in a post-gender world" (1991: 150), and thus undermines humanist notions of selfhood as stable, coherent and unitary. More importantly, Haraway's theorising of the cyborg links it with feminine agency. The cyborg has become a central figure in posthumanism because of its subversive hybridity and, since the 1990s, representations of cyborgs have also become increasingly popular in literature produced for adolescent readers. In many of these cases, cyborgian subjectivity is explicitly aligned with femininity and, in these narratives' examination of the effects of technology on feminine perceptions of self, embodiment plays a central role.

As outlined in my discussion of posthuman subjectivity in Chapter 2, the liberal humanist relegation of the body to a position of inferiority in comparison with the mind has become a critical issue in posthumanism. This marginalisation of the body has been particularly disenfranchising for women, among other groups, because, as Vint comments:

> The ability to construct the body as passé is a position available only to those privileged to think of their (white, male, straight, non-working class) bodies as the norm. This option does not exist for those who still need to rely on the work of their bodies to produce the means of survival, for those who lack access to technologies that can erase the effects of illness, and for those whose lives continue to be structured by racist, sexist, homophobic, and other body-based discourses of discrimination.
>
> (2007: 8–9)

Posthumanism is, accordingly, particularly relevant to women and girls, whose bodies have generally functioned as a sign of their "otherness". An obvious intersection between posthumanism and feminism lies in the way that each discourse seeks to deconstruct the essential, unified humanist subject in favour of a more fluid conceptualisation of subjectivity. This shared purpose is apparent in posthuman YA fiction that centres on the processes of identity formation as experienced by female subjects, and how technology can affect such processes. Focusing on the role of embodiment in the construction of adolescent feminine subjectivity, the texts I examine here explore the effects of technology on the female body and pose complex questions about the relationship between mind, body, selfhood and identity. One of the major themes in fiction for children and adolescents concerns the autonomy of the individual self and the quest for agency within a social context. Fictions that are set in a technologically advanced future provide a new system of social institutions and discourses within which to explore the development of subjectivity and the conditions for achieving subjective agency. In fictions produced for children and adolescents, agency is typically conceptualised in humanist terms as the capacity to act autonomously and independently; but the concept itself is not intrinsically linked to humanism. The sense in which I apply it to these texts is Bakhtinian and thus refers to the broad sense in which action can transcend its material context. My examination of these narratives is concerned with the extent to which the technologically advanced social settings of each story can facilitate intersubjective social interactions for female subjects.

The female body: Culture vs nature

The novels selected for discussion in this chapter canvass a range of topics that are pertinent to the impact of technology on feminine subjectivity. Westerfeld's *Uglies* trilogy (2005–2006), of which *Uglies* is the first book, takes issue with the continuing emphasis placed on feminine physical appearance in the modern world, envisioning a future where women and men are forced to undergo extreme cosmetic surgery at the age of 16 to make them uniformly attractive. Doctorow's "Anda's Game" (2004) redresses the prevalence of male characters and masculine points of view in science fiction through its story of a female online gamer and her quest for social and economic equality in the virtual world. Each text rejects the idea of mind/body separation, highlighting the integral role of the body in constructing subjectivity. Yet the way in which these narratives ideologically represent technology is highly oppositional. While "Anda's Game" constructs computer technology as an enabler of subjective agency for young women, *Uglies* takes a more conservative approach by demonising technology. Developments in biotechnology (specifically related to cosmetic body modification) are equated with a loss of agency for both men and women and it is only by returning to the natural world that Tally, the story's 15-year-old heroine, can rebuild her fractured subjectivity. Wasserman's *Skinned* (2009) and Pearson's *The Adoration of Jenna Fox* (2008), which are like *Uglies* in that they are also the first books in series, arguably offer a more provocative and complex representation of feminine subjectivity because they are narrated in the first person by subjects who can more appropriately be classified as cyborgs, rather than as human beings. The novels are strikingly similar: both tell the story of teenage girls who discover that their bodies have been artificially re-created after they were involved in car accidents. Jenna and Lia's awakening after their accidents functions on both a literal and figurative level (each regains consciousness after being in a coma and is also "reborn", to the extent that her mind and body are essentially brand new) and their struggle to define themselves as subjects is a fundamental renegotiation of the mind/body binary. It is important to mention at this point that *Uglies*, *Skinned* and *The Adoration of Jenna Fox* all comprise the first books in YA sci-fi series. The *Uglies* series, which also includes *Pretties* (2005), *Specials* (2006) and the related (but not strictly part of the series) *Extras* (2007), is set in a futuristic and environmentally devastated world where people undergo mandatory cosmetic surgery at the age of 16 in order to become uniformly attractive. Both the *Skinned* trilogy (which is comprised of *Skinned* (2008), *Crashed* (2009) and *Wired* (2010) and has been renamed the *Cold Awakenings* trilogy) and the *Jenna Fox Chronicles* (*The Adoration of Jenna Fox* (2008), *The Fox Inheritance* (2011) and *Fox Forever* (2013)) take cyborgian subjectivity as their focus and each series considers how individual selfhood is affected when the organic human body is replaced with an artificial and mechanistic one. My analysis of the first books of these series must therefore be evaluated in light of the fact that they form part of larger narratives about the dynamic interplay of technology and posthuman subjectivity. Within the scope of this chapter it is not possible to address each entire series, which is why the first books have been chosen as emblematic of the series' main themes and their ideological orientation towards the effects of technology on the body.

Uglies, "Anda's Game", *Skinned* and *The Adoration of Jenna Fox* each address the issue of embodiment and how it affects feminine subject formation, inventively and provocatively using technology for the purpose of posing an array of philosophical questions about the human body and its impact on our concept of self. The resulting thematic exploration of the mind/body relationship in these texts lays bare many of the cultural anxieties surrounding technology and the human body in the modern era. Vint argues that the body functions as a type of threshold, occupying "the liminal space between self and not-self, between nature and culture, between the inner 'authentic' person and social persona" (2007: 16). The body's capacity to disrupt such binary distinctions relating to the definition and construction of selfhood is clearly articulated in each of these YA fictions. Addressing the interaction of the material body with the cultural discourses that allow us as individuals and as a society to make sense of this body, Vint also refers to the anxiety that may result from technological changes to the body, which then amount to the challenge of those categories routinely used to define the human body:

> The human body, like the human subject, is a product of both culture and nature. Both body and subject must maintain a sense of natural and stable boundaries by continually marking out the distance between what is self and what is not. The natural body is maintained through a number of boundary lines: that between male and female bodies, that between my body and the rest of the world, that between the natural body and artificial supplements to this body. These boundaries have always been unstable, and the recent abilities of technology to modify the body in radical ways make anxiety about these boundaries all the more apparent.
>
> (2007: 17)

The YA novels discussed here all represent the human body in a manner that subverts the boundaries of which Vint speaks. In doing so, these texts also reveal a plethora of anxieties about the female body and its relationship to culture. Although *Uglies*, "Anda's Game", *Skinned* and *The Adoration of Jenna Fox* all set out to examine the significance of the female body in the production of feminine identity, they achieve varying degrees of success in challenging conventional ways of thinking about the body (as in mind/body dualism) and in attributing intersubjective agency to embodied female characters.

Uglies offers the most extreme representation of the body as both individual and social in its depiction of an imagined future where people are divided into either "uglies" or "pretties". Although "ugly" is a term that can be used in everyday speech to refer to either women or men, the word "pretties" is much more gendered in the sense that it is generally used only in relation to female bodies. The novel's use of "pretties" as an adjective that has become ungendered in its imagined future is a clever critique of contemporary gender politics: the world has become less fixated on gender difference, but this has not produced the type of gender equality feminists might have hoped for. Instead, the patriarchal discourses that historically acted to limit feminine agency (such as the equation of female physical beauty with goodness and virtue) are now applicable to men as well. In the fictional world of *Uglies*, children and adolescents below the age of 16 are called by the derogatory term of "uglies" because they have yet to undergo compulsory cosmetic surgery. After the surgery has been performed, they are known as "pretties" because their facial and other physical features have been "corrected" to look as symmetrical and aesthetically pleasing as possible. Westerfeld's novel portrays a society that has used fictional advances in biotechnology to formulate and impose a uniform version of physical perfection. This could be construed as an egalitarian step towards social harmony, because as Tally explains in the novel, it means that no one can be considered "privileged because of a random twist in their genes" (Westerfeld, 2005a: 277). However, the novel is clearly critical of the impact of such a practice both on society as a whole and also on individuals. This criticism is conveyed through Tally's exposure to and interactions with the Smokies, a renegade group of individuals living outside the city that is vehemently opposed to the compulsory surgery. These men and women challenge Tally's culturally constructed views regarding her body and its relationship to her subjectivity, as evident from this exchange between Tally and David (the son of the Smokies' founding members):

> 'Listen, Tally. That's not what's important to me. What's inside
>   you matters a lot more.'
> 'But *first* you see my face. You react to symmetry, skin tone, the
>   shape of my eyes. And you decide what's inside me, based
>   on all your reactions. You're programmed to!'
> 'I'm *not* programmed. I didn't grow up in a city.'
> 'It's not just culture. It's evolution!'
>
>   (Westerfeld, 2005a: 278; emphasis in original)

This conversation canvasses a complex range of ideological positions regarding the body and its relationship to the self. David's initial statement frames subjectivity within a liberal humanist model, with the body conceptualised as separate from the mind, which is responsible for producing a unique and individual self.

Tally counters this philosophical notion of the self by referring to science, calling attention to how human beings respond in certain ways to certain facial features (that is, they respond more positively to symmetrical faces). These two positions are diametrically opposed – one discounting the body in the production of identity, the other emphasising its significance in intersubjective social relationships – yet Tally's admonition that David is "programmed" to respond to certain bodily and facial features adds another dimension to this debate. Tally uses the word "programmed" to suggest that it is a biological impulse that prompts humans to respond to facial symmetry, but David quickly indicates that concepts of beauty are also culturally constructed and therefore variable. The irony of Tally's choice of language is that the term "programmed", a word that has come to be associated with computers in the modern digital age, is being used as a metaphor for biology – and in this sense invokes a cyborgian hybridity in the way that the boundaries between nature/artifice and human/machine are linguistically blurred.

This discussion is also noteworthy because of the varied (and conflicting) ideas about embodiment that it raises, but the novel never genuinely offers multiple subject positions from which to evaluate the body and its relationship to human subjectivity. Tally's beliefs about the importance of the body, particularly in the context of social interactions, are effectively invalidated by her discovery that the reasons behind the government's policy of compulsory surgical modification are sinister and self-serving: as well as making its citizens universally attractive, the surgery also affects their brains and renders the general populace docile and complacent. *Uglies* thus constructs a subject position for its readers that is highly critical of Tally's perfection-obsessed society and, accordingly, represents the relationship between technology and human subjectivity as hazardous, debilitating and prone to unethical or irresponsible outcomes.

Nevertheless, the novel's valorisation of Cartesian mind/body dualism is subtly undermined by the representation of the very characters who supposedly advocate a concept of self that is distanced from the physical body: David and his fellow Smokies. This is because of the way in which the Smokies' corporeality is constantly emphasised in Tally's focalisation of them. She describes their leader as "wrinkled, veined, discoloured" (2005a: 197) and upon touching David's hand, feels that it is "as rough as the wood grain of the table in the dining hall" (2005a: 217). She also reflects upon their physical strength and huge appetites (2005a: 207), repeatedly focusing the reader's attention on the physicality of these particular characters. As the novel is primarily focalised by Tally, her point of view necessarily reflects the ideologies about the desirability of physical perfection with which she has been indoctrinated. At the same time, the almost exaggerated corporeality of the Smokies (as perceived by Tally) disrupts the narrative's attempts to endorse the liberal humanist view (as articulated by the Smokies) that the body is irrelevant to the production of identity. As such, in the fictional future in which *Uglies* is set, there is a pronounced confusion between "what is self and what is not". The surgically enhanced bodies of people in Tally's world all look physically similar, but they also behave in a corresponding fashion because their brains have been affected by the operation. The differences between male and female bodies are also less overt – or perhaps less relevant – because the quest for physical perfection, an established attribute of patriarchal discourses of femininity, is reconstructed as a gender-neutral and collective desire. Technological interference with the natural human body results in the diminishing of subjective agency, as individuality is all but erased. Differences between "my body and the rest of the world", as expressed by Vint, are in effect eradicated in *Uglies*. The compulsory operation is performed under the auspices of the state to ensure that the population is homogeneous, rather than heterogeneous. The only boundaries specified by Vint that are maintained throughout the novel are the differences between the natural body and artificial supplements to this body – and this is because of the hierarchical way in which Tally's society is structured. Tally's focalisation helps to maintain this hierarchy, because as an "ugly" her status is that of a marginalised outsider. However, she yearns for her own physical transformation and an end to what she calls her "ugly purgatory" (Westerfeld, 2005a: 128). Her experiences with the Smokies gradually change her point of view, but also act to strengthen the binary relationship between natural and organic human bodies (Tally and the Smokies) and the unnatural, technologically altered bodies of the "pretties".

Technology and feminine empowerment

"Anda's Game", *Skinned* and *The Adoration of Jenna Fox* each investigate the role that technology can play in challenging conventional definitions of "the body", differentiating themselves from *Uglies* in that they construct technology as potentially liberating for female subjects. In concentrating on the effects of technology on the female body and feminine subjectivity, they also actively disrupt those patriarchal discourses that conventionally associate technology with masculinity. These novels illustrate Haraway's assertions about the fundamental ways in which technology transforms the world, in that the "difference between machine and organism is thoroughly blurred; mind, body and tool are on very intimate terms" (1991: 165). In *The Adoration of Jenna Fox*, the distinction between the organic and artificially constructed components of Jenna's body is deliberately ambiguous. Although readers are told that only 10 per cent of her brain could be recovered (Pearson, 2009: 117), the novel's use of first-person narration means that readers are only able to access Jenna's point of view – and the issue of which parts of Jenna are authentic or original, and which have been re-created or rebuilt, is impossible for her to resolve. Jenna's reflections on this very question consequently perform a key function in the representation of her subjectivity. The same is true of *Skinned*, although this novel appropriates Hans Moravec's concept of downloading human consciousness into a machine: none of Lia's new body or brain is organic. While Lia is perhaps less self-reflexive about her subjectivity than Jenna, the novel uses her status as cyborg to draw parallels with historical discourses of "othered" femininity (such as the social marginalisation of witches in the Middle Ages). Lia's artificial body negates her formerly privileged social status as a wealthy white woman, but it is only by becoming an abject subject that she can actively reconstruct her identity in more intersubjective terms.

"Anda's Game", *Skinned* and *The Adoration of Jenna Fox* also accord with Susan Honeyman's views about the ways in which science-fiction narratives can empower adolescent readers. The adolescent protagonists of these texts are embodied female subjects who are remarkably adept at using technology to assist in self-transformation, and speak to Honeyman's claim that in science fiction, "children become the vehicle for the improvement of the species – emblems of what we are striving, whether consciously or not, to become" (2004: 353). These narratives thus make a substantial investment in their adolescent female protagonists, suggesting that the nature of their relationship with technology is emblematic of the empowerment that technology can potentially engender for women.

Skinned offers the most overt meditation on the limitations of the humanist subject, as it makes repeated reference to the Cartesian paradigm of mind/body dualism. The novel opens with a parody of humanist rationalism that immediately invokes the transgressive figure of the cyborg and its propensity to subvert established categories of being – in this case, the difference between being alive and dead:

> Lia Kahn is dead.
> I am Lia Kahn.
> Therefore – because this is a logic problem even a
>   dim-witted child could solve – I am dead.
> Except, here's the thing: I'm not.
>
> (Wasserman, 2008: 1)

Lia's use of deductive reasoning in this opening foregrounds the novel's thematic exploration of posthuman subjectivity in its demonstration that humanist principles of reason cannot be applied to the hybridic and ambiguous figure of the cyborg. As is the case with *The Adoration of Jenna Fox*, the use of first-person narration in *Skinned* restricts the novel's ability to destabilise in a radical fashion the humanist concept of a unified and autonomous self (a cohesive narrative is, after all, constructed out of Lia's perceptions), but the novel places a much greater emphasis on the role of the body in the reconstruction of Lia's subjectivity. It achieves this through Lia's realisation that her human body has been replaced by a completely artificial one, and her experience of this is defined by profound loss:

> It wasn't even that I couldn't *feel* my legs. It was that, with
>   my eyes closed, I couldn't have said whether I had legs or not.
> Or arms.
> Or anything.
> *I think therefore I am*, I thought with a wave of giddiness. I would
>   have giggled, but I couldn't feel my mouth.
>
> (2008: 2, emphasis in original)

This passage is an excerpt of Lia's first thoughts as she regains consciousness after her "download procedure", and it demonstrates how these thoughts all revolve around her body (or lack of one). Her focalisation becomes increasingly anxious because of her loss of sensory perceptions: not only can she not feel her legs, but she cannot see them either, leading her to question the exact nature of her existence. This phenomenological perspective of subjectivity as defined by experience and perception is decidedly at odds with the humanist concept of self as based on reason and science. Lia's subsequent quotation of Descartes' famous dictum, "I think therefore I am", is accompanied by an assertion of how her body would have ordinarily reacted to such a statement ("giggled"). The choice of the verb "giggled" is indicative of the body's ability to convey emotional states, but it also points to Lia's perception of Cartesian mind/body separatism as worthy of ridicule – and the combination of these effects works to resituate the body, calling attention to its role in both personal expression and communication. Lia's organic human body has been destroyed, so it is not possible for it to be "restored" in any sense; the narrative suggests that the only way for her to recuperate a meaningful sense of self (that is, one that is not defined by loss and abjection) is to embrace her new material form and to acknowledge its difference from her previous, organic body.

The Adoration of Jenna Fox also explores the interaction of mind and body in the development of subjectivity, making a detailed study of how subjectivity is manifest through the physical body (which in Jenna's case has been almost entirely re-created using technology, constituting it as "artificial" instead of natural or organic). One of Jenna's first conscious memories after waking from her coma is of overhearing a comment made by her grandmother, who has been frightened by the cries Jenna first made after opening her eyes: "It sounds like an animal" (Pearson, 2009: 4). Lily's refusal to use the personal pronoun "she" when referring to Jenna makes it clear that she does not perceive Jenna to be a girl, or even a human being. The sounds that Jenna's body produces are "non-human" according to Lily's use of the pronoun "it", and Lily continues to regard Jenna with suspicion and hostility. Jenna herself feels at once alienated and separate from those around her, and the body and world she inhabits feel both strange and new. Nothing is recognisable to her – she cannot remember her past life and has forgotten the meaning of certain words (2009: 6) and common human behaviours, such as physical expressions of emotion, like smiling (2009: 1). Jenna's physical body plays a key role in this process, yet it is largely her body's failure to conform to the traditional definitions of what a human body is and how it should function – Jenna's gait is unnatural (2009: 64), living creatures such as birds are afraid of her (2009: 50) and she cannot digest organic food (2009: 35) – that informs her newly emergent sense of self. The strangeness of Jenna's body is clearly perceptible to others, as is made clear by her grandmother's open hostility, her parents' exaggerated assurances that there is nothing wrong with her and the responses of her classmates to her "oddness". Their discomfort in Jenna's presence conveys the cultural angst that is typically generated in the face of human bodies that transgress established categories of being.

The role of technology in female subject formation

The human body is not clearly defined in "Anda's Game", *Skinned* or *The Adoration of Jenna Fox*. Indeed, these narratives strive to blur traditional definitions of what constitutes the natural human body and what does not. Anda, Lia and Jenna are acutely aware of their bodies, an awareness that is chiefly born from the recognition that these physical forms transgress the conventional standards of how human bodies should look and behave. The transgressive or uncontrollable elements of each young woman's physical appearance are attributable to technology: Jenna and Lia's surgically altered, cyborgian bodies are a direct product of technological intervention, while Anda's obese body is the result of physical inactivity occasioned by long periods spent in a virtual, computer-generated reality. When exploring the role that the body plays in the construction of subjectivity, these fictions pay particular attention to the ways in which the human body is gendered. "Anda's Game" focuses on the feminist issue of body size in its portrayal of an adolescent girl whose subjectivity is radically fractured: in the virtual world of online gaming Anda's avatar is a strong and powerful warrior, but in the real world her body is actually morbidly obese. Doctorow's text revolves around the process that enables Anda to achieve a coherent subjectivity – reconciling the shame and self-loathing that characterise her subjectivity in the real world with the sense of empowerment she feels in the virtual world.

Skinned and *The Adoration of Jenna Fox*, on the other hand, lay bare the process of feminine subject formation as Lia and Jenna struggle to (re)construct their selfhood. In *The Adoration of Jenna Fox*, language clearly plays an integral role, but the novel places equal emphasis on the body in the production of feminine identity. Jenna's emergent sense of self is based entirely on sensory perceptions, as her "installed" memories seem to have little connection with the world she experiences, as if she is a newborn baby. *Skinned*, on the other hand, creates analogies between cyborg subjectivity and the discourses of discrimination that have precluded certain social groups from humanist constructs of selfhood, such as women and people of non-white racial origin. The "otherness" that suddenly defines Lia's life is used to undermine what have come to be understood as traditional modes of identity development for women. These include a preoccupation with physical appearance, the initiation of (hetero)sexual desire and a conception of feminine identity as collective, rather than individual. *Skinned* uses Lia's non-human, cyborg status to undermine and transform such paradigms. Both of these YA novels are connected through their use of the cyborg body to defamiliarise the relationship between mind and body, and by doing so each one queries conventional models of female subject development.

In "Anda's Game", the computer is represented as an extension of Anda's self, and the way that she thinks and behaves while online plays a crucial role in the construction of her subjectivity. It is a positive tale of how virtual reality can function as a site of social co-operation for young adolescent women. Yet this story does not advocate a total retirement from the real world. Instead it suggests that the physical human body is of equal importance to the mind, and it is only when Anda can reconcile the virtual and "real" aspects of herself that she can achieve an agentic subjectivity. Contrary to popular assumptions about virtual reality constituting a site that is divorced from physical reality, "Anda's Game" specifically draws attention to the role of the body within this fantasy or "non-realistic" setting. Instead of associating virtual reality with fantastically exaggerated versions of the human body (as tends to happen in masculine online gaming environments, which are populated with impossibly proportioned female characters such as Lara Croft), the lure of Anda's particular online game is that it offers a more realistic alternative: "Anda didn't really start to play the game until she got herself a girl-shaped avatar. When Anda was twelve, she met Liza the Organisa, whose avatar was female but had sensible tits and sensible armor and a bloody great sword that she was clearly very good with" (Doctorow, 2008a: 173). Anda's avatar is described as "girl-shaped" rather than "female", a phrase that emphasises the parallels between Anda and the fictional character that represents her in the online gaming world (and suggests that the avatar physically resembles a young girl, rather than an adult woman). Doctorow's repeated use of the term "sensible", which is applied to both the breasts and armour of Liza's avatar, humorously references the visual appearance of female characters in computer games – which is usually blatantly sexual due to their exaggeratedly large mammary glands and skimpy, impractical clothing. However, the story's thematic exploration of the female body and its cultural signification is not confined to virtual reality. "Anda's Game" simultaneously draws attention to the female body as it exists in the "real" world, contrasting the highly active and authoritative behaviour of Anda's avatar with the physical reality of her human body: she is overweight and what she refers to as her "podge" (the ring of fat around her belly) (2008a: 183) continues to grow as a result of her passive and unhealthy lifestyle. Because body size is an important Western signifier of social value and status, "women and girls face far more stringent standards of appearance than their male counterparts, so that normal, healthy body types, not just obesity, create social disadvantages" (Crosnoe et al., 2008: 1191). But rather than focusing on Anda's weight as an explicitly feminine and feminist issue, the text treats the issue of body size from the angle of health and mental well-being and suggests that, as Anda loses weight, the gap closes between her body in real life and "in-game".

Body and subjectivity are immediately and intimately connected in "Anda's Game", as the narrative pivots on the disjunction between Anda's real body and her virtual one and how these differences affect her subjectivity. The self-loathing and shame that Anda feels in relation to her physical body – "Liza came to school after PE, when Anda was massaging her abused podge and hating her entire life" (Doctorow, 2008a: 173) – subside when she is gaming. In this digital world her "body" is capable of doing almost anything she wants it to: "She reached the fifth man as he was trying to draw his dirk and dagger and lopped his bloody head off in one motion, then backflipped off the high branch, trusting to her shield to stay intact for her impact on the cottage roof" (2008a: 179). Anda can not only wield a sword with great skill and perform acrobatic feats with ease, but she can fight on equal terms with her male opponents. The text's construction of the digital world as a space in which young women can experience empowerment on both an individual and collective level is underpinned, however, by an acknowledgement that virtual reality is not a substitute for real life. Indeed, Anda can only achieve intersubjective agency when she is able to unite the two disparate elements of her subjectivity (the virtual and the real). Once she embarks on a process to heal her physical body (eating healthily, exercising and taking medication for the type of obesity-related diabetes she has developed), Anda's emergent sense of well-being and competency also manifests itself in her online existence. Her initial response to the discovery that multinational companies have begun to exploit underage girls in the Third World, forcing them to play the game in unbearable conditions and for very little pay, reflects her lack of power and agency in the physical world where, as a child, she can do little to prevent such capitalist exploitation of Third World workers: "im just a kid, theres nothing I can do about it" [sic] (Doctorow, 2008a: 190). Nevertheless, as she begins to take responsibility for her body (and self) in the real world, her developing subjectivity also becomes apparent in the digital context. The process of healing her physical body is mirrored in her attempts to "heal" the online world. Joining together with her Clan Fahrenheit members, she takes action to stop the oppression of these young women, an intersubjective gesture designed to restore a sense of equality and community to the digital world.

The role of the body in relation to subjectivity is made even more explicit in *The Adoration of Jenna Fox*, because Jenna awakes from her coma with no knowledge of who she is or what has happened to her. If subjectivity is constructed dialogically, as Bakhtin suggests, through interactions and exchanges with other selves, then Jenna has no basis on which to form her sense of self. When Jenna awakes from the coma she has no memory of her previous life (she has yet to "retrieve" these memories), so she depends on her body to help reconstruct her identity: her thoughts all revolve around what she has observed, heard and touched. Instead of communicating principally through language (which is difficult for Jenna because she cannot remember the meaning of certain words), Jenna's focus is the body – her own and those belonging to other people: "She puts her arm around me and squeezes. I lift the corner of my mouth. Then the other: a smile. Because I know I am supposed to. This is what she wants" (Pearson, 2009: 1). This interaction with her mother makes it clear that Jenna understands how and when it is appropriate to use the body to communicate with others. Her detachment and lack of spontaneity, however, are produced by the absence of an intersubjective relationship with the woman she recognises as her mother, but of whom she has no memories. The social construction of subjectivity is usually an implicit or invisible process, but in Jenna's case this process becomes transparent. She regularly practises moving her body, trying to make it look like the other bodies around her and hence emphasising that the physical gestures we take for granted as being "natural" might actually be culturally produced; acquired instead of inherent. The novel thus reflects the claim made by Elizabeth Grosz that the human body is a product of social and cultural discourses: "the body, or rather, bodies, cannot be adequately understood as ahistorical, precultural or natural objects in any simple way; they are not only inscribed, marked, engraved, by social pressures external to them but are the products, the direct effects, of the very social constitution of nature itself" (Grosz, 1994: x). Jenna's new cyborg body is, consequently, unmarked by the cultural discourses that conventionally act upon a body throughout its existence and render certain cultural ideologies as "natural". Her "otherness" as a cyborgian subject is produced through her body's unfamiliarity with the cultural discourses of femininity, for example, making it impossible for her to perform the role of daughter as desired by her mother.

Skinned offers its readers a less contemplative representation of Lia's attempts to negotiate her manufactured body, owing to her experience of this material form only in terms of deficiency and loss. For Lia, at least initially, the loss of her organic body serves to construct her as an abject subject:

They turn me off at night – I'm supposed to call it "sleep", but why bother? – and turn me on in the morning... Asa monitors me, Asa dresses me. Asa turns me off and on, and off again. It's how I know one day has passed. And another. I play catch with Asa and I stare at the ceiling and I wait and I try not to wonder whether I would rather be dead or whether I already am.

(Wasserman, 2008: 44)

Although this passage is closely focalised by Lia, she constructs herself as an interpellated subject. She has no agency or control over what happens to her (and here her lack of selfhood is constituted primarily because she has no connection to her body), indicated by the combination of the impersonal pronoun "they" (which later reverts to the name of her therapist, "Asa") and the sentence structure that repeatedly positions her as an object ("me"). The repetition that characterises this extract and its meandering construction, especially of the last sentence with its repeated use of the conjunction "and", serve to construct Lia's existence as one that is passive and lifeless. This idea is concretised when she leaves hospital and finds herself confronted by an angry mob of protesters, whose vehement objection to her new status as a cyborg draws on the historical discourse of religious persecution to which witches were subjected in the Middle Ages. Vilified because their bodies and behaviour transgressed patriarchal codes for femininity, these women were denounced by the all-powerful Church as heretical. Once branded with the name of "witch" such women were often murdered or executed. *Skinned* appropriates this discourse in its representation of the public hostility that Lia's body generates:

"An abomination! We shall all be punished for her sins!"

(2008: 84)

GOD MADE MAN. WHO MADE YOU?
FRANKENSTEIN ALWAYS BURNS.

(2008: 86)

The reference to Frankenstein on the protesters' banners is especially pertinent, given that the novel of this name written by Mary Shelley – the full title of which is *Frankenstein; or, The Modern Prometheus* (1818) – has often been interpreted as a feminist critique of science. This literary allusion creates a double-barrelled effect: on the one hand it casts Lia as a monster who has been created by an unethical scientist; but on the other it positions her as a character with whom women might emphathise (as they have with Shelley's tragic creation), possessing a body that is deemed "unnatural" and "uncontrollable" in accordance with the way female bodies have regularly been positioned by patriarchal discourses throughout history. Facing much more extreme opposition and hostility than Jenna (she is also ultimately rejected by her family because she fails to give an authentic performance of the Lia they knew), Lia's response is to seek out other cyborg subjects like herself, and it is her interactions with this marginalised group of "skinners" (the pejorative name used by humans to refer to these cyborg subjects) that gradually enable her to progress away from her alienated state.

Posthuman reconfigurations of the female body

The relationship between physical appearance and feminine subjectivity remains one of paramount importance in the modern era, where "the aestheticization of the body is, in our culture, the very core of being a woman" (Ganetz, 1995: 92). The motif of the female "make-over" is enduringly popular in literature and films directed at adolescent girls, where it frequently functions as a metonym for subjective agency (Stephens, 1999). Both *Skinned* and *The Adoration of Jenna Fox* disrupt the conventional paradigm of feminine identity development as it relates to the female face and body, each novel attempting to resignify how the female body contributes to the production of feminine subjectivity. *Skinned* takes a rather radical approach to this issue, as Lia's anxiety about her new mechanical body is manifest in evasion: she simply tries to ignore its existence. While once she was obsessed with clothes and looking attractive, she now loses interest in her exterior appearance: "I stayed away from mirrors" (Wasserman, 2008: 95). But this evasiveness does not mean that her body becomes irrelevant: on the contrary, the novel constructs the concept of pain as the primary means through which Lia is able to renegotiate a relationship between her mind and body. Pain is also what unites the marginalised cyborg community: their experience of extreme pain confirms their "otherness", as such pain does not affect a mechanical body in the same way it does an organic one. Although the physical sensation of pain is real, the cyborg body is designed to withstand any kind of accident or malfunction, as it is made of replaceable parts. The attraction of pain, therefore, is that it takes the body to the limits of its endurance – and in the context of a cyborg body, these limits can be continually pushed. Pain is closely related to posthuman conceptualisations of embodiment because, as Leigh Gilmore argues in her study of pain as it relates to the practice of life-writing, it affects the production of identity. She suggests that sufferers of chronic pain produce narratives of their experiences that interrogate humanist concepts of a unitary and autonomous self, because: "pain emerges at the boundaries of selves, and calls for ways of representing identity when one is interpenetrated and altered by disease and pain. Relationality emerges as an important focus here as pain shapes the relationships we have to our bodies and with others" (2012: 84). The relationality that pain engenders in *Skinned* functions as a key tool in the (re)formation of Lia's subjectivity. Pain enables Lia to engage with her mechanical body for the first time, as it creates a sensory experience that finally creates a link between her mind and body.

Lia experiences pain as a relinquishing of control, which again accentuates the novel's ideological opposition to the humanist concept of an autonomous subject. Her narration also acknowledges that language is inadequate for expressing the physical sensations that she has endured:

> It was just another thing I couldn't explain to him, the way it felt to go over the falls, to know that I had absolutely no control and to just let it happen, let myself fall – and to survive.
>
> (Wasserman, 2008: 321)

The absence of detailed experiential description in Lia's narration of this event is incongruous with its eventual significance within the narrative (it enables her to repair her fractured relationship with Auden, the one friend she has made since becoming a cyborg but whose romantic advances she has rejected, and also cements her ties with the cyborg community), but it is precisely this lack of linguistic explanation that best conveys the body's unique contribution to the production of identity.

The female body takes centre stage in *The Adoration of Jenna Fox*, although the body subject to scrutiny in this novel is notable primarily because of its dysfunction. Jenna's experience of moving her body, and her attempts to practise moving it in such a way that it looks similar to other bodies, are indeed constituted as a type of performance and, as such, can be interpreted as an illustration of non-representational theory. Non-representational theory is a critique of representation, so to speak, which focuses on processes of performance and enactment. Embodied expression and affect are central to the construction of Jenna's subjectivity, yet her attempts to narrate and represent the precise nature of how her physical movements are strange and unconventional – or what she must do in order to correct them – are vague and indistinct. While her narration stresses the importance of her body in constructing her subjectivity, she is extremely inarticulate in specifying how this is achieved. This idea of performance being unpredictable and even unknowable is acknowledged by Nigel Thrift, who writes that performance "is unwritable, unsayable, and unstable. And that is its fascination: it is a living demonstration of skills we have but cannot ever articulate fully in the linguistic domain" (2008: 138). Jenna's philosophical narration frequently ponders existential questions about the nature of being – "How many definitions of *human* can one person find? And how do you know which one is correct?" (Pearson, 2009: 128; emphasis in original) – yet her mind is unable to provide the answers she so desperately seeks. Instead it is her body that plays the primary role in the construction of her subjectivity – alerting her to her own oddness, but simultaneously demonstrating that she can learn to behave like other human beings. Jenna gradually learns to assert herself as an autonomous subject not through language (over which she has an inexpert command) but with her body. Determined to disobey her grandmother and parents, Jenna expresses her anger with actions: she slams kitchen drawers, smashes plates and deliberately eats organic food, which her parents have told her is strictly forbidden. The occasions on which Jenna conquers her fears about who she is and how to make sense of the world are directly attributable to bodily experiences:

> Our kisses grow heated, and everything that is curious and odd and funny and wrong about me disappears and I am no longer thinking about me, but everything about Ethan, because the warmth of Ethan, the scent of Ethan, the touch of Ethan, is all about who I am *now* ...
>
> (Pearson, 2009: 100; emphasis in original)

This kiss also functions as an expression of intersubjectivity, as indicated by the use of the pronoun "our" and also by Jenna's momentary ability to project her attention and empathy outwards, focusing all of her attention on the "otherness" of a different human being.

Pearson's use of a cyborgian figure as the narrator-focaliser of her novel enables a rich and complex ideological construction of subjectivity – particularly since the employment of first-person narration (in both the prose and poetry components of the text) means that readers are already intimately aligned with Jenna's character before it is revealed that she is not quite human. Embodiment plays a central role in Jenna's sense of self, as indicated above, but cognition is equally important to her subjective development. Jenna's artificially created brain does not function in the same way as human brains, making the development of her subjectivity a process that destabilises conventional models of subject formation. Although she initially has no recollection of her past, memories gradually start to come back – but they are "unnatural" ones: Jenna clearly remembers the sound of her mother's heartbeat from when she was a foetus (Pearson, 2009: 173), for instance. And while she has forgotten the meaning of certain words, she can easily recall information that has been specifically "uploaded" into her mind (such as data about historical events). Jenna's disjointed memories and abnormal brain processes accordingly produce a form of subjectivity that directly challenges the humanist concept of selfhood as unified and coherent. Further, Jenna's concept of selfhood throughout the novel is constantly measured against the person that she thinks she might have been prior to the accident. This causes Jenna to reflect on the issue of authenticity, as she wonders whether the 10 per cent of original "brain matter" uploaded into her new brain has created a genuine version of Jenna Angeline Fox or a replica, which is both similar to and different from the original: "Which is the real me? The one in the closet or the one here on the forest floor?" (Pearson, 2009: 188). The novel innovatively uses the idea of technological body modification to embrace the fragmented and fluid subjectivity associated with posthumanity.

It must be pointed out, however, that neither *The Adoration of Jenna Fox* nor *Skinned* is able to abrogate the liberal humanist concept of selfhood entirely. The focus of both novels on embodiment is predominantly underscored because both Jenna and Lia's subjectivities are constructed exclusively through their first-person narration. Their subjectivities are therefore represented purely through language.

The Adoration of Jenna Fox is more reluctant to abandon humanist assumptions about selfhood than *Skinned*, as demonstrated in the novel's closure: Jenna's final act of rebellion against her parents is to destroy the computer back-up of her original brain, legitimising the humanist notion of subjectivity as essential and unique, rather than plural or divided. Nevertheless, Jenna's behaviour does suggest that individual subjectivity is not static or fixed but in a constant process of transformation, a construction of subjectivity that reflects posthuman ideology. She is aware that subjectivity is socially constructed, pointing out in the novel's conclusion: "The world has changed. So have I" (Pearson, 2009: 248). This conclusion is also significant because it takes place 260 years after the date on which Jenna was "re-created". Jenna reveals that she now has a daughter, Kayla, who has Ethan's "coloring, wit, love of literature and sometimes his temper" (2009: 251) – but obviously Kayla's birth was in no sense "natural". Despite this, Jenna's attitude to Kayla is overwhelmingly maternal: "My breaths begin and end with her" (2009: 251). Jenna's identification of herself as a mother is of interest here, chiefly because the figure of the cyborg generally repudiates any sense of natural gestation or birth. Instead, the cyborg is representative of ectogenesis (conception outside the womb), as noted by Susan Merrill Squier, and the "denial of the relationship between fetus and gestating woman" (1994: 95) is one reason why women might choose to reject the cyborg as a liberatory symbol. The specific articulation of a mother–daughter relationship between Jenna and Kayla in this novel, even if such a relationship is not biological, is decidedly posthuman in its redistribution of human behaviours and roles to non-human subjects. The novel uses the cyborgian character of Jenna to destabilise traditional ideologies of identity, suggesting that technology can produce radically new ways of being in the world.

The female body's engagement with technology is a topic that offers limitless ways of rethinking concepts of the self. The three YA narratives discussed here reflect upon the significance of the body and the self within technologically advanced societies. *Uglies*, *Skinned* and *The Adoration of Jenna Fox* use advances in biotechnology and the concept of body modification as a context for exploring the relationship between subjectivity and the body, while "Anda's Game" contrasts the unlimited freedom of the body in virtual, computer-generated worlds with a more sombre physical reality (the human body in a state of disease as a result of the Western lifestyle), evaluating the impact of this split on individual subjectivity. In examining the impact of technology on the status of both the body and the self, these YA fictions engage with the ideologies associated with posthumanism, which is similarly concerned with how technology produces "reworkings of the subject" (Toffoletti, 2007: 165). In particular, the narratives discussed here focus on the female body by addressing the issue of whether technology is empowering or oppressive for the female subject. The intersection of technology and feminine subject formation yields varied results in each of the focus texts. *Uglies* ultimately confirms the traditional humanist paradigm of mind/body dualism, yet employs certain representational strategies (such as Tally's point of view) that simultaneously destabilise this conceptualisation of subjectivity. "Anda's Game", *Skinned* and *The Adoration of Jenna Fox*, on the other hand, demonstrate an explicit awareness of the limitations of humanist constructions of the subject for women and girls. These texts represent technology as both enabling and empowering for female subjects, and in doing so endorse the posthuman conceptualisation of subjectivity as fragmented and plural, with a focus on the processes of becoming (rather than being). At the same time, however, none of these YA narratives is prepared to abandon humanism entirely. Their eventual representation of feminine subjectivity is consequently constructed dialogically, drawing from both humanist and posthuman discourses. These YA fictions make a significant contribution to feminist thought in the sense that they demonstrate how narratives produced for adolescents attempt to make sense of feminist ideology relating to embodiment and technology, creatively (and often provocatively) asking important questions about what it means to be a young woman living in a technological age.

5
Surveillance Societies: Privacy and Power in YA Fiction

Noga Applebaum (2010) and Farah Mendlesohn (2009) both argue that science-fiction writing for children overwhelmingly endorses an anti-technology position, depicting technology as a "corrupting force" (Applebaum, 2010: 1) that must be carefully monitored and controlled. This chapter takes specific issue with this notion, using the subject of surveillance and its portrayal in five works of YA fiction to propose that an emerging group of contemporary authors is exploring in complex and innovative ways the concept of what it means to live in a "surveillance society": either by envisaging empowered responses to oppressive forms of surveillance or considering the concept of "participatory surveillance", a term designed to describe an individual's willing submission to surveillance through online activities such as shopping and social networking. These narratives suggest that adolescent subjects are supremely adept at engaging and interacting with digital media. Further, as a result of being exposed to digital technologies since birth – an exposure that determines technological proficiency – these narratives imply that children and adolescent subjects may conceive of surveillance differently to adults. The concept of "private space" has undergone multiple transformations over the past 30 years, owing to the significant impact of digital technologies such as computers and the internet on human life. The ubiquity of modern-day surveillance is intensely evident in the way that these narratives treat the concept of being watched and monitored. Rather than trying to escape or overthrow surveillance regimes, the most noteworthy aspect of these novels is their desire to educate readers about surveillance and its varied purposes. Such stories suggest that individuals can choose to be agentic – not inter-pellated – surveillance subjects, thus reshaping a concept that has conventionally been associated with disempowerment.

If posthumanism is an ideology that investigates the myriad ways in which technology has become entwined in the production of human subjectivity (Hayles, 1995, 1999; Bukatman, 1993), then the concept of electronic surveillance offers an ideal arena for an explo-ration of the effects of technology on concepts of selfhood. Foucault's seminal theorising of surveillance in his discussion of the panopticon (which remains pervasive in modern surveillance discourses) revolves around the idea that prisoners in this particular model of a jail would be visible at all times, and that the awareness of being watched would "induce in the inmate a state of conscious and permanent visibil-ity that assures the automatic functioning of power" (1977: 201). The notion of "being watched" has been almost totally transformed by digital technology in the modern age, to the extent that writ-ers such as Roger Clark (1988) and David Lyon (2006) have used the term "dataveillance" to denote the shift from surveillance as it has been traditionally performed by human beings to the much more omnipresent type of monitoring that can be achieved by digi-tal technologies such as computers and CCTV. The varied nature and function of modern surveillance, coupled with its increasing ubiq-uity, undermines some of the central tenets that underpin Foucault's work. Kevin Haggerty suggests that Foucauldian models of surveil-lance need to be critically re-evaluated, particularly in the context of assertions that surveillance "serves a single coherent purpose, such as 'social control'" (2006: 28). Haggerty asserts that:

> Outside of the prison, surveillance is used for a plethora of projects, including deterrence, consumption, entertainment, titil-lation, health promotion, education, governance, accountability, child-rearing and military conquest (Haggerty, 2006; Dandeker 1990). While surveillance regimes are designed with particular purposes in mind, they often evolve in unanticipated ways. Uses are not necessarily established in advance, but are emergent, resulting from the creative insights of individuals who envision novel possibilities for systems developed for entirely different purposes.
>
> (2006: 28)

Haggerty's comments are germane to my reading of surveillance as it is represented in literature for adolescents. The following YA novels illustrate the widespread nature and function of contemporary surveillance, each envisioning the act of surveillance as performed by different subjects or institutions and for divergent purposes: *Feed* (2002), by M.T. Anderson, provides a satirical examination of the interpellating effects of corporate surveillance on individual consumers; *Little Brother* (2008), by Cory Doctorow, explicitly references George Orwell's *Nineteen Eighty-Four* (1949) in its critical depiction of intrusive government surveillance; *The Hunger Games* (2008), by Suzanne Collins, the first book of the hugely popular YA series, draws on the discourse of reality television programmes and offers readers a surprisingly complex representation of surveillance as both an aspect of institutional power and public voyeurism; *Useful Idiots* (2004), by Jan Mark, is a futuristic fantasy that uses the concept of race to explore the relationship between marginalised subjectivities and surveillance; and *serafina67 *urgently requires life** (2008) (referred to hereafter as *serafina67*), by Susie Day, is a novel written in blog format, which reveals how cyberspace encourages individuals to voluntarily offer up parts of their lives for public surveillance.

These five novels have been selected as the corpus for this chapter because they canvass the broad range of responses that surveillance can occasion – responses that range from outrage and hostility to acceptance and then, perhaps, pleasure and satisfaction (in relation to the act of blogging and its construction of an online audience). More importantly, however, these fictions function as a representation of the experiences of people who are the subjects of surveillance. In terms of policing and social sorting, surveillance functions as an act of power. It therefore stands to reason that children, who are generally less empowered than adults, are most typically in the position of being watched, rather than doing the watching themselves. Children's fiction, which uses child characters as narrators and focalisers, thus represents surveillance by exploring the significance of "being watched" within a range of different social and political contexts and examining how such surveillance affects the construction of individual subjectivity and social relationships. The argument offered here is not that these fictions provide "new" posthuman representations of surveillance that constitute a rupture with surveillance experiences in the past. Instead, my purpose is to investigate the relationship between surveillance and digital technology and articulate how this relationship is transforming modern concepts of selfhood – especially in the context of how subjects make sense of the visual spectatorship of their virtual bodies in surveillance scenarios. For this reason I have extended my discussion to incorporate texts such as *The Hunger Games*, which is not posthuman in a direct sense, but does thematise the role of the corporeal body in digital surveillance regimes and demonstrates how such regimes produce subjectivities that blur the distinctions between real and virtual selves.

Power and surveillance: Shifting spectatorship

One of the most interesting features of surveillance as it is depicted in these five works of YA fiction is the shifting notion of spectatorship. The question of who (or what) is watching whom is answered in multiple and sometimes conflicting ways. The relationship between power and surveillance is an established one, as is evident from David Lyon's definition of surveillance as "the focused, systematic and routine attention to personal details for the purposes of influence, management, protection or direction" (2009: 14). Lyon also asserts that surveillance "usually involves relations of power in which watchers are privileged" (15). Traditionally, governments have been the group that is most interested in collecting data about individuals, but this is a situation that has been substantially transformed in contemporary society, as is evident from the narratives under examination here. Government surveillance is certainly an issue in novels such as *Little Brother*, *Useful Idiots* and *The Hunger Games*, but each represents the experience of surveillance subjects as more complex than a simple desire to overthrow an oppressive gaze. *Little Brother* focuses explicitly on the computer technology that is used to perform surveillance activities by unscrupulous governments with little concern for individual liberties – a fairly familiar plot device, but Doctorow's novel is innovative in its portrayal of computer hacking as a valid type of resistance to this type of surveillance. *Useful Idiots* similarly portrays surveillance as the provenance of a government with totalitarian inclinations, but its thematic exploration of surveillance is cleverly unique for two reasons: first, it interrogates surveillance from a position of complicity; second, it appraises the function of surveillance as a form of social sorting that targets particular racial groups.

The Hunger Games is distinctive because it tackles surveillance from the angle of shifting spectatorship. When Katniss (the adolescent protagonist of this speculative fantasy) enters the Hunger Games arena, she is acting as a participant in a deadly sport where the young players are expected to engage in a battle to the death. She is the subject of constant surveillance – but the identity of her "watcher" is plural and unfixed, rather than singular and stable. Cameras are fixed on her every move, transmitting data about her location and behaviour not just to government representatives, but also to corporate sponsors (whose finances provide her with much-needed food and medicine) and the general public, who view the games as entertainment. Katniss' perceptions of being watched while in the arena therefore reveal a range of different attitudes to surveillance: hostility towards the repressive government referred to as "the Capitol"; a desire to please and act appropriately in order to attract generous gifts from her sponsors; and even a reaction that verges on pleasure or comfort, stemming from the knowledge that her mother and sister are also viewers of the surveillance footage in which she features. Collins draws heavily on the discourse of reality television in *The Hunger Games*, where the concept of being perpetually watched by the public (a public that includes family, partners and friends) is an integral component of this particular television genre.

Willing surveillance subjects: Participatory surveillance

In contrast to *Little Brother*, *Useful Idiots* and *The Hunger Games*, narratives such as *Feed* and *serafina67* intentionally subvert the perception of surveillance as an act of governmental power. It is to these two novels that I will first turn, as they provide a clear indication of how the concept of surveillance has evolved in a contemporary context. Each narrative acts as a sharp counterpoint to traditional conceptions of surveillance, due to their portrayal of subjects who willingly surrender themselves to "being looked at". *Feed* represents an ethically corrupt futuristic world where corporate power is paramount – to the extent that individuals each have a "feed" (akin to an internet feed) hardwired into their brains. This enables their very consciousness to be regularly interrupted by media broadcasts and advertisements. The corporations that control the feednet possess the ability to perform surveillance on such an extensive and intimate level that their influence is profound, affecting every facet of human existence.

Feed has been the subject of widespread critical discussion since its publication, with many writers focusing on the passivity that characterises the dystopian, hyper-surveilled futuristic society it represents. Clare Bradford and Raffaella Baccolini make note of protagonist Titus' "overall apathy" (2011: 54); Elaine Ostry describes Titus as character who is lulled into complacency (2013: 105), while Bradford et al. write that the feednet is expressly designed to "deny individual subjectivity" (2008: 166). This societal passivity is key to the novel's negative depiction of surveillance (which is necessarily equated with repression, and hence constructed as an incursion upon individual liberty). What is remarkable about this novel, however, is that the power to watch and monitor citizens shifts from government institutions to corporate entities. The popular conceptualisation of surveillance as crime prevention is thus turned on its head in *Feed*, where the most mundane of activities – shopping – is the motivating principle behind all data collection performed.

The rather pessimistic (and paranoid) approach to surveillance evident in *Feed* is deftly countered by a novel such as *serafina67*. The internet is represented here as a space of peer interaction and adolescent agency – but it shares something in common with *Feed* in that it depicts virtual reality as a space of voluntary or invited surveillance. An important structural feature of *serafina67* is the inclusion of multiple "comments" made to Sarah/Serafina's blog by a community of online and real-world friends. This enables what is essentially a first-person narrative to become polyvocal. Sarah/Serafina regularly posts seemingly intimate details about her life and relationships (in the confessional and intimate style associated with diary entries), but in posting them online she openly acknowledges that her private life is made public. She invites public scrutiny of her writing, as is evident from the way in which she engages with the people who leave comments about her posts – she often joins the "comments" discussion that appears after each post. In terms of surveillance, blogging is a practice that is obviously quite different from traditional surveillance contexts, such as a prison, a workplace or the military. Whereas Lyon defines surveillance as "the focused, systematic and routine attention to personal details for purposes of influence, management, protection or direction" (2009: 14), such a definition seems at odds with blogging, which is essentially a peer-oriented social activity. However, Lyon also points out that human life is subject to surveillance every day, and in many ways individuals today have become more and more accustomed to having their lives digitally monitored. This awareness of "being watched" is the exact appeal of activities such as blogging – where participants solicit peer surveillance, voluntarily offering up glimpses of their private lives in the hope that these contributions will be widely noticed. The representation of surveillance as experienced through the practice of blogging in *serafina67* is the most overtly posthuman in its depiction of individual subjectivity as something that encompasses both the material and virtual selves. Sarah/Serafina's conception of selfhood depends on an acknowledgement of the role that both her material body and virtual self play in the production of her identity – and although she reflexively makes distinctions between the two domains she inhabits (cyberspace and social reality), it is actually virtual reality that is privileged within the construction of her narrative, since the narrative is constructed entirely out of her blog posts.

In response to the increasing popularity of online social networking (which developed as a consequence of Web 2.0, a set of web applications that enabled greater levels of online interactivity), two new terms have emerged to describe the way in which higher levels of online participation facilitates new forms of surveillance: these are "participatory surveillance" and "lateral surveillance" (which in some ways is a subcategory of "participatory surveillance"). Participatory surveillance, a concept first developed by Mark Poster (1990: 68), refers to surveillance that is consensual. The exact nature of participatory surveillance is a matter of some debate, as is evident from the different contexts in which the term is deployed. Richard Rogers defines participatory surveillance with specific reference to consumer society, and his comments are applicable to both *Feed* and *serafina67*:

> Participatory surveillance describes how the consumer must leave traces and thereby becomes subject to dataveillance, as Roger Clark has termed it, the current state of which is described below. Click-and-agree as well as click-and-buy have an intermediary step, however, where it is noted in the scroll down what information is collected about you ... To participate in consumer society, you have to be watched. It is not so much that resistance is futile. It has more to do with the fact that there is just too much interactivity.
>
> (2008: 288–89)

The fantasy setting of *Feed* functions as an explicit contradiction of Rogers' comments about the function of surveillance in reality – as in Anderson's satirical novel it becomes very clear that resistance is completely futile. The notion of voluntary participation is also problematic, as the character of Violet poignantly demonstrates that the cost of resisting the interpellating effects of the feed is death. Hence *Feed* serves to remind the reader that although modern individuals might willingly consent to certain forms of surveillance, the potential for exploitation and abuse remains.

In *serafina67* the highly interactive nature of the internet is emphasised through its use of the blog genre, but the act of blogging is not necessarily an act of consumerism. Nevertheless, Sarah/Serafina's blogging perfectly illustrates Rogers' comments about the "interactivity" of the internet, and the notion that modern users of the internet necessarily leave data traces whenever they participate in online activities. The novel's closure involves the revelation that one of Sarah/Serafina's online friends, who has regularly posted supportive comments on Sarah/Serafina's blog under the pseudonym Daisy13, is in actual fact her father. The narrative doesn't deal with this aspect of the story particularly effectively, effacing the significant issue of whether such parental surveillance is appropriate (or constitutes a breach of privacy, which is perhaps the more interesting and ethically complex issue). However, this aspect of the story emphasises that digital technologies such as the internet can function in multiple and seemingly contradictory ways: as a vehicle for freedom of expression, but with the capacity for data to be closely monitored (and linked to certain individuals); as a space that can be perceived as simultaneously private (in terms of social networking sites and the private information that individuals routinely post on such sites) and public, in that the connected, communal nature of the internet means that information can flow in an unrestricted fashion (O'Hara and Shadbolt, 2008: 112–15).

Lateral surveillance

A central concern throughout Sarah/Serafina's story is the concept of "lateral surveillance". Like "participatory surveillance", "lateral surveillance" is consensual. As Mark Andrejevic states, lateral surveillance "is not the top-down monitoring of employees by employers, or citizens by the state, but rather the peer-to-peer surveillance of spouses, friends, and relatives" (2004: 481). Peer-to-peer surveillance is crucial to *serafina67*, as numerous events occur precisely because of Sarah/Serafina's blogging: she writes a post in which she expresses concern for a friend who she suspects has anorexia or bulimia, and is then treated with hostility by that friend and bullied at school; she also discovers that her boyfriend has cheated on her after seeing photos of him with another girl that have been posted online. The internet and its associated practices and behaviours is not presented in this novel as a virtual space that is somehow separate from reality; instead, virtual reality interacts with the real world, and in this instance the internet forms an extension of the school playground. The type of peer-to-peer surveillance conventionally associated with the school playground has been translated into the digital world – where the most significant transformation is that the rumours and innuendo of the traditional physical playground can now be documented and proved, a consequence of each online user's digital footprint.

The novels *serafina67* and *Feed* add a unique dimension to critical discussions about surveillance as it is represented in YA fiction, as both depict surveillance as a modern practice that many individuals are very willing to invite upon themselves. The manner in which the two novels depict the act of consenting to surveillance is vastly different – each represents opposing ends of a broad spectrum (*Feed* is ideologically opposed to corporate surveillance; *serafina67* is more ambiguous, but does explore some of the positive effects of peer-to-peer surveillance). The divergence of the two novels is beside the point, however, as each plays an important role in challenging established perceptions about surveillance and its effects on individual subjectivity and social relations. In conjunction with novels such as *Little Brother*, *The Hunger Games* and *Useful Idiots*, these narratives paint a complex picture of modern surveillance and its effects.

Surveillance as social discrimination

An important thematic concern in each of the novels discussed in this chapter is the relationship between surveillance and power. *Feed* and *serafina67* make a unique contribution to such a debate as they reimagine traditional surveillance hierarchies. *Little Brother*,

The Hunger Games and *Useful Idiots*, while being slightly more conventional in their deployment of the concept of surveillance, are nevertheless also enlightening in terms of the way that they skilfully deconstruct more traditional forms of surveillance. A primary function of modern surveillance is its ability to perform what Lyon calls "social sorting" (2003, 2007) – and *Little Brother, The Hunger Games* and *Useful Idiots* are highly attuned to this phenomenon in their thematic exploration of how class, race and age can affect one's status as a "surveillance target". In *Discipline and Punish*, Foucault asserts that surveillance is a repressive process that "produces homogenous effects of power" (1977: 200). The individual who is the subject of surveillance, according to Foucault, "is seen, but he does not see; he is the object of information, never a subject in communication" (1977: 200). Of course Foucault's comments were made in relation to a prison, which is a very different context from the much more expansive uses of surveillance in the modern world. One of the more pressing issues to arise in contemporary critical discourses of surveillance is its capacity to categorise people:

> For surveillance today sorts people into categories, assigning worth or risk, in ways that have real effects on their life-chances. Deep discrimination occurs, thus making surveillance not merely a matter of personal privacy but of social justice.
>
> (Lyon, 2003: 1)

The discriminatory effects of surveillance are a central theme of *Useful Idiots, The Hunger Games* and *Little Brother*, each of which is concerned with the experiences of surveillance subjects. Perhaps more importantly, each suggests pathways of resistance to oppressive surveillance – and in doing so constructs its adolescent protagonist as an agentic, rather than disempowered, subject of surveillance. *Useful Idiots* draws the reader's attention to the notion of surveillance as crime prevention, a model that often results in racial profiling. However, the narrative uses the strategy of defamiliarisation to interrogate the concept of the racialised body as being immediately suspicious within a surveillance context. In *The Hunger Games*, surveillance is a tool of class oppression. In accordance with Foucault's pronouncements, this produces a paranoid subjectivity that is permanently conscious of being watched – as indicated through Katniss' first-person narration, which routinely admits to self-censure in order to escape the attention of "the Capitol" (the ruling body). Surveillance of this nature, Lyon writes, "constrains us and encourages us to comply with the social order" (1994: 19). Yet Katniss does not remain an interpellated subject of surveillance. As the novel progresses, she becomes adept at manipulating surveillance to her own advantage. She remains on camera at all times, as it were, but this does not allow the Capitol to control her. A similar type of resistance is depicted in *Little Brother* – although the discriminatory nature of this surveillance is slightly different because the target group is so much broader: adolescents. Decidedly middle class and from a variety of different ethnic backgrounds, the teenagers that come under suspicion for a terrorist attack in this novel attract attention because of their technological expertise, as all are skilled in computer hacking. The novel highlights the creative ways in which technology can be used to outwit surveillance – and as such reshapes technology into a means for achieving empowerment and autonomy, rather than simply functioning as an act of government repression. In effect, technology becomes the means through which individuals can fight for their privacy – a space that is safe from government spying and intervention.

The subject of surveillance is intimately connected to race. Critical discussions of surveillance (a discourse that gained momentum in the early 1990s) are, according to John McGrath, "almost always framed in terms of crime prevention (now very much extended to terrorism prevention) and privacy rights" (2004: 2). The "crime prevention" aspect of surveillance involves monitoring "suspicious" subjects – and, as McGrath asserts, "suspicion is often dependent on skin colour" (2004: 22). That surveillance operates by targeting specific groups is crucial to the work of David Lyon, who contends that a primary goal of surveillance is "social sorting" (2009: 63), a process that involves the specific targeting of racial groups. In this context, Mark's decision in *Useful Idiots* not to make the Oysters (a derogatory name given to the indigenous population) the target of governmental surveillance is an interesting and enlightened one, because it enables her to explore the effects of surveillance on individuals in terms of their compliance with it. Mark's novel therefore implicitly addresses two issues associated with posthumanism: first, it considers the impact of technology on subjectivity through its exploration of Merrick's surveillance complicity; second, it engages with the way in which humanist concepts of subjectivity have sought to exclude certain groups of subjects on the basis of their bodies – in this case, the racialised bodies of the Oysters.

When Merrick, the novel's young protagonist, first enters the Briease Moss (the name given to the Oyster Reserve) it is the lack of surveillance (amongst a range of things that he perceives as different) that causes him most consternation:

> There seemed to be no code, no key, no scanner. He could not get into his own apartment, even into his own height, ['height' refers to the level of the building] without pausing for the doors to recognise him. He looked round for an eye but if one existed it was very well concealed.
>
> (Mark, 2004: 156)

Merrick's initial perception of the Oyster settlement is thus characterised by attention to lack, through the repeated use of "no" and emphasis on what is missing ("no code, no key, no scanner") in his focalisation. Merrick has come to the Briease Moss with Frida, an indigenous dancer whom he has only recently met. When he expresses his dismay at the lack of surveillance there, his point of view is quickly countered by Frida:

> 'But anyone could get in.'
> 'Who'd want to?'
> 'You have no crime?'
> 'One of the advances we've elected to live without? No, the advance we've elected to live without in this instance is surveillance. My apartment in the city – the one I've been living in while I've worked at the Ayckbourn – it has a record of every person who has ever lived in it, how many times they went in and out, who they brought with them, how long they stayed, a record of every visitor, maintenance worker, every ancillary robot – it must be like that where you live, where you work. Nobody needs that information but it's there, it keeps growing. And when you go to the theatre, the parc, to a shop – if anyone wanted to they could

access every building you'd ever been in from the moment you were born, and when, and for how long. The same for me when I'm in the city, but not here. That's part of our charter, we choose what to record of ourselves'.

(Mark, 2004: 157–58)

Frida's comments transform the entire tenor of the conversation, moving it away from concepts of civilisation (or lack of it, which is how Merrick interprets the Oysters' refusal to use surveillance technology) to an assertion of rights and agency. Frida is patently aware that the collection of seemingly unimportant personal data has the potential to be (mis)used in ways that might limit individual freedom. The lack of surveillance technology in the Briease Moss is therefore not an accident, but a premeditated and legal assertion of individual rights, as indicated by her reference to "our charter".

Frida and Merrick's discussion reflects the nature of debates about surveillance, which pivot on issues of crime prevention and safety versus the protection of individual privacy. The irony of Frida's words lies in Merrick's inability to conceive of himself as a target of surveillance, which is exactly what he becomes over the course of the narrative. Merrick's dismay at the lack of surveillance technology on the Reserve arises from his previous compliance with such technology (the novel suggests that it is simply a normal part of his life). While surveillance can be perceived in negative ways, as an invasive tool of Big Brother-like institutions or agencies, it can also be viewed in a positive light, as intimated by Merrick when he tells Frida of the crime-prevention benefits of such practices. Lyon's description of the ubiquity of surveillance in the modern world offers an effective rationale for Merrick's complicity:

Today's social and economic world is so deeply permeated by surveillance practices and processes that it is simply impossible to know about all that happens using personal data, let alone respond intelligently or imaginatively to it.

... Few stop to think what the surveillance might mean or where the data go. They simply acquiesce with the system. Indeed, if people did hesitate, let alone withdraw willing cooperation, everyday social life as we know it today would break down.

(2009: 164)

It is not until Merrick becomes a target of surveillance that his views change. Merrick's gradual acquisition of the status of "surveillance target" culminates in an assassination attempt – but Mark carefully evades a polarised representation of surveillance technology as intrinsically evil. This is partly because Merrick is never able to pinpoint with any confidence exactly who (or what) is trying to target him. The suggestion is that it may be a corporation or governmental authority, but this is never completely confirmed (although whoever is responsible has access to data about Merrick's movements at home, at work and in public spaces). The negative construction of technology (as an invasive recorder of personal data) is also mediated by Merrick's own video-recording activities. Merrick makes a video diary of the creation of his own pearl, a testament of what he has endured (which involved substantial pain). Although this record is eventually stolen, along with the pearl, the process of making the record is constructed as significant – as it is this very process that enables the development of Merrick's subjectivity, profoundly altering his perceptions of self and other.

Useful Idiots thus destabilises the relationship between race and surveillance. The novel's exploration of the impact of surveillance technology on individual subjectivity circumvents the typical categorisation of racialised subjects as targets of suspicion in a surveillance environment. Instead, the narrative places the Oysters outside of the surveillance sphere and reflects on the nature of complicity. In depicting Merrick's evolution from "invisible and unnoticed" to surveillance target, Mark thus enables Merrick to experience the process of "othering" as it is performed by surveillance technology – and his dawning consciousness of what it means to occupy the subject position of alienated Other.

The representation of surveillance as a form of social sorting that discriminates against particular groups is not as sophisticated or nuanced in *The Hunger Games* or *Little Brother*, but both of these novels share several key features with *Useful Idiots*: first, they also show how surveillance data can be used to disadvantage people who are identified as a member of a group with certain characteristics. More importantly, these two novels also explore how subjects can resist or manipulate surveillance, and they are also similar to *Useful Idiots* in their unwillingness to demonise the technology that enables surveillance data to be collected (in fact, all three novels suggest that technology can actually assist in the acquisition of subjective agency for adolescent subjects).

The relationship between class and surveillance in *The Hunger Games* initially conforms to a Big Brother-type paradigm: a centralised regime (the "Capitol") maintains its power through the repressive surveillance of its citizens. The actual "Hunger Games" are an annual form of punishment for the 12 districts that surround the Capitol, a harsh reminder that a previous attempt at rebellion was unsuccessful. Each district must sacrifice two adolescents to the games each year, a selection made using a lottery system called "the reaping". The games act as a metaphor both for the brutality of this fictional world and its strict surveillance regime, as the competitors' fight to the death is filmed and then broadcast to every home in Panem. The class implications of being selected as a participant in the games (which is really the "ultimate surveillance space", as it is an arena that has been specially designed to allow television cameras to record each and every movement made by the competitors) are made explicit very early in the narrative, when Katniss explains how the supposedly democratic process used to select the two competitors is heavily geared towards choosing poorer individuals: "But here's the catch. Say you are poor and starving, as we were. You can opt to add your name more times in exchange for tesserae [a year's supply of grain and oil for one person]" (Collins, 2008: 15).

The routine surveillance that Katniss experiences as a lower-class inhabitant of District 12, a region associated with coal mining, is a function of the authoritarian control that the Capitol exerts over the districts of Panem. (An awareness of being watched and listened to is mentioned constantly in the introductory stages of the narrative, as a way of establishing the structures of the fictional society in which Katniss lives.) In this respect, *The Hunger Games* offers a fairly conventional portrayal of surveillance. Katniss' internalisation of the Capitol's surveillance is a rather predictable outcome of such pervasive state monitoring, as commented upon by Kelley Wezner, who writes: "Katniss and others, aware that they are always being watched and judged, internalize the normative gaze and are controlled by it" (2012: 154).

The surveillance paranoia that Katniss habitually experiences as a citizen of Panem is transformed, however, once she begins to participate as a competitor in the games. The surveillance that Katniss experiences in the arena becomes even more omnipresent (she has a GPS tracker implanted, via a needle, under her skin), as well as more ambiguous. No longer does surveillance simply represent the Capitol's totalising power. Instead, Katniss has become a reality television star and the surveillance to which she is subjected has an altogether different focus. Instead of positioning her as a criminal subject, this surveillance alternatively constructs her in voyeuristic terms as a "spectacle". Katniss' response to this diversification of surveillance is equally complex: she becomes aware that surveillance is no longer just a function of institutional power, but an avenue for self-construction. She begins to perform for the television audience, aware that she is capable of fashioning her own subjectivity for this audience:

> "Prim, let go," I say harshly, because this is upsetting me and I don't want to cry. When they televise the replay of the reapings tonight, everyone will make note of my tears, and I'll be marked as an easy target. A weakling. I will give no one that satisfaction.
>
> (Collins, 2008: 27–28)

The surveillance that Katniss experiences here produces a performative response, motivated by her understanding that she is being watched and monitored as part of a public television broadcast. The "harshness" of her voice, the visible part of her performance, thus contrasts with her emotional state ("this is upsetting me") and an internal awareness that she must control and hide her emotional interiority. Despite the violence and brutality of the games they are considered popular entertainment, providing what John S. Turner calls an "opportunity to celebrate the spectacle elements invested in surveillance" (1998: 94). Turner suggests that spectacle and surveillance have become increasingly entwined in popular culture, and his comments are especially pertinent to *The Hunger Games*, which draws on the discourse of reality television in order to play with the relationship between the two. Turner's discussion is focused on the use of surveillance in popular film, where he argues that surveillance is typically used as a "narratival device to promote suspense and, subsequently, violence" (1998: 94). The connection between surveillance, suspense and violence is an issue that is taken up by Shannon

Mortimore-Smith in relation to *The Hunger Games*, which she discusses from the perspective of the spectator's gaze. She argues that the popularity of US reality television programmes such as *Jersey Shore*, whose ratings thrive on overt displays of violence and intoxication, is dependent on viewer interactivity: the programmes reflect exactly what viewers wish to see (2012: 161). For Mortimore-Smith, *The Hunger Games* therefore functions as a cautionary tale about viewer practices: "Criticising the cruel appetite of twenty-first century viewers, Collins' dystopia forecasts the brutal outcome of any society that loses sight of the 'reality' that drives its entertainment" (2012: 164). The correlation of surveillance and violence in the films and television programmes that Turner and Mortimore-Smith analyse, which then function as a form of entertainment, is indeed prevalent in *The Hunger Games* – although the question of who is being entertained by the violence that Katniss experiences in the arena is more complex. Katniss' "audience" is comprised of three distinctive groups: the population of Panem, the gamemakers and the Capitol, and the actual reader of the narrative. The novel assumes an implied reader who is familiar with the format of reality television and the concept of surveillance performativity, but uses Katniss' first-person narration to immediately align readers with her critical appreciation of how the viewers of reality television can be easily manipulated.

An obvious distinction between *The Hunger Games* and reality television programmes is that Katniss has not volunteered or given her consent to be placed under surveillance – but she does rely on her own knowledge and experience of what it is like to watch the games on television in order to respond appropriately to the audience. The most obvious example of what Lyon calls "acting out" in the context of reality television (2009: 137) occurs with the manufacture of a romance between Katniss and Peeta (the other competitor from District 12). The romance is a strategy engineered by Haymitch, Katniss and Peeta's coach, to make them more appealing to the television audience – and it is hugely successful. Katniss' final gesture in the arena shows a clear and sophisticated understanding of how to use surveillance to her own advantage – although, again, her performance is one that acknowledges both the "gamemakers" (the officials who preside over the game and are implicitly attributed with some kind of institutional authority) and the wider audience watching her on their television screens. She and Peeta perform a "Romeo and Juliet" death pantomime, spreading out poison berries on their hands for the benefit of the cameras – Peeta whispers to Katniss, "I want everyone to see" (Collins, 2008: 418). Their ploy is a success – and their careful manipulation of their own images and behaviour on camera produces a unique result: for the first time in history, the gamemakers announce that there are two winners of the Hunger Games. The novel's thematic exploration of surveillance therefore suggests that surveillance has been transformed from an exercise of institutional power to something much more multifaceted and oblique. The notion of "being watched" has become an aspect of everyday life, but the identity of "the watcher" is now plural. The effect of this "surveillance multiplicity" is to disrupt the conventional assumption that surveillance necessarily equates to repression. Although the novel does depict institutional state surveillance of this nature, it also reveals that surveillance in the modern world can have more benign functions – as Katniss discovers in the arena. Instead of constructing surveillance – or the technology that enables it – as inherently evil, *The Hunger Games* suggests that individuals who are subjected to surveillance must be canny about its presence and agenda. If they are able to educate themselves about how and why they are being watched, they, like Katniss, may also be able to use it to their own advantage.

Educated and empowered surveillance subjects

The idea of "reacting" to surveillance in an empowered way is central to the novel *Little Brother*. In terms of the discriminatory effects of surveillance, this novel depicts a fairly broad category of individuals that is targeted as "suspicious": adolescents. The story directly examines the surveillance state that emerged as a result of the terrorist attacks that took place in the United States on 11 September 2001. After these attacks the US government hugely increased its use of surveillance (now purposefully targeted at men from the Middle East) and passed emergency laws that allowed government agencies to subvert normal criminal procedures when it came to terrorist suspects (such as detaining them without needing proper grounds for arrest). Doctorow's novel is rather ingenious in its depiction of Marcus as the archetypal "ordinary boy" – he is white, he is middle class, he is not even an adult – but he suddenly finds himself under suspicion for committing a violent terrorist act. Marcus' intimate, engaging first-person narration creates an immediate alignment with the reader, and as his story progresses, its thematic significance depends on the implied reader realising that Marcus' situation, wherein he becomes a surveillance target, could perhaps happen just as easily to him or her. Like *The Hunger Games*, *Little Brother* is thematically concerned with how to resist oppressive surveillance. Perhaps its most innovative achievement is its depiction of computer hacking as not simply antisocial or intrinsically destructive, but as a legitimate and agentic way for individuals to respond to invasive technological surveillance. More specifically, *Little Brother* focuses on an individual's right to privacy and Marcus' hacking is reframed in this context as justifiable behaviour because it is a response to what is depicted as the unlawful surveillance of his body, his home and his computer. *Little Brother* is accordingly distinctive from the other novels thus far discussed, as it does not simply accept the fact the surveillance is ubiquitous in modern life. Doctorow's novel actively defies such a pronouncement:

> There's something really liberating about having some corner of your life that's yours, that no one gets to see except you. It's a little like nudity or taking a dump. Everyone gets naked every once in a while. Everyone has to squat on the toilet. There's nothing shameful, deviant or weird about either of them. But what if I decreed from now on, every time you want to evacuate some solid waste, you'd have to do it in a glass room perched in the middle of Times Square, and you'd be buck naked?
>
> ... It's not about doing something shameful. It's about doing something private. It's about your life belonging to you.
>
> (Doctorow, 2008b: 22)

Marcus makes an extremely plaintive appeal to the reader here, using the analogy of having to go to the toilet in a highly public, visible space in order to convey the extent of the intrusion produced by the Department of Homeland Security's surveillance in the narrative. He is adamant that individuals should have some part of their lives that is beyond the reach of surveillance (note the strategic shift to second person in the latter part of this extract, directly engaging the reader to think about Marcus' assertions). To a certain extent, Marcus' reaction to the surveillance that he is placed under is fairly simplistic and limited. Lyon writes that "struggles over surveillance frequently refer to the idea of privacy" (2009: 174), but the problem with this type of response is that privacy is a historically and culturally relative concept (Lyon refers to cultural differences that exist in countries such as Japan, where salary details are more "public" than in Western countries, and in rural India, where bathroom facilities are similarly more "public"). O'Hara and Shadbolt concur, asserting that "the privacy which a person could have experienced in the 1900s has gone forever, swapped for a plethora of powers, skills and opportunities undreamt of a century ago" (2008: 232). For writers such as Lyon, O'Hara and Shadbolt, it is not particularly useful or enlightening to reduce discussions about surveillance to the issue of privacy, since it ignores more pressing concerns: such as the ethical processing of surveillance data and the potential for this data to be used for social sorting purposes, which have a discriminatory effect on particular groups of people.

The irony of Marcus' appeal to privacy is that it was born in response to the type of unethical processing of surveillance data that Lyon suggests is a much more pertinent issue. The Department of Homeland Security (DHS) is depicted within the novel in exaggeratedly negative terms: when Marcus and his friends are being interrogated (without being properly charged for any crime), Marcus is subjected to treatment that is directly associated with torture. He is blindfolded and denied access to a bathroom, forcing him to urinate on himself. Within the context of this heavy-handed and obviously unethical surveillance (Marcus has done nothing wrong apart from being in the wrong place at the wrong time), Marcus' reaction is presented as appropriate and justified. The paradox of his response, however, lies in its outright breach of individual privacy. One of Marcus' rebellious initiatives, designed to disrupt the DHS surveillance of people's movements around the city, is to reprogram the codes associated with "Fast Passes" and "FasTraks" (the electronic cards used to pay for public transport and motorway tolls). But to do this, he needs to clone existing cards:

> as I brushed up against him, I triggered my arphid cloner, which was already loaded in the pocket of my leather jacket. The cloner sucked down the numbers of his credit cards and his car-keys, his passport and the hundred-dollar bills in his wallet.
>
> (Doctorow, 2008b: 46)

This interaction constitutes a rather severe invasion of privacy (of which Marcus seems ignorant), but also demonstrates an illogicality of the narrative: that to participate in online culture, as hacking and programming necessitate, means to surrender certain aspects of more traditional concepts of privacy. The nature of the internet is that it creates a digital memory that can outlast any other physical forms of data storage – and it is the existence of this memory that allows Marcus to hack into systems such as those for public transport and motorway payments. *Little Brother* constructs this breach of privacy as behaviour that clearly produces subjective agency. Marcus' act of cloning his fellow passengers' credit card and travel pass numbers allows him to disrupt the gratuitous surveillance of the San Francisco police and throw the entire transport system into complete chaos. This act is implicitly justified because the police surveillance that the city is subjected to is so extreme – but Marcus does not engage in any overt self-reflection on the implications of his own surveillance activities.

The internet, as noted by O'Hara and Shadbolt, is an odd space in that it is "neither fully public nor fully private" (2008: 112). This ambiguity is highlighted in *Little Brother*, where the internet plays a pivotal role in enabling the adolescent hacker community to come together and organise a collective resistance to the DHS and their so-called security measures. Notwithstanding Marcus' repeated assertions of his right to privacy, *Little Brother* perfectly illustrates the arguments of Lyon, O'Hara and Shadbolt, each of whom acknowledge that modern surveillance is unavoidable and suggest that the real challenge is "one of democratic practice in the information age: to oblige organisations to handle personal data responsibly and fairly" (Lyon, 2009: 177). Marcus, of course, is confronted with a totalitarian surveillance regime, but instead of becoming a passive surveillance subject he is able to use his hacking skills (in a manner that typically breaches traditional concepts of privacy) to thwart the DHS surveillance programme and bring its corrupt agents to justice. The celebratory nature of this story closure is perhaps not especially realistic, but it does exemplify the key arguments of surveillance theorists such as Lyon: namely, that surveillance regimes need to be much more transparent (as opposed to the secretive surveillance conducted by the DHS in *Little Brother*) and that individuals need to educate themselves about the kinds of surveillance they are routinely subjected to, so that they can maintain some agency in the context of how much information about themselves they choose to reveal. This need has become more urgent since the 2013 revelations about the existence of PRISM, the USA's clandestine mass electronic surveillance data-mining program. Presumably there will be responses to this information in YA fiction that is published in the future.

Subjectivity and surveillance in the posthuman era

My discussion of *Little Brother* in this chapter has focused principally on the concept of agency, and how individuals can attain such agency in the face of perpetual surveillance. By way of conclusion I would now like to turn to the concepts of subjectivity and agency in order to explore how they are affected by surveillance in the narratives under examination here. As outlined at the beginning of this chapter, posthumanism offers an apposite way in which to make sense of the effects of digital surveillance on individual identity. Many of the novels under consideration here use surveillance as a means for formulating alternative, non-traditional forms of subjectivity. Kim Toffoletti describes the humanist conceptualisation of subjectivity in the following way:

> the modern subject is an autonomous agent whose sense of being remains constant, regardless of the factors that impact on the experience of day-to-day living. In a human-centred universe, external factors count for very little when seeking to understand the "essence" of being human. For the Enlightenment subject, understanding the fundamental characteristics of humanity demands a transcendence of historical and social contexts in favour of an interpretation of the self as self-mastering and universal.
>
> (2007: 13)

In contrast to this notion of the self as fixed and essential, novels such as *The Hunger Games*, *Little Brother*, *Useful Idiots*, *Feed* and *serafina67* construct the surveillance subject as fragmented and necessarily plural, thereby engaging with a posthuman model of subjectivity. An awareness of being under surveillance is to be conscious that an image of yourself (or package of data containing personal information pertaining to you) is being watched and/or tracked. Such an awareness produces an immediate destabilisation of the unitary humanist subject, as it necessitates the realisation that several versions of the subject simultaneously exist. *The Hunger Games* offers a particularly nuanced representation of this phenomenon, as Katniss is perpetually conscious of being watched. Katniss' success in the games arises partly from her capacity for intersubjectivity. Although she is the subject under surveillance, she constantly places herself in the position of the watcher so as to determine her own behaviour. The actual practice of watching is always foremost in her mind, as demonstrated by the following extract of narration: "...and I feel Gale's grey eyes watching me watching Peeta, all the way from District 12" (Collins, 2008: 379). The structure of this sentence, which contains three verbs ("feel", and the repeated "watching"), is indicative of the way in which surveillance technology creates a profusion of spectral images. What is most interesting is the way in which Katniss positions herself as both the object and the subject of the gaze (she is watching Peeta, yet she can also perceive herself as the recipient of Gale's surveillance, via the television cameras discreetly pointed at her). This is ultimately the key to her success in the games: her sophisticated knowledge of viewing practices enables her to give the surveillance cameras a performance that leads to her victory in the competition.

Little Brother is similarly effective in demonstrating how surveillance technologies produce a fluid construction of subjectivity: the narrative uses the internet and the avatars that act in this online environment to suggest that subjectivity is no longer fixed or stable. On an overt level this is achieved through Marcus' use of multiple virtual identities. When the narrative commences he explains that "W1n5t0n" is the code name he uses for his hacking, but once the DHS starts to track his behaviour more closely, he adopts the new online moniker of "M1k3y". The distinctions between Marcus, W1n5t0n and M1k3y are initially clear: Marcus is "real", W1n5t0n and M1k3y are not. However, in the narrative's closure, when Marcus is about to be tortured by DHS agents, they repeatedly refer to him as "M1k3y" (2008: 121). M1k3y also plays an instrumental role in sabotaging the DHS surveillance operation – and the novel thus subtly blurs the distinctions between Marcus' three personas. Doctorow is able to disrupt the conventional meanings of "real" and "unreal", confusing what Toffoletti calls "the very categories of virtuality and reality" (2007: 18). This closure proposes that human interactions with technology (whether they be related to surveillance or otherwise) result in new and unconventional forms of subjectivity, which are necessarily ambiguous and unfixed.

The representation of agency is perhaps more explicit in *The Hunger Games* and *Little Brother*, as both of these novels are principally concerned with how adolescent subjects might achieve agency within a society where they are placed under constant surveillance. The conditions for achieving an agentic subjectivity in a surveillance context are less apparent or harder to fulfil in *Useful Idiots*, *Feed* and *serafina67*. The development of Merrick's subjectivity in *Useful Idiots* does not occur until he becomes cognisant of himself as a complicit surveillance subject. It is only when he finds himself free of this surveillance (as he does when entering the Oyster Reserve) that he is able to contemplate its effect on his subjectivity. The role of the body in the production of subjectivity is of paramount importance in this novel (Merrick injects his wrist with horsefly venom and then waits for a "pearl" to grow, proving that the myth behind the Oysters' name is based on reality). It is through bodily experience that Merrick acquires an intersubjective appreciation of Oyster history and his own indigenous ancestry, adopting the subject position of the racially marginalised Other in a process that allows him to recuperate his own damaged subjectivity. This creative interrogation of Cartesian mind/body dualism is inherently posthuman in orientation, as it reformulates established categories of being.

The human body is also important to the novels *Feed* and *serafina67* – but only because of its diminished presence or absence in the production of subjectivity. In *Feed*, bodily experience has been relegated to the fringe. Titus' interaction with the world around him is achieved primarily through his feednet: he talks to friends over the feed (feed chatting has replaced actual dialogue) and when he attends parties, his feed regularly informs him how to purchase the clothes he sees others wearing and the music he hears being played. Even the typical adolescent behaviour of experimenting with illicit drugs has been appropriated by the feed: Titus and his friends access illegal online sites for the purpose of experiencing a feed "malfunction" (Anderson, 2003: 101). Anderson's novel takes the concept of "participatory surveillance" to an exaggerated level in this satire of consumerism and communication technology: the inhabitants of Titus' world have been so willing to participate in a technologically advanced consumer society that they have completely surrendered their own individuality and subjective agency. This societal capitulation – and the pervasive nature of the surveillance that Titus (pleasurably) experiences – is conveyed most effectively through the novel's structure. Titus' first-person narration is constantly interrupted (in a manner that replicates his experience of the feed) by advertisements, snatches of songs, special news broadcasts, or magazine-type headlines such as "20 Hot Sex Tips for Girls" (2003: 203). The use of this fragmented narrative structure inevitably produces a representation of Titus' subjectivity as similarly disjointed – yet this fragmentation is a sign of abjection, rather than agency. Perhaps the most interesting conundrum posed by *Feed* lies in the subject position it creates for adolescent readers. These readers are expected to read and interpret the randomness and proliferation of meaning (typically associated with postmodernism) that permeates every level of the narrative. Such a requirement presumes a sophisticated and agentic reader, one who actively constructs meaning and significance through a reflective engagement with the text. However, the story's closure offers the adolescent implied reader a radical criticism of adolescent subjectivity that is inherently lacking in agency. The two positions are never reconciled.

The surveillance experienced by Sarah/Serafina in *serafina67* is of an extremely different nature. Unlike the other novels discussed in this chapter, this novel is realist rather than a fantasy. However, the "reality" depicted is virtual, as the narrative is comprised of blog posts. Sarah/Serafina willingly offers up parts of her private life for public scrutiny in her blog posts in a context that Mark Andrejevic suggests is not actually a new phenomenon:

> Surely, there is nothing particularly new and earth-shattering about the fact that peers develop strategies for keeping track of one another, and those who write about new media might even go so far as to suggest that contemporary strategies for mutual monitoring merely rehabilitate, in technological form, the everyone-knows-everyone-else's-business world of traditional village life, undoing the anonymity of urbanized modernity.
>
> (2004: 481)

Andrejevic's benign phrase "keeping track of one another" is a very appropriate description of the type of surveillance that Sarah/ Serafina experiences as a result of keeping a blog. Her blog has enabled her to build a small community of online friends, all of whom monitor her blog posts and offer comments and messages of support in response to her virtual musings (which document typical adolescent crises such as cheating boyfriends and parental divorce). Sarah/Serafina's experience of surveillance through blogging produces subjective agency through its intersubjective potential: it enables her to enter into numerous intersubjective relationships with her online friends. As she says at one point, "Sometimes I think we can be closer to people online than the people we see all the time" (Day, 2008: 120), a comment that attests to the liberation that anonymity can occasion. Sarah/Serafina does not disclose her real name on the blog, so the pseudonym "Serafina67" (itself an indication of how many other "serafinas" are active in the same cyberspace domain) does afford her some privacy (although it must be mentioned that some of her "commenters" are friends who know her in reality, so her online identity is not completely anonymous). As is the case with *Little Brother*, the use of an online pseudonym serves to destabilise unitary humanist constructions of the subject because it attests to the plurality of subjectivity, but *serafina67* takes this one step further in its eradication of the "real". The reader can only access Sarah/Serafina's subjectivity through its virtual presence.

One of this novel's greatest successes is its exploration of the inter-relationship between gender and the practice of lateral surveillance, as well as its acknowledgement that the types of social surveillance to which marginalised social groups are routinely subjected (for example, women or people whose race or ethnicity mark them as Other) can be just as oppressive as technological surveillance. Sarah/ Serafina reflects that virtual reality as she knows it is a welcoming and decidedly feminine space: "I think most of the people on here are girls" (2008: 133). The action of publishing her thoughts online is therapeutic for Sarah/Serafina, functioning as an escape from the real world:

> But then part of what's nice about ULife [the name of the novel's fictional blogging host site] is the bits where I am not that girl.

I am not in my horrid body or hearing my whiny voice or wishing I could hide the bad bits.

(2008: 119)

Serafina's subjectivity is thus constructed as a more agentic subjectivity than Sarah's, because it is constructed at a distance from the type of destructive feminine surveillance that women and girls experience on a daily basis in the real world, as a result of patriarchal ideology that locates feminine subjectivity in the female face and body. Accordingly, *serafina67* uses the idea of online lateral surveillance (as it applies to the practice of blogging) to interrogate conventional assumptions about the relationship between the human body and mind, providing a representation of subjectivity that engages with many of the central ideologies of posthumanism.

In the modern world, surveillance has become an inevitable part of human existence. The novels discussed within this chapter forthrightly acknowledge the omnipresence of surveillance, but instead of railing against its use, these narratives (with the exception of Anderson's *Feed*) explore the possibilities for achieving an agentic subjectivity within a surveillance society. What is perhaps most remarkable about this particular group of texts is the diversity that is evident in their representation of surveillance: each narrative offers an inherently distinctive vision of the purposes for which surveillance is used, how it affects subjectivity and how individuals can retain a sense of autonomy in the face of such intense scrutiny. Lyon uses a rather poetic turn of phrase to describe the diversity of modern surveillance, suggesting that "unlike the fixed spaces of the Panopticon, surveillance now shifts and undulates, expands and contracts like the swell and tides of the ocean" (2009: 180). Yet the mutable nature and function of surveillance is not cause for dismay in these novels. Instead, they focus on representing protagonists who are knowledgeable about surveillance practices and who can use such knowledge to their own advantage. The representation of digital surveillance in these narratives thus functions as an extremely effective vehicle for a posthuman critical lens, as each uses surveillance as a means through which to explore and better understand the transformative effects of digital technology on the human subject.

6
Subjectivity in Cyberspace: Technorealism and the Merging of Virtual and Material Selves

Children and adolescents now spend increasing amounts of their daily lives online and, despite media hysteria about its detrimental effects, a rising number of children's authors are using fiction to explore the ways in which cyberspace can enrich young lives. Building on the argument established in Chapter 5 with reference to lateral surveillance and blogging, this chapter seeks to demonstrate that, within narratives produced for children and adolescents, cyberspace often functions as a communal, nurturing space that enables young people to achieve subjective agency. Over the past ten years, the textual representation of cyberspace in novels produced for adolescent readers has emerged as a new genre of printed books: technorealism. Narratives that can be classified as "technorealism" employ a range of linguistic and graphic techniques that mimic the use of online social media such as blogs, instant messages, chat rooms and message boards. This particular subgenre incorporates significant textual innovation (fragmented narratives, polyfocalised narration, genre mixing, linguistic experimentation and so on), but is also remarkable because it heralds a significant ideological shift in terms of how virtual reality is conceptualised. Hayles (1999) warns that the conventional dichotomisation between virtual reality and materiality will have the detrimental effect of devaluing physical presence. A preferable ideological direction would be to conceive the disembodied nature (or "pattern") of electronic data and embodied materiality as complementary. This, I propose, is exactly how a small yet steadily increasing group of contemporary YA novels constructs the relationship between physical and digital selves. Within the novels selected

155

for discussion in this chapter, virtual reality is presented as a very "real" space for the acting out of identity development and peer relationships. Such fictions depict cyberspace as collective, heterogenous and empowering for adolescent subjects and demonstrate that many of the rites of passage associated with the transition from adolescence to adulthood are now being played out in virtual reality.

The propensity for cyberspace (a networked system of computers) to reshape human identity and culture has been a key element of posthuman ideology since the mid-1980s. For Hayles, cyberspace is a deeply ambiguous realm that has the potential simultaneously to "expose the presuppositions underlying the social formations of late capitalism and to open new fields of play where the dynamics have not yet rigidified and new kinds of moves are possible" (1993: 175). The status of cyberspace as a site of ambiguity, with the capacity to shed new insight into human social formations, is an idea that is also taken up by Mark Nunes (1999). Following Baudrillard's theory of simulation, which interrogates traditional Western paradigms of the relationship between representation, subjectivity and signification, Nunes argues that the move towards "hyperreality" (in which the mind can no longer distinguish between reality and simulation) constructs cyberspace as an "increasingly real simulation of a comprehensible world" (Nunes, 1995: 5). The "comprehensibility" of the world that opens up to children and adolescents through their use and experience of computers, the internet and virtual reality is clearly articulated in narratives that deal with the online practices of blogging, instant messaging and visiting chat rooms. In most of the fictions under consideration in this chapter, cyberspace is not represented as something that is experienced "separately" from the young protagonists' social reality. Instead, it is experienced in conjunction with their everyday lives, and the behaviours that they engage in while online are as integral to the construction of their individual subjectivities as anything else. Nunes confirms this phenomenon, writing that cultural representations of "computer mediated communication" are frequently conceptualised in terms of space, a process that "writes place and distance onto the medium". The naming of cyberspace thus:

> reveals and creates a virtual location for actual experiences. This popular acceptance of cyberspace as a space has not needed to wait

for the arrival of bodysuit-and-goggle "virtual reality"; for literally millions of users, cyberspace already "exists" as a *place*, as real as the work and play conducted "in" it. That is not to say that only *one* virtual topography exists. Rather, we see in government documents, in the media, in scholarly journals, and in popular reports signs of cyber*spaces*: multiple and competing spatial figurations.

(Nunes, 1999: 61)

The perception that cyberspace is a "place", as real as any other physical space that children and adolescents inhabit as embodied subjects, is evident in literary representations of cyberspace where child protagonists segue from the physical world to virtual reality with the greatest of ease. It is perhaps young people's insatiable appetite for online interactions that is responsible for adults' concern about the negative consequences of such behaviour. Several recent studies suggest that children, and particularly teenagers, in countries such as the United States, Great Britain and Australia, spend large portions of time on the internet each day. A US study conducted in 2012 found that "95% of teens are online, a percentage that has been consistent since 2006" (Madden et al., 2013: 3). This is consistent with the situation in the UK, with Livingstone and Bober reporting that 75 per cent of 9- to 19-year-olds had accessed the internet from a home computer in a given period of 2004 (2006: 93). A similar survey conducted in 2012 by the Australian Bureau of Statistics about children's internet usage in Australia states that, within a 12-month period, 90 per cent of children "aged 5 to 14 years [had] accessed the internet" (ABS, 2012).

The ubiquity of the internet in the lives of young people today – and the fact that children's use of computer technology (and competency in this area) far outstrips comparable adult behaviour – has, unsurprisingly, garnered much public attention and resulted in a conceptualisation of the "child internet user" that is ideologically contradictory:

In academic and policy debates over the management of internet diffusion and appropriation, children and young people tend to be regarded with ambivalence, being seen both as the *digital generation*, pioneers in developing online competencies, yet also vulnerable and potentially at risk. Parents seem to share this ambivalence, especially given their children's apparently greater expertise with the internet.

(Livingstone and Bober, 2006: 93)

The types of "risks" that the internet poses for children and teenagers include exposure to inappropriate (or illegal) content and potential encounters with paedophiles, amongst other concerns – but the very nature of this debate has parallels with the more general concept of "youth" in the modern era, a category that is problematic because it is subject to ideological impulses that are antithetical to one another. On the one hand, Romantic ideologies of children as innocent, playful and vulnerable remain dominant in Western societies. Yet these idyllic visions of childhood are under constant attack, threatened by an image of today's youth as dangerous, violent, oversexualised and out of control (Brooks, 2003: 1). The internet exemplifies this ideological paradox: because children are innocent and in need of protection, they are vulnerable to the many dangers (pornography, paedophilia) that may be lurking online. At the same time, however, prolonged internet usage has been linked (particularly in the media) to antisocial and dysfunctional behaviours in children – such as violence (as a result of playing computer games), or the recent phenomenon of cyber bullying.

The relationship between children and cyberspace is thus conceptualised in ambiguous and conflicting ways in Western societies. A contributing factor to this ambiguity is that researchers often find it difficult or problematic to survey children's internet behaviour because it is either unsupervised or covert. Livingstone and Bober state that "one fifth (19 per cent) of 9- to 19-year-olds have internet access in their bedroom (particularly boys, middle-class children and teenagers), and fewer than half of the computers online in homes with children are located in a public room" (2006: 94). However, the "anxiety" surrounding children's internet usage is, largely, an adult construct, as research also suggests that children themselves experience little, if any, concerns about participating in online activities. Instead, adolescent internet users report that the internet "has improved their relationships with friends", and current research also indicates that they are attuned to privacy issues, to the extent that they are able to exert "a great deal of control over who views their profiles, who views what they upload"(Subrahmanyam and Greenfield, 2008: 123). It is to children's positive encounters with cyberspace that I now turn, focusing specifically on how children's literature ideologically represents cyberspace in narratives for adolescents as a place that is free of the normative constraints of "reality" (particularly for girls), which enables empowered forms of self-expression and also facilitates relationship building with peers.

Cyberspace and narrative form

In addition to transforming traditional understandings of identity, cyberspace has, in turn, begun to affect narrative forms. Children, especially teenagers, are sophisticated and highly adaptive users of new technologies – and it might therefore have been anticipated that children's literature would be quick to replicate the linguistic and generic forms common to cyberspace. (Although, as Applebaum and Mendlesohn repeatedly attest, children's fiction has conversely demonstrated a real reticence for pro-technology themes.) What is more unexpected, however, is the way in which the children's narratives selected for this chapter's primary corpus depict online practices such as blogging and instant messaging in a way that substantively deviates from the traditional standards of novel writing. These novels, all of which are aimed at adolescent audiences, are in the process of establishing a genuinely new mode of literature: one that uses radically hybridised generic forms (imposing narrative structures upon the collective, dialogic communication exchanges typical of online social media) and innovative linguistic expression (using acronyms for idiomatic phrases, emoticons and pictographic keystrokes).

While children's literary criticism has addressed, to an extent, the issues that arise when books are transferred into a digital context (see Erica Hateley's (2013) discussion of interactive picture-book applications for the iPhone and iPad or Dorothy Clark's (2006) analysis of what she calls "electronic reading", which focuses on children's literary narratives that have been adapted into interactive CD-Rom format) only minimal critical attention has been paid to the myriad ways in which digital technologies have started to affect the form and style of literary narratives. Eliza Dresang and Noga Applebaum are notable exceptions here, as both have explored some of the ways in which more traditional media – such as books – have been affected by the profound changes brought about by the advent of the computer. Dresang is renowned for the development of "radical change theory", a concept used to describe those works of children's literature that embrace the characteristics of digital technology, such as "interactivity", "connectivity" and "access" (1999). Integral to radical change theory is the idea that such literature is not just a modern phenomenon:

> It is important to note that the word "change" does not indicate a break with the past. Radical change, as a concept, has utility for identifying pre-digital age books that demonstrate these characteristics, which may have gone largely unnoticed. Experimentation with the forms and formats of words on the page is one manifestation of radical change...
>
> (Dresang and McClelland, 1999: 160)

Dresang's theory is, in essence, a celebration of children's books that use experimental forms and techniques in a fashion that mimics the interactive, collaborative and non-linear nature of cyberspace, rather than a theory that interrogates the textual representation of technology in children's books, which is my purpose here. This is not to say that Dresang's work is ill-suited to the children's books selected for discussion here. In fact, many of her arguments about interactivity are particularly germane to the primary corpus of this chapter. In an article entitled "Radical Change Revisited: Dynamic Digital Age Books for Youth" (2008), Dresang looks back at the intervening ten years since she published *Radical Change: Books for Youth in a Digital Age* and writes that children's books which embody the principles of radical change theory "are continuing to appear in more and more sophisticated forms and formats, promoting more and more active engagement of the user/participant/reader, just as is happening with other dynamic media" (2008: 295). The synergy between digital and traditional media that Dresang argues is becoming much more prevalent in contemporary children's fiction is also the central thesis of this book, but a noticeable discrepancy between our positions emerges in relation to the issue of narrative structure. For Dresang, non-linearity is one of the defining features of narratives that produce reading behaviours that accord with radical change theory principles. However, none of the novels that I have chosen to focus on in this chapter employs non-linear plots or structures. This is because the novels that make up the primary corpus of this chapter are all realist in orientation. Although these novels embrace digital technology – replicating the genres of blog writing, chat rooms, emails and instant messages – and do so within a narrative framework that is characterised by more traditional principles of causality. Each narrative has a clear beginning, middle and end, and time progresses in a linear, temporal fashion, without recourse to flashbacks or flash forwards. While it could be argued that such a narrative structure is ideologically conservative (or one that places digital and traditional media in a hierarchical relationship, with digital media designated as inferior), this is not necessarily the case. Alternatively, what arises in these fictions is a genuinely hybridised narrative form – where online behaviours and formats can co-exist with novelistic conventions in (to borrow Dresang's phrase) a synergistic fashion. The novels considered in this chapter, despite their use of generic forms associated with digital media, are also highly intertextual, constructing relationships with other literary texts. This intertextuality functions to create a dialogue between various forms of writing practice, both online and off, illustrating the contentions of Sorapure (2003) and McNeill (2012) that the internet is a space that encourages non-traditional forms of autobiographical self-expression.

The realist orientation of my primary corpus, which includes *Being Emily* (Rachel Gold, 2012), *Train Man* (Hitori Nakano (translated by Bonnie Elliott), 2004), *Entr@pment: A High School Comedy in Chat* (Michael Spooner, 2009), *ttyl* (Lauren Myracle, 2004) and *Eyeleash: A Blog Novel* (Jess C. Scott, 2009), also puts it at odds with Noga Applebaum's (2010) evaluation of the impact of modern technology on narrative structure. Applebaum's self-professed focus is the genre of science fiction, yet even so she is hard-pressed to find more than three examples of narratives that engage with technology at the level of discourse, rather than just story or theme. She cites *The Night Room* (E.M. Goldman, 1995) and *Ultraviolet* (Lesley Howarth, 2001) as examples of novels that "try to achieve resemblance to electronic games" (Applebaum, 2010: 77) and her emphasis is therefore on these novels' use of techniques such as multiple character perspectives and non-linearity. She concludes by discussing M.T. Anderson's *Feed* (2002) and its innovative use of language as a metaphor for social and technological dysfunction. The novels that Applebaum considers are all fantasies, and it is important to point out here that fantasy literature positions readers very differently to realism. John Stephens writes that fantasy and realism are literary genres that are constituted linguistically, and as such the types of language conventionally associated with each of these modes of literature can have varying ideological effects (1992). Stephens' comments are particularly apt for my purposes in this chapter, as one of the reasons why Applebaum's work has only minimal resonance with the narrative depictions of cyberspace in my own primary corpus is because of a difference in genre. The use of realist subject matter and linguistic conventions in novels such as *Train Man, ttyl, Entr@pment: A High School Comedy in Chat* (hereafter referred to as "*Entr@pment*") and *Eyeleash: A Blog Novel*, which are all realist YA romances (of a sort), also produces stark ideological dissimilarities in relation to the types of sci-fi fantasies considered by Applebaum, as this group of realist texts frequently depicts fluid boundaries between cyberspace and social reality. Unlike Applebaum's corpus, these novels construct cyberspace as directly comparable with social reality, emphasising that the digital arena has started to play an increasingly significant role in the development of adolescent identity and the rites of passage (such as romance) that herald the transition to adulthood.

Applebaum's work on technology and narrative structure depends on primary texts that were all published pre-2005. However, the relationship between digital technology and printed children's books has changed radically over the past decade, and although Applebaum's comments are important – in that they mark one of the first critical attempts to explore the impact of technology on narrative forms – they no longer apply to a wide range of children's texts, which, more and more frequently, are depicting cyberspace behaviours and experience as a normalised part of modern childhood and adolescence.

The origins of the term "cyberspace" are, in fact, literary. The word "cyberspace" first appeared in William Gibson's seminal sci-fi novel, *Neuromancer* (1984). This provenance implies a close and intimate relationship between printed books and digital technology – both enable forms of human expression and communication, after all – and it therefore may have been anticipated that the widespread adoption of digital media over the past decade would have flow-on effects for more traditional media, such as books. Perhaps less expected is the rather dramatic fashion in which conceptualisations of cyberspace have also changed over a corresponding period. Writing in 1999, Hayles characterises cyberspace as defined "by a regime of representation within which pattern is the essential reality, presence an optical illusion" (1999: 36). She reflects that "the emphasis on information technologies foregrounds pattern/randomness and pushes presence/absence into the background", an eventuality that has serious implications because it will result in "a systematic devaluation of materiality and embodiment" (1999: 48). My contention, however, is that printed books for children and adolescents that ideologically embrace cyberspace now construct the relationship between pattern (cyberspace) and presence (materiality) as harmonious and relational. They act as confirmation of Hayles' assertion at the cusp of the twenty-first century that the most productive development for theories pertaining to cyberspace would be to "open up the possibilities of seeing pattern and presence as complementary rather than antagonistic" (1999: 49).

The synergy between digital and physical "selves" is clearly apparent in children's texts. The novels I discuss in this chapter offer representations of cyberspace as a primary site of communication and peer interaction for adolescent subjects. The digital sphere now plays a pivotal role in the development of child subjectivity, particularly since it is a realm that makes social interactions highly visible. As Subrahmanyam and Greenfield remark: "society's traditional adolescent issues – intimacy, sexuality, and identity – have all been transferred to and transformed by the electronic stage" (2008: 139–40). But how does a printed book emulate this online experience? *Train Man*, *ttyl* and *Entr@pment* use narrative forms that mimic the structural conventions of chat rooms and message boards, where multiple individuals post synchronous messages and interact with each other in a collective space. *Eyeleash: A Blog Novel* is a narrative comprised of two blogs (one belonging to the primary character and the other to the boy she likes), while *Being Emily* depicts a transgendered teen who finds solace in various online activities – group forums, the virtual game World of Warcraft, and information searching/collecting about transgender experience. Each novel demonstrates that the divide between cyberspace and reality is becoming increasingly blurred, as cyberspace has begun to function in similar ways to social reality for children and teens. Subrahmanyam and Greenfield contend that "teens now conduct a higher *proportion* of their communication through writing in an electronic medium rather than face-to-face or voice-to-voice" (2008: 136) and novels for young readers support such a proposition through their attempts to re-create a digital environment within the traditional format of the printed book.

Polyphony in the technorealist novel

The most notable feature of novels that seek to adopt online modes of expression and communication is that they are "polyphonic", offering readers multiple character perspectives. The potential for literary narratives to be polyphonic, a concept attributed to Bakhtin, predates the emergence of digital technology – but what is remarkable about contemporary narrative depictions of cyberspace for young readers is their rapacious capacity for polyphony, to the extent that the format of a "chat-room novel" such as *Train Man, ttyl* or *Entr@pment* is initially disorienting to readers because it contains so many characters' voices represented on a single page. In contrast to polyfocalised novels of the past (for example, Melvin Burgess' much-lauded *Junk* (1996), which is composed of alternating first-person narration from approximately ten characters, each of whom focalises for two or three pages on each occasion), these chat-room novels take polyphony to a much more extreme degree. Such novels are thus completely dialogic, in a similar vein to a drama script.

A signature distinction between the polyphony that characterises these chat-room narratives and that which is typical of a theatrical script is that the novels are never meant to be performed in any sense. They exist only on the page, but this does not mean that they lack performative qualities. Indeed, the nature of cyberspace as an environment that enables playful experimentations with subjectivity (as illustrated by online game avatars or the multiple subject positions enabled by different forms of social networking media) is conveyed through typographic experimentation in these novels. *Entr@pment* combines four generic forms: blog posts (publicly available, posts are stored in a log), instant messages (private, synchronous communications using online technology that are non-permanent) chat-room posts (also public, but non-permanent) and text messages (which take place outside cyberspace, are private and can be stored). These forms are used interchangeably, yet each has distinct typographic features. In the chat-room posts, each character adopts a different font (and some characters' posts appear in bold, serving as further contrast). Instant messages are delineated from other sections by a heading, for example "IM from Gothling", and the same standard-ised font for both sender and recipient, while the blog entries most closely resemble a conventional narrative form – in that they are a sustained piece of first-person narration. Text messages appear as quite distinct communications. They are presented in small, grey-shaded boxes, accompanied by a pictogram of a mailbox. As the rest of the novel is comprised of brief (one or two lines) interactive com-ments from an assortment of characters, the blog posts stand out for their linearity and cohesion, in what can otherwise be described as a chaotic narrative presentation. Interestingly, the blog posts perform an altogether different ideological function. They belong to a blogger named "Uncle Jerry", who adopts the position of older, wiser adult in a narrative about young romance. (The plot revolves around two girls who attempt to dupe their boyfriends into cheating on them, by masquerading as exotic foreign-exchange students in a high-school chat room.) Uncle Jerry's blog posts frame the entire novel (as well as appearing throughout at regular intervals), and the post that func-tions as the opening of the narrative adopts an attitude of cynicism to youthful romantic idealism through its use of hyperbole and sarcastic humour:

> And there is nothing – nothing – more entertaining than the flash of fury in a young girl's eye when she finds her boy in the arms of her own best friend. Cruel, you say? Heartless? Not at all. I enjoy this only because I know it is the prelude to wisdom. Ah, yes, young lovers. I've had a love of my own. Worst eight hours of my life.
>
> (Spooner, 2009: 1–2)

The sharp use of satire in Uncle Jerry's blog posts is most pertinent in relation to his intertextual quote of both the title and lyrics from the song, "Hello, Young Lovers", which featured in the 1951 Rodgers and Hammerstein musical, *The King and I*. The song was extremely popular when covered by Frank Sinatra in 1954 and again in 1965, and is a sentimental love song in which the speaker reminisces about youthful romance. He urges young lovers not to cry because he is alone, assuring them that he is happy because "I've had a love of my own". The speaker's nostalgic memories of past love construct youth as a time of romantic experience and joy, while older years are associated with loneliness and memories. Uncle Jerry's use of the line "I've had a love of my own" is therefore highly ironic when accompanied by the comical explanation: "Worst eight hours of my life." Together these sentences denigrate love as ephemeral – a marked contrast to the romantic lyrics of the pretext, which focus on the capacity of young lovers to "be brave and faithful and true" ("Hello, Young Lovers", Rodgers and Hammerstein, 1951).

The tone of Uncle Jerry's narration is much more formal than the exchanges that take place in the instant messages or chat room. He adopts a dramatic style (the sequential repetition of the word "nothing" for added emphasis, use of the melodramatic phrase "flash of fury" to describe an emotional state, the inclusion of rhetorical questions and comic irony) and his intention is to construct a hierarchical distinction between the follies of youth and the wisdom that comes with age and experience. His use of language is extremely different, for example, to this exchange between "gothling" (real name: Annie), Ms T (real name: Tamra) and bliss4u (real name: Bliss):

> **gothling:** \<snore>
> Ms.T: what?
> **gothling: u campers need 2 get a grip. haven't u done this before?**
> bliss4u: done what?
> **gothling: u know. worn a mask online. had a different e-dentity**
> Ms.T: have you?
> **gothling: all the time**
> bliss4u: oh right. Like when?
> **gothling: like ur talking to uncle jerry clarkson of bloomington minnesota**
>
> (Spooner, 2009: 87)

In comparison with Uncle Jerry's post, which is in the form of a cohesive monologue, this chat-room dialogue is characterised by the alternating voices of multiple characters, a lack of conventional punctuation, the use of shorthand abbreviations ("u" for "you", "ur" for "your") and the brevity of each participant's response (which is limited to just a few words, rather than the much more expressive sentences crafted by Uncle Jerry). The exchange reveals that "Uncle Jerry" is actually an "e-dentity" invented by Annie/Gothling, one of the female protagonists who masterminds the plot to tempt the boys into cheating on their girlfriends. The novel is a retelling of Mozart's opera *Cosi Fan Tutte* (1790), which centres on fiancé-swapping, although Annie/Gothling's role as the mastermind of the scheme also suggests that a possible literary pre-text is Jill Paton Walsh's 1989 novel *A School for Lovers* (itself an adaptation of Cosi Fan Tutte), in which a university lecturer masterminds (and finances) an elaborate plot to demonstrate to a group of students that true love is an illusion (and he wins his bet). Uncle Jerry's use of a more conventional, extended first-person mode of expression creates the impression of narrative comprehensibility and adult wisdom, especially in comparison with the frenzied, collective communication that is used by the characters in the chat rooms and instant messages. However, this effect is undermined by the events of the narrative, which eventually discredit his cynical views – narrative closure that also overthrows the outcome of Cosi Fan Tutte and *A School for Lovers*. The non-collective nature of Uncle Jerry's blog posts is exposed as artifice, or at least devalued, in favour of communal, negotiated discourse. Uncle Jerry's cynicism about young love, his status as a pseudo-adult and his proclivity for dramatic, monologic narration are all destabilised in the novel's closure, which suggests that the couples might just survive gothling/Annie's deception (the narrative is fairly ambiguous, and although all parties are upset, the damage does not seem irreparable). The final chapter shows Big J/alfonso asking gothling/Annie out on a date, which she accepts – and this causes Uncle Jerry to leave the building, so to speak. The novel closes with a final blog post from Uncle Jerry, which is titled "Under Construction". This phrase is generally used on the homepage of websites that are in the process of being built and are therefore unready for operation, and it suggests that something is awry with the blog. The text of the final post simply states: "Your Uncle Jerry is currently taking leave of his senses. Peace and joy" (Spooner, 2009: 308), and is accompanied by a simple black-and-white pictogram of a curving path, leading away from the viewer. This combination of text and image must be interpreted with the knowledge that "Uncle Jerry" is also gothling/Annie, so it accordingly works as a double-entendre. When read in the context of the heading "Under Construction", this statement functions as the symbolic death of Jerry. The image and accompanying text produce an effect of ambiguity, because they deliberately collapse the distinctions between Annie and her e-dentities. That Uncle Jerry is "currently taking leave of his senses" can also be interpreted as Annie taking leave of her senses by flirting with the possibility of love – an ending that is essentially a celebration of cyberspace and its potential for enabling human relationships and interactions, because it is precisely because of their online interactions that gothling and alfonso have developed feelings for each other.

Like *Entr@pment*, the celebrated Japanese novel *Train Man* is also chaotically polyphonic. This narrative is unique, however, because the novel contains posts from what appear to be hundreds of different contributors. A key distinction between the two novels is that *Train Man* does not seek to invest these contributors with recognisable markers of identity. For the most part they remain anonymous, and even the main character never provides an indication of what his real name might be. He simply goes by the moniker, "Train Man". This novel also varies from the purely digital domain of *Entr@pment* by incorporating short passages of omniscient narration in order to impose a cohesive narrative frame on the message board posts made by a community of "otaku" (a Japanese word that refers to technology geeks with minimal social skills). The novel's plot is minimal: a young man stops a drunk from harassing a group of women on a train and then makes a post about it, whereupon he is eventually urged by this online community to develop a romantic relationship with one of the women. *Train Man* has a much more meandering narrative pace than novels like *Entr@pment* or *ttyl*. It is supposedly based on real events, the novel's back-cover blurb stating, "*Train Man* is lifted directly from Japan's 2-Channel chat forum, the world's largest message board and the most popular website in Japan" (Nakano, 2006). The phrase "lifted directly" corresponds with the notion that realist literature offers readers a transcription of reality (an idea that discourages readers from identifying realist writing as a carefully constructed representation, much like any other genre of narrative production). One of the narrative conventions of realism is the incorporation of detailed information about everyday experiences that appears to be superfluous (as opposed to fantasy, which is generally action-driven and, as a consequence, employs more transparent processes of narrative causality), and *Train Man* exploits this in rather explicit ways. It lacks the momentum of a novel like *Entr@pment*, which has a clearly developed plot; instead, much of *Train Man* is comprised of the message-board geeks waiting around for Train Man to make a post about his experiences with Hermes (the girl he met on the train, referred to on the message boards as "Hermes" because this was the brand of teacup she gave to Train Man as a thank-you gift). The posts (from an assortment of identities) are often repetitive and banal, simply congratulating Train Man on his awkward and drawn-out wooing of Hermes. An example of this interaction occurs on page 313, which is made up of seven posts that say, "I think I'm gonna cry . . . ", "Shit, forgot to get my ASCI ready", "way to go!", "way to go, you did a really great job", "my heart aches", "I'm already crying" and "Right back atcha". In the context of these multiple posts from a host of different contributors to the message board, the brief interjections from an omniscient third-person narrator are significant in shaping the cacophony of posts into something that resembles a narrative. These passages are extremely short, but they do propel the story forward:

> The curtains lift to reveal the miraculous final chapter.
>
> (Nakano, 2006: 249)

> We find Train Man calling Hermes when she returns from her trip. He is happy one moment and then gasping for his last breath another. The Geeks gather and . . .
>
> (2006: 257)

> The countdown to the final battle continued as Train Man and the netizens of the thread fidgeted about restlessly.
>
> (2006: 263)

These interruptions impose narrative shape on the otherwise quite random and circular posts of the online community. They are dramatic in nature, akin to the stage directions contained within a theatrical script. The first two examples provided above use present-tense verbs (which is still largely unconventional in literary narratives), and because they are interspersed with Train Man's exchanges with the other posters, suggest that writing practices in the modern era blend elements of both digital and traditional genres. These short passages of narrator focalisation also create links between groupings of posts (filling in "time gaps" between series of posts), as well as maintaining suspense and reader interest – alerting readers, for example, that they are about to encounter "the final chapter". The narration also establishes connections between Train Man and the other online contributors, most obviously through the use of language that reinforces the idea of a cyber community through terms that refer to the message board posters as "The Geeks" or "the netizens". The issue of nomenclature is particularly relevant in this instance, as a definite tension exists between the naming conventions of literary narratives and online message boards. To the reader of *Train Man* this becomes obvious in the novel's opening, as although there are multiple posts represented on each page (ostensibly made by different people, differentiated graphically by lines that separate the text posted by each contributor), none of the authors of these posts are given a unique identifier (the reverse is true in novels such as *Entr@pment* and *ttyl*, where each character not only has a distinct name, which in the case of *Entr@pment* offers insight into that character's personality, but also a distinct typographic style). Instead, each post in *Train Man* is attributed to "Anonymous" and identified from other posts only by a post number and a date/time stamp. "Train Man" himself initially posts under the title "Anonymous", but in the opening of the narrative this quickly morphs into the number "731", and then "731 aka Train Man", until it finally settles on "Train Man". In terms of literary conventions, characters who are not named can be problematic, as the naming of characters assists in the process of distinguishing one from the other. *Train Man's* refusal to identify subjects with unique names, in conjunction with the main character's shifting moniker, adheres with the nomenclature conventions of cyberspace, where identity is mutable. In *Entr@pment*, the same feat is achieved somewhat differently: single characters have multiple names and identities. The two techniques have a single thematic effect, which is to emphasise that identity is mutable and fluid in cyberspace. Interestingly, both novels focus on the role that cyberspace can play in the acting out of teen romance. Although they take different approaches to the issue, both suggest that some of the awkwardness that is typically experienced by teenagers in the first rush of sexual desire might be obliterated (or at least alleviated) in the dematerialised realm of cyberspace. Such a position also depends on these adolescent subjects being able to express their feelings linguistically, rather than physically (which can pose difficulties for adolescent bodies that are awash with hormones and perhaps do not always respond appropriately). The dialogic and polyphonic nature of online social media is thus presented to adolescent readers as a boon, something to be celebrated rather than feared or approached with caution.

In *ttyl* (a popular online acronym for "talk to you later") readers are offered yet another variation of the polyphonic dialogue enabled by cyberspace. As with *Entr@pment*, this novel tells its story using a combination of digital generic forms: instant messages and chatroom exchanges. The innovation in this case lies in the graphic manipulation of the page for the purpose of representing multiple, synchronous conversations. This results in a page layout that initially contains a dialogue between two participants, where the dialogue extends across the whole page. One of the participants then indicates that they are about to begin a conversation with another character – "hey, zoe just popped up on my buddy list...hold on, I'm gonna check in with her real quick" (Myracle, 2004: 30) – whereupon the page layout changes: the first conversation is pushed to the left-hand side of the page, and the second conversation takes place on the right.

The layout is not particularly sophisticated or detailed (the two conversations simply appear as text on a white page, without any kind of graphic distinction between the two) but the novel does succeed in conveying the multilayered, synchronous nature of communication in cyberspace. Such a representation is also effective at showcasing the type of "multitasking" that often occurs online, with individual users frequently participating in many different activities (messaging, Facebooking, game playing and so on) at the same time.

Collective identity in cyberspace

The extreme polyphony that characterises these technorealist novels works on a very overt level to promote and revel in the collectivity of cyberspace. Within novels such as *Train Man*, *Entr@pment* and *ttyl*, which employ collaborative generic forms such as chat rooms and instant messages, individual identity develops in a collective rather than autonomous fashion. In a discussion about the networked autobiographical writing practices fostered by online social media sites such as Facebook, McNeill asserts that such sites have transformed traditional concepts of personal identity and her comments are germane to the YA novels under consideration here:

> In so doing, this networked self [that is created on sites such as Facebook] emphasizes the collective nature of subjectivity, challenging the perceived autonomy of the human subject as championed by liberal humanism (Hayles 3). It makes manifest concepts of relationality that have revised contemporary theories of auto/biography to argue that life narratives are not produced by individuals in some sort of social vacuum, but that identities and the stories that shape them are intertwined with others...
>
> (2012: 73)

Individuals can, of course, strive to construct their own life narratives, but this process will always be subject to interruption and comment from others, which may ultimately propel the course of such a narrative in different directions. Intersubjectivity thus becomes more communal, and also more overtly negotiated. *Entr@pment* is a good example here, where online collectivity and collaboration are advocated through the development of gothling/Annie/Uncle Jerry's character. In *ttyl*, the collectivity of cyberspace is specifically gendered as feminine. The three female characters use the online space to discuss their desires and hopes (which the novel implies might be more difficult in face-to-face situations), and reflect on their daily lives. Cyberspace is designated, for the most part, as a nurturing and supportive space for young women. As mad maddie comments in the novel's close, "It's funny how some things r easier to talk about over the computer, isn't it?" (Myracle, 2004: 208). In the case of *Train Man*, this collectivity is also gendered – but in this case, it is gendered as masculine. When the protagonist begins to post regular messages about Hermes (the young woman he helped to rescue on the train), articulating his lack of experience with women and asking for advice, the virtual community (which is predominantly male) responds with surprising enthusiasm. They cheer him on, offer guidance and suggestions (what to make of her gift, how to select an appropriate restaurant for a date) and eventually come to think of Train Man as an extension of themselves: a symbol of what might happen to a shy individual when a community gets behind him and generously provides their support. Pierre

Lévy, a French philosopher and cultural theorist whose work focuses on social relations in cyberspace, points to "collectivity" as an integral feature of online communities. He proposes that identity be understood as fluid and multiple in cyberspace, arguing that computers are now responsible for producing what he terms "collective intelligence". Unlike physical manifestations of identity, Lévy asserts that cyberspace engineers a different type of social bond, which allows:

> another kind of subjectivity to develop, one that pulverizes the signs of knowledge or identity, enabling them to flow, blend, and run together, grow strong, expand, and intermingle. It does not shatter identities but liberates them.
>
> (1997: 159)

Lévy's views about cyberspace are definitely utopian, but a somewhat idealised perception of online collectivity is indeed evident in the represented relationship between Train Man and the unidentified contributors who respond to his posts. As the narrative progresses, the net community becomes increasingly invested in Train Man's adventures with Hermes. When he is absent from the thread, the other contributors interact with each other as they wait for him to make a post, and at these times the collective nature of online storytelling becomes apparent. The main character of the narrative temporarily disappears from the story at regular intervals, whereupon each of the minor characters has the power to manipulate the story in varied directions, revealing snippets of information about their own lives and experiences: at one point a contributor discusses his own encounter with a drunk on a train (Nakano, 2006: 228); while another mentions his quest to locate the tea that Train Man described being served at Hermes' house (2006: 230). These incidents invest the narrative with rich potential, as they suggest that it has the ability to travel in myriad directions. This interconnectivity also implies that Train Man's experiences are turned into collective experience through the act of posting descriptions about them online. He writes about what happens to him and Hermes, and later the contributors post about similar and related experiences of their own. Most importantly, this technosociality is not confined to the digital stage, but conflates the boundaries between cyberspace and the real world, suggesting that the two are interrelated in the production of identity and community.

Typographic experimentation and intertextuality

Earlier I indicated that the polyphony that characterises chat-room novels for adolescent readers is often manifest on the physical page through variations in typographic font, which enable readers to distinguish between characters, or through page layout, which can be manipulated to give the impression that multiple conversations are taking place simultaneously. It is to the issue of how text is arranged on the page, and the ideological significance of such arrangements, that I now turn. Current incarnations of online social media (as used by children and teenagers on a daily basis) enable regular viewing and sharing of digital images. This remains a key point of distinction between the current digital environment and traditional printed novels. Narrative representations of cyberspace for children have nevertheless found ingenious techniques to approximate this visual quality. *Train Man* provides an excellent example of how characters (letters, numerical digits and punctuation marks, as commonly located on a computer keyboard) can be used in unconventional formations to create images – more properly referred to as ASCII art. Images produced in this way appear regularly throughout the novel as part of posts made by Train Man's supporters, and they include crude pictures of a bunch of flowers, captioned "Train man, way to go you bastard!" (Nakano, 2006: 314); a man who is running (2006: 313); and two cats sitting side by side, captioned "all happiness to you" (2006: 315). These rather crude images appear regularly throughout the novel and have an important thematic function. First, Train Man himself never posts any images. The images are a contribution of the wider message-board community and therefore signal the participatory nature of narratives that take place within the realm of cyberspace. Second, the images themselves hark back to a time when online social media did not allow users to post images as message content. The images contained within *Train Man* represent a new form of digital language but they simultaneously situate the novel in a particular historical moment (ASCII art developed during the 1970s and 80s but declined in the 1990s due to the development of computers with more sophisticated graphics capabilities). The act of transforming the characters conventionally associated with written language into a means of visual communication is metonymic of the monumental shifts in communication that have occurred since the mid-1980s as a result of the internet. And even though the images in *Train Man* might initially look old-fashioned and crude to young readers accustomed to high-quality graphics when online, it is difficult not to be impressed by the creativity and attention to detail required to produce an image from the limited number of characters available on an average keyboard.

One of the more memorable character-created images in *Train Man* is of a Moomin, a fantasy creature from Tove Jansson's much-loved series of books for children (which have been very popular in Japan). The image has little relationship to the narrative about Train and Hermes – but this is precisely the point. *Train Man*'s intertextual quotation of a popular Finnish children's book series, for no apparent reason, serves as a reminder that printed books that engage with cyberspace (its generic forms, its modes of expression) are inherently intertextual. Marie-Laure Ryan comments on intertextuality as it applies to cyberspace, writing: "In postmodernism, the ideal of the total work gives way to the idea of universal intertextuality: every individual text is linked to countless other ones, and the whole is reflected in every of its parts, as in fractal images. In the electronic age, thanks to the hyperlink, the text literally becomes a matrix of many texts and a self-renewing entity" (1999: 14). Such a statement is obviously problematic if applied to a representation of cyberspace in a printed book, where any reference to a hypertext link can only be a symbolic reference, rather than a functioning link to another text. However, as the inclusion of the Moomin image in *Train Man* shows, cyberspace narratives for children still seek to create relationships between cyberspace textuality and more traditional forms of narrative. Such intertextual quotation is also evident in *Entr@pment*, which uses Cosi Fan Tutte as a pretext (but subverts the outcome of the traditional story) and in *Eyeleash: A Blog Novel*, where intertextuality functions more broadly on a genre level, as the novel provocatively blends memoir, YA fiction and erotica in a narrative that destabilises many of the ideological conventions pertaining to representations of sex, personal expression and female adolescent identity. The function of intertextuality in these novels is to create associations between various forms of linguistic expression, particularly in the sense that the brief, colloquial and shorthand language of cyberspace (which is, in actuality, a specific youth discourse) is linked to forms of writing that are regarded as belonging to high culture. As Ryan reminds us, texts produced in cyberspace "are less durable and therefore less binding than handwritten and printed messages" and the nature of such texts is that they "encourage informality, brainstorming, and the throwing of ideas on the forum for the pure sake of testing the reactions of the audience" (1999: 5). Regardless of these distinctions, novels such as *Train Man, Entr@pment* and *Eyeleash: A Blog Novel* encourage readers to think about the similarities and overlaps between cyberspace texts and more traditional forms of writing – a process that in each of these novels complements the thematic blurring of the distinction between digital and material subjectivities.

Adolescent identity in cyberspace

In the final part of this chapter I focus on the connection between cyberspace and adolescent identity, examining how cyberspace might be used to produce positive experiences for young adults. Reflecting on the relationship between cyberspace and self-identity, Kevin Robins writes: "the exhilaration of virtual existence and experience comes from a sense of transcendence and liberation from the material and embodied world" (2000: 79). Robins is, in actuality, suspicious of attempts to position virtual reality as a fantastic alternative to the banality of the real world and, like Hayles, would prefer to see a more synergistic relationship between digital and material contexts. One example of how such synergy might be achieved is provided in YA fictions that depict cyberspace as a site for exploring adolescent feminine subjectivity, particularly in relation to the female body and emerging feminine sexuality. Such fictions portray cyberspace as a site that is situated at one remove from reality, but this distance is not used simply as a means through which adolescent girls might escape their status as embodied subjects. Rather, the construction of cyberspace as transitional or liminal space allows it to function in a non-normative manner. In practice, what this means is that teenage girls view cyberspace as a site that is free from parental surveillance and certain negative forms of peer judgement. They are also attuned to the internet's capacity for private and public exchanges, utilising both functions in the process of expressing and reflecting upon their desires and anxieties in online spaces. In *Eyeleash: A Blog Novel, ttyl* and *Being Emily*, cyberspace is represented as playing a significant role in the development of adolescent sexuality and body image.

While cyberspace has traditionally been viewed as disembodied and immaterial, newer forms of online social media routinely involve the networked sharing of photographic images of human faces and bodies. This is one form of cyberspatial embodiment, but what the YA novels examined in this chapter point out is that virtual embodiment can take a plethora of different forms. On a thematic level, cyberspace functions as a realm that is safe, private and supportive for adolescent protagonists who wish to take temporary shelter from the real world and the damaging forms of peer pressure that can characterise adolescent interactions therein. This is most apparent in Rachel Gold's *Being Emily*, a novel that focuses on a male-to-female transgender teen's quest for parental and social acceptance. The narrative deals with Chris/Emily's process of coming out as a transsexual, a difficult and traumatic experience for an individual living in a relatively remote and conservative community. Chris/Emily's isolation is mediated, however, by her experiences in virtual reality. Online, she finds various forms of support (from trangender sites and discussion forums) and also platforms for expressing her feminine subjectivity (she is an avid player of World of Warcraft, where her female avatar enables her to inhabit – virtually – a female body). Privacy is of pivotal importance to Chris/Emily, as her computer is located in her bedroom and is thus safe from parental surveillance. Yet the public and networked capabilities of cyberspace are simultaneously presented as valuable, as they allow Chris/Emily to get in contact with other transgendered individuals and seek advice about issues related to the transgendered physical body: such as sex-reassignment surgery and hormone therapy. Unlike the other novels considered within this chapter, *Being Emily* is not set in cyberspace, nor does it attempt to replicate the generic forms associated with communication in cyberspace. Nevertheless, the novel is thematically preoccupied with the non-normative (transgendered) human body. A dilemma for transgendered subjects is the reconciliation or remediation of a body that does not accord with one's perceived gender identity. *Being Emily* thoughtfully explores this issue and deliberately constructs cyberspace as a realm that assists transgendered subjects in attaining subjective agency. One of the novel's most ingenious strategies for representing transgendered subjectivity is to render social interactions (as perceived by the protagonist) as computer code:

> I hardly have to think about it anymore. My larynx is programmed with all the appropriate responses, and I don't even pay attention. It's like I wrote all the code years ago and now my brain just reads it:
>
> /run: greet teammate
>
> 1. speak: "Hey man, how's it going?"
> 2. joke about a) sports, b) cars, c) weather, d) class
> 3. make inarticulate sound of agreement
> 4. run line 2 again
> 5. make gesture: a) grin, b) shrug, c) playful hit
> 6. repeat 3–5 until bell rings
>
> (Gold, 2012: 6)

This extract shows a sophisticated understanding of the interplay between the mind and body in a conversational exchange, using the analogy of computer programming to illustrate the brain's processing of spoken words and gesture. The conceptualisation of subjectivity evident here is inherently posthuman, as it demonstrates what Kim Toffoletti refers to as "a body that emerges from the eradication of any critical distance between the human subject and information and media systems" (2007: 108). As I have argued throughout this chapter, technorealist literature for children adopts this exact premise in its portrayal of child subjects for whom cyberspace is an intrinsic part of daily life. What is perhaps most interesting about the passage reproduced above is that the computer has become a metaphor for human subjectivity – the two have become completely amalgamated.

The passage is also an exaggerated illustration of gender performativity, a comic satire of hegemonic masculinity and the words and gestures used to naturalise this gender category. The actions and expressions are so artificial to Chris/Emily, that she declares that the actual moment of interaction requires no independent thought, as her "larynx is programmed" to respond in this scripted manner. The passage heavily emphasises the role of the body in the production of gender identity (the inarticulate grunts and gestures associated with conventional masculinity; violence – such as a "playful hit" – as an appropriate masculine social response), and by using a programming analogy the novel reveals, in a decidedly posthuman fashion, how digital technology opens up new ways of thinking about the self, and how many of these ways of "being" are embodied.

A novel that accentuates cyberspace as an "embodied" domain is *Eyeleash: A Blog Novel*, self-published by the young (born in 1986) Singaporean writer Jess C. Scott. The novel's provocative account of adolescent sexuality is highly unconventional, but it is perhaps the combination of the novel's generic form – the narrative is constructed purely out of blog posts and instant messages – with this lusty portrayal of adolescent female desire that made it appear so unviable to commercial publishers. (Scott has a highly visible online presence, as she is the author of multiple blogs, and describes receiving hundreds of rejection letters when she approached publishers with the *Eyeleash* manuscript.) The novel is thematically aligned with the fairly predictable romance metanarrative found in most YA fiction. According to Roberta Seelinger Trites, this metanarrative takes the following form in YA novels:

> Generally speaking, two teenagers feel sexually attracted to one another in a standard YA romance. The action is occasionally blocked during a stage in which each character thinks the attraction is unrequited. The characters eventually communicate and express their attraction. Then the action is blocked while they make decisions about consummating their passion. More often than not, they express their passion with some sort of sexual contact.
>
> (2000: 84–85)

This is an exact plot summary of the romance between 17-year-old Jade Ashton and Novan Chang, but where the novel distinguishes itself is in the construction of Jade's sexuality. On her blog, Jade regularly documents engaging in masturbation. The documenting of these sexual experiences serves to undermine the otherwise conservative narrative about sexuality, which is based on the idea of "waiting for the right one", so that sex can be meaningful. One of the most popular forms of self-representation in cyberspace is the personal blog. The primary difference between a blog and other more traditional forms of autobiographical writing, such as keeping a diary, are that a blog is both public and interactive. (These are key features of the novel *serafina67 * urgently requires life**, which was discussed comprehensively in Chapter 5, with reference to its engagement with the concepts of participatory and lateral surveillance.) Jade's blog functions quite differently, however, as it is private and not available to anyone. In this respect, the immateriality of cyberspace is of central importance, as the secrecy of Jade's autobiographical writing can be maintained much more effectively than if she were writing in a physical book. The potential for cyberspace to be characterised as a domain that is simultaneously public and private is cleverly invoked in *Eyeleash*, which opens with an instant message from Jade to Novan, stating:

> Since you asked for it, I'm sending you a copy of my personal blog. I know I said I didn't blog, but I do – just that it's a private one. So it's very personal.
>
> (Scott, 2011: 1)

Jade's use of the term "private", and her admission that she lied previously about maintaining a blog, indicates that she perceives her blog in similar ways to a secret diary, yet the action of being able to send the entire diary electronically to another person simply by clicking a button is a reminder that a blog is very different to the material artefact of a diary. Even a private blog can be transferred to or accessed by another person extremely easily – and, for that matter, the "privacy" of Jade's blog (in comparison with the more common form of public blog) is presumably something she could also change at the click of a button, simply by updating the access criteria on the host site. This ambiguity is brought to the forefront of the reader's mind due to its placement on the opening page, and acts as a thematic reminder that digital technology has exerted a profound host of changes on traditional forms of self-expression. In the context of technorealist literature produced for teenagers, *Eyeleash* also marks itself as unique because of its sustained engagement with the conceptual relationship between cyberspace and sexuality. For many adults, cyberspace is intimately connected with sexuality. The most typical reason for this is the easy accessibility of pornography online, but the internet also offers a vast array of online matchmaking sites, as well as sex shops that take the anxiety out of ordering sexual toys or aids. The internet also offers a surplus of information about sex, so it would seem logical that teenagers (given the statistics which show that such large numbers of them have internet access) would use cyberspace as a means for exploring their emergent sexuality. This does not seem to be the case so far in YA fiction, and *Eyeleash* is the only YA novel currently available, to my knowledge, that deals with adolescent sexuality in a digital world. (*Being Emily* tentatively suggests that the internet can be used for this purpose, but Chris/Emily's sexuality is not represented in any detail, as the narrative focuses solely on gender.) In *Eyeleash*, Jade's blog is essentially a private place for her to express and explore her sexual desires. Thus although cyberspace is technically disembodied space, Jade's blog posts constantly focus on her body in her descriptions of what sexually arouses her, how she stimulates herself and what she finds most attractive about Novan.

Needless to say, this novel is not a conventional work of YA fiction. Its highly charged sexual content is, on occasion, extremely provocative – particularly statements such as "I think good sex should hurt" (Scott, 2011: 14) – but for the most part the novel endorses a healthy attitude to adolescent sexuality in its normalisation of both masturbation and sexual desire. Jade, after all, is not being sexually promiscuous, she is simply skilled at articulating her desires and pleasuring herself (achievements that should see her celebrated as a feminist sexual role model for teenage girls). And, as opposed to a material diary, cyberspace enables this articulation of physical desire to be interactive. At one point in the narrative, Jade and Novan exchange nude digital photographs of themselves and each then uses the photographs of the other as a stimulus for more masturbation. This is, again, a provocative inclusion in a novel aimed at adolescent readers, because much adult panic around young people's use of the internet stems from a perception that they lack awareness of the internet as a "public" domain. Jade is aware of this possibility but the experience is shaped quite differently into an empowering (and sustained) performance of sexual desire. Jade's self-representation of her sexuality in her blog posts depends, to a certain extent, on cyberspace as immaterial and disembodied, as these very qualities afford her the luxury of self-creation. Unlike the realities of first-time adolescent sex (discomfort or pain, anxiety, performance issues, mess), Jade's recounting of her experiences situate her as in control of her sexuality: proud of her body, aware of what arouses her, and up front about her desires in online message exchanges with Novan. Reflecting on the process of taking nude photographs of herself, Jade is surprised by how much she approves of the results: "I think the pix look quite nice. I've an hourglass figure, to my surprise" (2011: 89). Her discovery that the images differ from her mental perceptions are indicative of how the act of self-styling one's own sexuality (particularly if the subject is sexually inexperienced) can have extremely beneficial results. The act of controlling the camera – "I took a lot of high-angle (more flattering) shots" (2011: 89) – enables Jade to control which parts of her body she wishes to sexualise, and to choose the exact images of herself that she is willing to share with Novan. The disembodied nature of cyberspace also enables Jade to communicate her desire to Novan effectively and articulately. She directs him, as it were, when it comes to taking photographs of himself that will please her, effectively communicating the intersubjective nature of this virtual sexual experience. Jade tells Novan what to wear in some of the photos, "take some like in some crisp-looking kind of outfit... smth that looks smart", as well as which body parts to focus on, "actually i'd like torso and back" (2011: 97). As a consequence, the resulting portrayal of sex as it is played out in cyberspace is one that allows Jade to construct herself as a consensual and autonomous participant, and also as a young woman with a clear appreciation of her sexual needs and desires, who takes an active role in sexual encounters. Such a positive representation of adolescent sexuality in literature directed at teen audiences is, to say the least, unusual.

Part of the appeal of Jade's sexual self-representation in cyberspace is the colloquial youth register in which she expresses herself. *Eyeleash* is written in the everyday, youth-oriented, shorthand style that characterises online interactions. The euphemistic, metaphorical language often used in literature for adolescents to describe the act of sex is replaced in this novel with language that is direct, plain and literal – and, above all, accessible to a young (and sexually inexperienced) adolescent reader. Readers don't need sophisticated interpretive skills to perceive Jade as a sexually empowered character, and the means through which she achieves much of this empowerment – the internet – is similarly within reach of most of these readers. Jade's recognisable and accessible form of self-representation also performs a thematic function, in that it helps to normalise adolescent sexual desire as a part of daily life.

The link between sex and cyberspace is now an established one, with many online channels dedicated to cybersex encounters. Gareth Branwyn's critical examination of sexuality in cyberspace, which was published in 2000 and focused on the emerging phenomenon of "text-based compu-sex" (2000: 402), is exploratory in nature, and thus concludes with a number of questions. More than a decade has now passed since Branwyn's work was published, and it seems suitable to revisit some of the questions that he raises in light of a novel such as *Eyeleash*, which deals with similar territory:

> Will on-line sex become a satisfying substitute for sex in the real world? What impact will all forms of computer-mediated relationships have on face-to-face relationships as virtual communities develop a wider spectrum of interactional possibilities? Is this line of questioning even relevant anymore? As more people spend greater amounts of their time in cyberspace and come to identify themselves increasingly with their various cyber-constructs and non-physical relationships, won't the boundaries between "real" and "imaginary" have less practical significance?
>
> (2000: 402)

Eyeleash provides a series of insightful answers to Branwyn's questions and, in many ways, acts as an exemplar for the corpus of technorealist novels for adolescents considered in this chapter. In *Eyeleash*, online sex is not portrayed as a substitute for sex in the real world, but it does play a vital role in the development of adolescent sexuality and also in the initiation of sexual relationships. The act of self-expression/ self-representation within cyberspace can have a positive impact on adolescent subjectivity, especially since this self-expression can occur in a virtual space that is free of many of the constraining phenomena (such as those that govern normative categories of gender and sexuality) that characterise social interactions in the real world. Branwyn's query about the blurring of the demarcation between "reality" and "virtual reality" is, of course, most pertinent to *Eyeleash* and similar works of YA fiction, but not for the exact reasons that Branwyn outlines. His expression suggests a privileging of cyberspace over social reality, underscored by a conceptualisation of cyberspace as a domain that is imaginary and immaterial. However, *Eyeleash* and novels like it present cyberspace as an extension of social reality within adolescent life, a technologically mediated realm that facilitates and enhances the social processes associated with adolescent identity development. Admittedly, Branwyn's analysis revolves around anonymous online sex, so is not wholly applicable to the online sexual scenarios that occur in *Eyeleash* between two individuals who have met in real life and use cyberspace as a platform for initiating a sexual relationship. Cyberspace is never completely "imaginary" or "anonymous" in *Eyeleash*, as it is closely linked with embodied reality. This is a crucial feature of *Eyeleash* and novels like it: cyberspace is not separate from social reality, but must always be considered in relation to it. Ideologically, the boundaries that separate cyberspace from real life are becoming much less clearly demarcated as more and more of the social interactions that characterise daily life are transferred to an online context.

The positive portrayal of cyberspace in *Eyeleash* and the other works of YA technorealism discussed here does not naively ignore that there are definite risks associated with online social interactions. *Eyeleash* acknowledges that the internet can be used to initiate sexual encounters with strangers (Jade meets "Tyler" in an online simulation after Novan has failed to show up to a date), but it presents such relationships as sleazy and shallow. *Entr@pment* similarly indicates that cyberspace can generate unwanted sexual attention for young women, through gothling's casual description of the internet site, Myspace, as a place where you have "so many losers hitting on u" (Spooner, 2009: 87). Gothling's clever response is simply to adopt a male avatar. The issue of nude digital photographs, and the internet's capacity to "share" such images on a massive scale, is also visited in *Eyeleash* and *ttyl*, with both novels suggesting that teenagers need to be aware of such possibilities and attuned to how to avoid them. In an ironic twist, the predatory adult male character of *ttyl* (a teacher who attempts to seduce Zoe) does not approach her online, but in the much more accessible space of his classroom – a reminder that such behaviour is not purely confined to the internet. Nonetheless, each of these novels endorses a thematic conceptualisation of cyberspace that focuses much more closely on the benefits that children and adolescents can gain from online interactions.

One of the most notable elements of novels such as *Eyeleash, ttyl* and *Entr@pment* is the sense of community that is produced, especially for young women, in cyberspace. (The same is true of *Train Man*, although the community is predominantly male.) These narratives, which are not only set in cyberspace but also use the narrative forms and youth-oriented modes of expression associated with virtual reality, emphasise the collective and liberatory nature of virtual reality for adolescent subjects. The production of online selves in the YA novels examined within this chapter is depicted as a routine part of contemporary adolescent existence. Importantly, the types of subjectivity produced in cyberspace challenge conventional understandings of human identity. The very concept of "social interaction" is fundamentally subverted in cyberspace, which offers a dialogic, polyphonic environment that individuals can enter, with the aid of a computer, while otherwise completely alone. The immaterial nature of cyberspace also allows individual subjects to participate in their own self-styled representation – and it is this aspect of cyberspace that literary authors have embraced with such gusto. The adolescent characters of these social media narratives are all "speaking subjects" who use first-person present tense: they speak for themselves, in the vernacular of youth, and are constantly engaged in chaotic, frenzied dialogue with each other. The resulting representation of adolescent identity is intrinsically posthuman in its production of digitally mediated, multiple and fluid subjectivities that transgress the binary of "real" and "virtual" worlds.

Conclusion

For children living in the Western world at the start of the twenty-first century, regular access to technology is simply a routine part of life. Computers are now omnipresent in classrooms and homes, and many of the social and practical aspects of daily living have been transferred online. Children are also highly proficient users of technology, their skills often surpassing those of their parents. Despite this reality, fictional narratives produced for young readers have continued to pursue an anti-technology agenda, representing technoscientific developments as something that should be regarded with fear and scepticism. This negative representational paradigm has been maintained for a number of decades – but since the mid-2000s has slowly started to shift, thanks to the emergence of a growing subset of novels that have sought to engage with children's positive real-life experiences of technology and represent it within narrative as having a constructive effect on human subjectivity and society.

These fictions show, in their exploration of the various relationships that arise between human subjects and technology, a preparedness to deconstruct traditional understandings of what it means to be human. As the preceding chapters have demonstrated, these fictional narratives use the theme of technology to interrogate the status of the human subject in the modern era – employing motifs such as robotics, cybernetics and digital surveillance to critique established humanist concepts of selfhood. In doing so, these YA novels demonstrate an ideological alignment with posthumanism, which strives to deprivilege humanist conceptualisations of the self through an examination of the different ways in which technology produces alternative formulations of the subject. Posthuman subjectivity is thus defined by its collective rather than individualistic nature, its fragmentation and plurality, and its emphasis on embodiment. A defining feature of posthuman ideology, as discussed in Chapter 2, is its attention to "otherness". In addressing how traditional definitions of human identity and experience can be destabilised by technology, fictions produced for adolescent readers frequently use non-human protagonists and narrators to interrogate ideas about subject formation from the position of an outsider. The non-human status of these robot and cyborg characters is used to comment on the exclusionary nature of humanist concepts of subjectivity and to endorse a more expansive and de-hierarchised understanding of selfhood. One of the more interesting developments in YA fictions that respond to the idea of a posthuman future is the recognition that such a shift in dominant ideological paradigms of identity formation cannot be represented through story and theme alone. These novels use a range of narrative techniques to reflect the fluid, networked and shifting nature of posthuman modes of subjectivity. Such narratives do not necessarily offer a utopian vision of the technofuture, but they nevertheless suggest that technology has the potential to enhance and deepen our understanding of what it means to be human in the modern era.

One of the criticisms that may be levelled at this book is that the collection of young adult novels that have been selected to demonstrate posthuman models of subjectivity often feature characters that could just as easily be interpreted as conforming to normative humanist paradigms of identity. Characters such as Marcus Yallow, from *Little Brother* and *Homeland*, Wade from *Ready Player One*, or even the cyborg Cinder (in the novel of the same name), are recognisably humanist in some senses: they are all individuals who achieve subjective agency; the narratives in which they appear are cohesive and coherent; and they each triumph over negative social forces. But this is precisely the point. Posthumanism does not entail a total rejection of the humanist traditions of the past. Instead, as I have argued throughout this book, it involves a reconceptualisation of selfhood and social relations that fit more readily with human experience in the digital age. The humanist subject is thus reformulated – rather than outright rejected – within posthumanism. Indeed, Tony Davies provides confirmation of this in *Humanism* (2008), a critical and historical exploration of the concept, which ends very fittingly with a discussion of posthumanism. Davies concludes: "though it is clear that the master narrative of transcendental Man has outlasted its usefulness, it would be unwise simply to abandon the ground occupied by the historical humanisms" (2008: 141). Such is the case with posthuman narratives produced for children and adolescents, which similarly do not entirely forsake the humanist traditions that have become so integral to the representation of subjectivity within the domain of children's fiction. Agency, a concept that is essential to humanist understandings of selfhood, also plays a significant role in the posthuman narratives analysed throughout this book. However, "agency" is transformed within these fictions and reconstituted as a collaborative rather than individualistic attribute. The same could be said for the way in which these narratives promote altruistic and intersubjective social relations. What makes such interactions distinctly posthuman is the way in which technology is constructed as their enabler: virtual reality functions as a communal and collaborative space, or the technologically enhanced female body is used to construct new and empowered forms of feminine subjectivity.

Teenagers are highly adaptive and proficient users of digital technology, and it is therefore hardly unexpected that printed books written for this demographic have been quick to appropriate the generic forms, visual style and shorthand linguistic discourse associated with cyberspace. One of the most exciting outcomes of my research into representations of the posthuman in YA fiction has been the discovery that such fictions are not just innovative in their thematic depiction of technology, but also in how they use narrative discourse to represent subjectivity in a technologically mediated world. These texts create a specific ideological link between youth and technology, using narrative form and discourse to complement stories that are about young protagonists who perceive and use technology as a form of self-expression and empowerment. Although the number of YA realist novels that present a genuine engagement with cyberspace is currently very limited, the few that do so are strikingly creative. Currently these narratives only represent a small portion of the digital media social interactions in which teenagers are involved on a daily basis – indicating that this is an area to watch with respect to future experiments in style and form.

The subject matter canvassed in this book provides a conceptual (although by no means comprehensive) introduction to the manner in which the genre of YA fiction has recently started to engage with the effects of technology on child and adolescent subjects. Technology has the potential to alter human existence on its most basic level: that is, in relation to how human beings think about their own selfhood and identity. This is exactly why the critical philosophy of posthumanism has so much relevance to children's literature: although it addresses "big" ideas, it applies these to a personal and individual context. Books produced for young readers frequently focus on the personal, as one of the ways in which the genre distinguishes itself from adult fiction is through its extensive focus on personal maturation and the formation of identity. Many of the novels discussed in the preceding chapters examine technology by taking a concept such as surveillance, artificial intelligence or genetic engineering and then exploring how such a concept would affect an individual character's perception of themselves, their relationships with others, and their understanding of the world and society they inhabit. This is especially relevant to narratives about cyborg characters, which deal with significant social issues – such as the prolongation of human life through the use of various medical technologies, including the replacement of organic body parts with artificial ones – yet do so in a pronouncedly personal manner. These fictions often involve the use of imagined technologies, but their focus is not on the exact nature of the technoscience. Instead, they concentrate on how it feels for an individual to manipulate prosthetic limbs for the first time, or how a computerised brain would affect one's memory of past events and relationships. By using non-human characters as narrators or focalisers, these YA novels creatively interrogate the very concept of "human", pushing readers to consider why the technologically-enhanced characters of these stories should not be afforded the same amount of dignity and respect as other human subjects. This philosophical agenda lies at the heart of posthumanism, as indicated by Elaine Graham's explanation of how the category of the posthuman seeks to deprivilege the status of the humanist subject:

My preferred usage of post/human denotes perhaps less a condition…than an intervention. By intervention, I mean that talk about representations of the post/human is an occasion for acknowledging what has always been the case – that talk about "human nature" is as much a piece of human artifice as all the other things human beings have invented.

(2002: 37)

The examples of YA fiction that form the primary corpus of this book are aligned with posthumanism in that they are involved in a comparable process of offering alternative and more expansive understandings of what it means to be human in the posthuman era. Modern technology is the incentive for such a project because, in a relatively short space of time, it has managed to drastically change human life. The invention of the computer, advances in medical science, the advent of pervasive digital surveillance and the increasing popularity of online social media are just some of the technological developments that have acted to transform the activities associated with daily living – and as such they have also affected concepts of selfhood and social organisation. Humanist conceptualisations of selfhood as coherent, stable and individualistic are ill-suited to life in the new millennium, which is characterised by simultaneous presence in both virtual and real worlds, omnipresent digital surveillance that depends on an awareness of one's image being replicated and advances in biotechnology that allow diseased or malfunctioning body parts to be replaced with genetically engineered or mechanical substitutes.

The literary trends that this book addresses are still only at an incipient stage. Although each of the YA fictions discussed in the preceding chapters offers a complex representation of how technology can affect the human condition, such texts have only arrived on the literary scene relatively recently, as prior to 2000 a technophobic paradigm of technological representation was the norm. A fundamental connection between the narratives discussed here lies in their represented awareness of the diverse ways in which technology can potentially empower child and adolescent subjects. It seems fitting to end this book with a quotation from Sherryl Vint, who argues for the necessity of an ethical posthumanism in response to the technological developments of the future:

While it seems inevitable that technoscience will change what it means to be human in the near future, this is not necessarily a cause for despair. It is imperative that we develop an ethically responsible model of embodied posthuman subjectivity which enlarges rather than decreases the range of bodies that matter.

(2007: 190)

It would seem that YA fiction is well on the way to developing and exploring such a philosophy.

Bibliography

Primary Sources

A.I. Artificial Intelligence. Directed by Steven Spielberg. DreamWorks Pictures, 2001.

Anderson, M.T. *Feed*. 2002. London: Walker Books, 2003. Print.

Beckett, Bernard. *Genesis*. 2006. Melbourne: The Text Publishing Company, 2008. Print.

Bukatman, Scott. *Terminal Identity: The Virtual Subject in Postmodern Science Fiction*. Durham, North Carolina: Duke University Press, 1993. Print.

Card, Orson Scott. *Ender's Game*. 1991. London: Atom, 2008. Print.

Cline, Ernest. *Ready Player One*. New York: Crown Publishers, 2011. Print.

Collins, Suzanne. *The Hunger Games*. London: Scholastic, 2008. Print.

Cusick, John M. *Girl Parts*. Somerville, Massachusetts: Candlewick Press, 2010. Print.

Day, Susie. *serafina67 * urgently requires life**. New York: Scholastic, 2008. Print.

Doctorow, Cory. "Anda's Game". 2004. Strahan, Jonathan (ed). *The Starry Rift: Tales of New Tomorrows*. New York: Penguin, 2008a: 173–206. Print.

———. *Little Brother*. New York: Tor Books, 2008b. Print.

———. *Homeland*. New York: Tor Books, 2013. Print.

Farmer, Nancy. *The House of the Scorpion*. New York: Simon and Schuster, 2002. Print.

Fox, Helen. *Eager*. London: Hodder Children's Books, 2003. Print.

Gates, Susan. *Dusk*. London: Puffin, 2004. Print.

Gibson, William. *Neuromancer*. New York: Ace, 1984. Print.

Gold, Rachel. *Being Emily*. Tallahassee, Florida: Bella Books, 2012. Print.

Harland, Richard. *Ferren and the Angel*. Ringwood, Victoria: Penguin, 2000. Print.

Hoffmann, E.T.A. "The Sandman". 1816. Web. *Project Guttenberg*. 02 January 2014. (http://www.gutenberg.org/files/32046/32046-h/32046-h.htm).

Huxley, Aldous. *Brave New World*. London: Chatto and Windus, 1932. Print.

Jansson, Tove. *Adventures in Moominland*. London: Penguin Books, 1974. Print.

Lee, Tanith. *The Silver Metal Lover*. 1981. New York: Bantam, 1999. Print.

———. *Metallic Love*. New York: Bantam, 2005. Print.

Mark, Jan. *Useful Idiots*. Oxford and New York: David Fickling Books, 2004. Print.

Meyer, Marissa. *Cinder*. London: Puffin, 2012. Print.

———. *Scarlet*. London: Puffin, 2013. Print.

———. *Cress*. London: Puffin, 2014. Print.

Myracle, Lauren. *ttyl*. New York: Harry N. Abrams, 2004. Print.

Nakano, Hitori. *Train Man*. Trans Bonnie Elliot. 2004. London: Constable and Robinson, 2006. Print.

Bibliography 193

Orwell, George. *Nineteen Eighty-Four*. London: Secker and Warburg, 1949. Print.

Pearson, Mary E. *The Adoration of Jenna Fox*. 2008. Sydney: Allen and Unwin, 2009. Print.

——. *The Fox Inheritance*. New York: Henry Holt and Co., 2011. Print.

——. *Fox Forever*. New York: Henry Holt and Co., 2013. Print.

Perrault, Charles. "Cinderella, or The Little Glass Slipper". Tatar, Maria (ed). *The Annotated Classic Fairy Tales*. New York and London: W.W. Norton, 2002. Print.

Peterson, Margaret Haddix. *Turnabout*. New York: Simon and Schuster, 2002. Print.

Rodgers, Richard and Oscar Hammerstein II. "Hello, Young Lovers". Rodgers, Richard and Oscar Hammerstein II. *The King and I*. New York: 1951.

Scott, Jess C. *Eyeleash: A Blog Novel*. 2009. Maine: jessINK, 2011. Print.

Spooner, Michael. *Entr@pment: A High School Comedy in Chat*. New York: Margaret K. McElderry Books, 2009. Print.

Walsh, Jill Paton. *A School for Lovers*. London: Weidenfeld and Nicolson Ltd, 1989. Print.

Wasserman, Robin. *Skinned*. New York: Simon Pulse, 2008. Print.

——. *Crashed*. New York: Simon Pulse, 2009. Print.

——. *Wired*. New York: Simon Pulse, 2010. Print.

Westerfeld, Scott. *Uglies*. New York: Simon Pulse, 2005a. Print.

——. *Pretties*. New York: Simon Pulse, 2005b. Print.

——. *Specials*. New York: Simon Pulse, 2006. Print.

——. *Extras*. New York: Simon Pulse, 2007. Print.

Secondary Sources

Albrechtslund, A. "Online Social Networking as Participatory Surveillance". *First Monday*, 13 March 2008. Web. 21 May 2012. (http://www.uic.edu/htbin/cgiwrap/bin/ojs/index.php/fm/ article/view/2142/1949).

Andrejevic, Mark. "The Work of Watching One Another: Lateral Surveillance, Risk, and Governance". *Surveillance & Society: "People Watching People"* 2.4 (2004): 479–97.

Applebaum, Noga. *Representations of Technology in Science Fiction for Young People*. Abingdon (Oxon) and New York: Routledge, 2010. Print.

Australian Bureau of Statistics (ABS). *ABS 4901.0 – Children's Participation in Cultural and Leisure Activities*. Australia, April 2012.

Bakhtin, Mikhail M. *Problems of Dostoevsky's Poetics*. Edited and translated by C. Emerson. Minneapolis: University of Minnesota Press, 1984. Print.

Balsamo, Anne M. *Technologies of the Gendered Body: Reading Cyborg Women*. Durham, NC: Duke University Press, 1996. Print.

Basu, Balaka, Katherine R. Broad and Carrie Hintz (eds). *Contemporary Dystopian Fiction for Young Adults: Brave New Teenagers*. New York and London: Routledge, 2013. Print.

Bhabha, Jacqueline. "The 'Mere Fortuity' of Birth? Are Children Citizens?" *Differences: A Journal of Feminist Cultural Studies* 15.2 (2004): 91–117.

Bostrom, Nick. "A History of Transhumanist Thought". Rectenwald, Michael and Lisa Carl (eds). *Academic Writing Across the Disciplines*. New York: Pearson Longman, 2011: 1–30. Print.

——. "Why I Want to Be a Posthuman When I Grow Up". Gordijn, Bert and Ruth Chadwick (eds). *Medical Enhancement and Posthumanity*. Dordrecht: Springer, 2008: 107–13. Print.

——. "In Defence of Posthuman Dignity". *Bioethics* 19.3 (2005): 202–14.

Bradford, Clare, Kerry Mallan, John Stephens and Robyn McCallum. *New World Orders in Contemporary Children's Literature: Utopian Transformations*. Basingstoke: Palgrave Macmillan, 2008. Print.

Bradford, Clare and Raffaella Baccolini. "Journeying Subjects: Spatiality and Identity in Children's Texts". Mallan, Kerry and Clare Bradford (eds). *Contemporary Children's Literature and Film: Engaging with Theory*. Basingstoke: Palgrave Macmillan, 2011. Print.

Branwyn, Gareth. "Compu-Sex: Erotica for Cybernauts". Bell, David and Barbara M. Kennedy (eds). *The Cybercultures Reader*. London and New York: Routledge, 2000: 396–402. Print.

Brooks, Karen. "Nothing Sells Like Teen Spirit: The Commodification of Youth". Mallan, Kerry and Sharyn Pearce (eds). *Youth Cultures: Texts, Images and Identities*. Connecticut: Greenwood, 2003: 1–16. Print.

Clark, Dorothy. "Hyperread: Children's Literature, CD-ROMS and the New Literacy". *The Lion and the Unicorn* 30.3 (2006): 337–59.

Clarke, Roger A. "Information Technology and Dataveillance". *Communications of the ACM* 31.5 (1988): 498–512.

Crandall, Nadia. "Cyberspace and the Gothic Novel". Jackson, Anna, Karen Coats and Roderick McGillis (eds). *The Gothic in Children's Literature: Haunting the Borders*. New York and Abingdon: Routledge, 2007. Print.

Crosnoe, Robert, Kenneth Frank and Anna Strassman Mueller. "Gender, Body Size and Social Relations in American High Schools". *Social Forces* 86.3 (2008): 1189–216.

Currier, Dianne. "Assembling Bodies in Cyberspace: Technologies, Bodies and Sexual Difference". Flanagan, Mary (ed). *Reload: Rethinking Women + Cyberculture*. Austin Booth: MIT Press, 2002: 519–38.

Davies, Tony. *Humanism: The New Critical Idiom*. 2nd ed. London and New York: Routledge, 2008. Print.

Didur, Jill. "Re-embodying Technoscientific Fantasies: Posthumanism, Genetically Modified Foods, and the Colonization of Life". *Cultural Critique* 53 (2003): 98–115.

Dobrowolsky, Alexandra and Jane Jenson. "Shifting Representations of Citizenship: Canadian Politics of 'Women' and 'Children'". *Social Politics* 11.2 (2004): 154–80.

Dresang, E.T. *Radical Change: Books for Youth in a Digital Age*. New York: Wilson, 1999. Print.

——. "Radical Change Revisited: Dynamic Digital Age Books for Youth". *Contemporary Issues in Technology and Teacher Education* 8.3 (2008): 294–304. Print.

Dresang, Eliza T. and Kathryn McClelland. "Radical Change: Digital Age Literature and Learning". *Theory into Practice* 38.3 (1999): 160–67.

Foucault, Michel. *Discipline and Punish: The Birth of the Prison*. Trans. Alan Sheridan. New York: Penguin Books, 1977. Print.

Ganetz, H. "The Shop, the Home and Femininity as a Masquerade". Fornäs, J. and G. Bolin (eds). *Youth Culture in Late Modernity*. London: Sage, 1995: 72–99. Print.

Gilmore, Leigh. "Agency Without Mastery: Chronic Pain and Posthuman Life Writing". *Biography* 35.1 (2012): 83–98.

Gooding, Richard. "*Clockwork*: Philip Pullman's Posthuman Fairy Tale". *Children's Literature in Education* 42 (2011): 308–24.

Graham, Elaine. *Representations of the Post/human: Monsters, Aliens and Others in Popular Culture*. Manchester: Manchester University Press, 2002. Print.

Grosz, Elizabeth. *The Nick of Time: Politics, Evolution, and the Untimely*. Durham, NC: Duke University Press, 2004. Print.

——.*Volatile Bodies: Toward a Corporeal Feminism*. Sydney: Allen and Unwin, 1994. Print.

Gurak, Laura J. and Smiljana Antonijevic. "The Psychology of Blogging: You, Me, and Everyone in Between". *American Behavioral Scientist* 52.1 (2008): 60–68.

Gutierrez, Anna Katrina. "Mga Kwento ni Lola Basyang: A Tradition of Reconfiguring the Filipino Child". *International Research in Children's Literature* 2 (2009): 159–76.

Guzzetti, Barbara and Margaret Gamboa. "Online Journaling: The Informal Writings of Two Adolescent Girls". *Research in the Teaching of English* 40.2 (2005): 168–206.

Haggerty, Kevin D. "Tear Down the Walls: On Demolishing the Panopticon". D. Lyon (ed). *Theorizing Surveillance: The Panopticon and Beyond*. Cullompton: Willan, 2006: 23–45. Print.

Haraway, Donna J. *Simians, Cyborgs, and Women: The Reinvention of Nature*. London: Free Association Books, 1991. Print.

Harfield, Timothy D. "Exposing Humanism: Prudence, Ingenium, and the Politics of the Posthuman". *Journal of Historical Sociology* 26.2 (2013): 264–288.

Harpham, Geoffrey Galt. "The Posthuman: Without It, Nothing Else Is Possible". *Interdisciplinary Science Reviews* 37.2 (2012): 101–12.

Hateley, Erica. "Reading: From Turning the Page to Touching the Screen". Wu, Y., Kerry Mallan and Roderick McGillis (eds). *(Re)imagining the World: New Frontiers of Educational Research*. Berlin and Heidelberg: Springer-Verlag, 2013: 1–13.

Hayles, N. Katherine. "The Seductions of Cyberspace". Conley, Verena Andermatt (ed). *Rethinking Technologies*. Minneapolis, MN: University of Minnesota Press, 1993: 173–90. Print.

——. *How We Became Posthuman: Virtual Bodies in Cybernetics, Literature, and Informatics*. Chicago: Chicago University Press, 1999. Print.

——. "The Life Cycle of Cyborgs: Writing the Posthuman". Chris Hables Gray (ed). *The Cyborg Handbook*. New York and London: Routledge, 1995: 321–35. Print.

Honeyman, Susan. "Mutiny by Mutation: Uses of Neoteny in Science Fiction". *Children's Literature in Education* 35.4 (2004): 347–66.

Huxley, Thomas. "On Descartes' 'Discourse Touching the Method of Using One's Reason Rightly and of Seeking Scientific Truth' ". *Method and Results: Essays by Thomas H. Huxley*. (1870). New York: D. Appleton and Co., 1896.

Kalil, Ariel and Patrick Wightman. "Parental Job Loss and Children's Educational Attainment in Black and White Middle-Class Families". *Social Science Quarterly* 92.1 (2011): 57–78.

Kidd, Dorothy. "Indiemedia.org: A New Communications Commons". McCaughey, Martha and Michael D. Ayers (eds). *Cyberactivism: Online Activism in Theory and Practice*. New York and London: Routledge, 2003: 47–70. Print.

Kovel, Joel. *White Racism: A Psychohistory*. 1970. London: Free Association Books, 1988. Print.

Lebert, Joanne. "Writing Human Rights Activism: Amnesty International and the Challenges of Information and Communication Technologies". McCaughey, Martha and Michael D. Ayers (eds). *Cyberactivism: Online Activism in Theory and Practice*. New York and London: Routledge, 2003: 209–31. Print.

Lévy, Pierre. *Collective Intelligence: Mankind's Emerging World in Cyberspace*. Trans. Robert Bononno. New York and London: Plenum Trade, 1997. Print.

Leydet, Dominique. "Citizenship". Zalta, Edward N. (ed). *The Stanford Encyclopedia of Philosophy*. 2006. Web. 03 September 2009. (http://plato.stanford .edu/entries/citizenship).

Livingstone, Sonia and Magdalena Bober. "Regulating the Internet at Home: Contrasting the Perspectives of Children and Parents". Buckingham, David and Rebekah Willet (eds). *Digital Generations: Children, Young People and New Media*. London and New Jersey: Lawrence Erlbaum Associates, 2006: 93–113. Print.

Lyon, David. *The Electronic Eye: The Rise of Surveillance Society*. Minneapolis: University of Minnesota Press, 1994. Print.

——. *Surveillance as Social Sorting: Privacy, Risk and Digital Discrimination*. New York and London: Routledge, 2003. Print.

——. (ed). *Theorizing Surveillance: The Panopticon and Beyond*. Cullompton: Willan, 2006. Print.

——. *Surveillance Studies: An Overview*. Cambridge, UK and Malden, MA: Polity, 2007. Print.

Madden, Mary, Amanda Lenhart, Maeve Duggan, Sandra Cortesi and Urs Gasser. "Teens and Technology 2013". *Pew Internet & American Life Project*. 2013. Web. 10 July 2013. (http://www.pewinternet.org/Reports/2013/Teens -and-Tech.aspx).

Mallan, Kerry. *Gender Dilemmas in Children's Fiction*. Basingstoke, Hampshire: Palgrave Macmillan, 2009. Print.

———. "All That Matters: Technoscience, Critical Theory and Children's Fiction". Mallan, Kerry and Clare Bradford (eds). *Contemporary Children's Literature and Film: Engaging with Theory*. Basingstoke, Hampshire: Palgrave Macmillan, 2011: 147–67. Print.

———. *Secrets and Lies and Children's Fiction*. Basingstoke, Hampshire: Palgrave Macmillan, 2013. Print.

Mallan, Kerry and Clare Bradford (eds). *Contemporary Children's Literature and Film: Engaging with Theory*. Basingstoke, Hampshire: Palgrave Macmillan, 2011: 147–67. Print.

Mallan, Kerry and Sharyn Pearce (eds). *Youth Cultures: Texts, Images and Identities*. Connecticut: Greenwood, 2003: 1–16. Print.

Martin, James. *The Meaning of the 21st Century: A Vital Blueprint for Ensuring Our Future*. 2006. London: Transworld Publishers, 2007. Print.

McCallum, Robyn. "Young Adult Literature". Zipes, Jack (ed). *Oxford Encyclopedia of Children's Literature*. New York: Oxford University Press, 2006, Vol. 4: 214–19. Print.

McCaughey, Martha and Michael D. Ayers (eds). *Cyberactivism: Online Activism in Theory and Practice*. New York and London: Routledge, 2003. Print.

McDuffie, Kristi. "Technology and Models of Literacy in Young Adult Dystopian Fiction". Basu, Balaka, Katherine R. Broad and Carrie Hintz (eds). *Contemporary Dystopian Fiction for Young Adults: Brave New Teenagers*. New York and London: Routledge, 2013: 145–56. Print.

McGrath, John. *Loving Big Brother: Performance, Privacy and Surveillance Space*. London and New York: Routledge, 2004. Print.

McNeill, Laurie. "There Is No 'I' in Network: Social Networking Sites and Posthuman Auto/Biography". *Biography* 35.1 (2012): 65–82.

Mendlesohn, Farah. *The Inter-galactic Playground: A Critical Study of Children's and Teens' Science Fiction*. Jefferson, NC: McFarland, 2009. Print.

Montgomery, Kathryn and Barbara Gottlieb-Robles. "Youth as e-Citizens: The Internet's Contribution to Civic Engagement". Buckingham, David and Rebekah Willet (eds). *Digital Generations: Children, Young People, and New Media*. London: Lawrence Erlbaum Associates, 2006: 131–47. Print.

Moravec, Hans. *Mind Children: The Future of Robot and Human Intelligence*. Cambridge: Harvard University Press, 1988. Print.

Morrissey, Thomas J. "Parables for the Postmodern, Post 9/11 and Posthuman World: Carrie Ryan's *Forest of Hands and Teeth* Books, M. T. Anderson's *Feed*, and Mary E. Pearson's *The Adoration of Jenna Fox*". Basu, Balaka, Katherine R. Broad and Carrie Hintz (eds). *Contemporary Dystopian Fiction for Young Adults: Brave New Teenagers*. New York and London: Routledge, 2013: 189–201. Print.

Mortimore-Smith, Shannon R. "Fueling the Spectacle: Audience as Gamemaker". Pharr, Mary F. and Leisa A. Clark (eds). *Of Bread, Blood and the Hunger Games: Critical Essays on the Suzanne Collins Trilogy*. Jefferson, North Carolina: McFarland and Company, 2012: 158–66. Print.

Mossberger, Karen, Caroline J. Tolbert and Ramona S. McNeal. *Digital Citizenship: The Internet, Society, and Participation.* Cambridge, MA: MIT Press, 2008. Print.

Nayar, Pramod K. *Posthumanism.* Cambridge and Malden, Massachusetts: Polity Press, 2014. Print.

Newcomb, Erin T. "The Soul of the Clone: Coming of Age as a Posthuman in Nancy Farmer's *The House of the Scorpion*". Basu, Balaka, Katherine R. Broad and Carrie Hintz (eds). *Contemporary Dystopian Fiction for Young Adults: Brave New Teenagers.* New York and London: Routledge, 2013: 175–88. Print.

Nunes, Mark. "Virtual Topographies: Smooth and Striated Cyberspace". Ryan, Marie-Laure (ed). *Cyberspace Textuality: Computer Technology and Literary Theory.* Bloomington and Indianapolis: Indiana University Press, 1999: 61–77. Print.

O'Hara, Kieron and Nigel Shadbolt. *The Spy in the Coffee Machine: The End of Privacy as We Know It.* Oxford: Oneworld, 2008. Print.

Ostry, Elaine. "Is He Still Human? Are You?: Young Adult Science Fiction in the Posthuman Age". *The Lion and the Unicorn* 28.2 (2004): 222–46.

——. "On the Brink: The Role of Young Adult Culture in Environmental Degradation". Basu, Balaka, Katherine R. Broad and Carrie Hintz (eds). *Contemporary Dystopian Fiction for Young Adults: Brave New Teenagers.* New York and London: Routledge, 2013: 101–14.

Pharr, Mary F. and Leisa A. Clark (eds). *Of Bread, Blood and The Hunger Games: Critical Essays on the Suzanne Collins Trilogy.* Jefferson, North Carolina: McFarland and Company, 2012: 158–66. Print.

Poster, Mark. *The Mode of Information: Poststructuralism and Social Context.* Chicago: University of Chicago Press, 1990. Print.

Putnam, Robert. *Bowling Alone: The Collapse and Revival of American Community.* New York: Simon & Schuster, 2000. Print.

Robins, Kevin. "Cyberspace and the World We Live In". Bell, David and Barbara M. Kennedy (eds). *The Cybercultures Reader.* New York: Routledge, 2000: 77–95. Print.

Robinson, Wendy. "Review of Digital Soul: Intelligent Machines and Human Values by Thomas M. Georges". *International Journal of Computational Intelligence and Applications* 7.1 (2008): 97–99.

Rogers, Richard. "Consumer Technology After Surveillance Theory". Kooijman, Jaap, Patricia Pisters and Wanda Strauven (eds). *Mind the Screen: Media Concepts According to Thomas Elsaesser.* Amsterdam: Amsterdam University Press, 2008: 288–96. Print.

Rose, Jacqueline. *The Case of Peter Pan: The Impossibility of Children's Fiction.* London: Macmillan, 1984. Print.

Ryan, Marie-Laure (ed). *Cyberspace Textuality: Computer Technology and Literary Theory.* Bloomington and Indianapolis: Indiana University Press, 1999. Print.

Sambell, Kay. "Presenting the Case for Social Change: The Creative Dilemma of Dystopian Writing for Children". Hintz, Carrie and Elaine Ostry (eds). *Utopian and Dystopian Writing for Children and Young Adults.* New York and London: Routledge, 2003: 163–78. Print.

Sanford, Stefanie. *Civic Life in the Information Age*. New York and Hampshire: Palgrave Macmillan, 2007. Print.

Seaman, Myra J. "Becoming More (than) Human: Affective Posthumanisms, Past and Future". *JNT: Journal of Narrative Theory* 37.2 (2007): 246–75.

Simon, Bart. "Introduction: Toward a Critique of Posthuman Futures". *Cultural Critique* 53 (2003): 1–9.

Smith, Sidonie and Julia Watson (eds). *Getting a Life: Everyday Uses of Autobiography*. Minneapolis: University of Minnesota Press, 1996. Print.

——. *Reading Autobiography: A Guide for Interpreting Life Narratives*. 2nd ed. Minneapolis: University of Minnesota Press, 2010. Print.

Sorapure, Madeleine. "Screening Moments, Scrolling Lives: Diary Writing on the Web". *Biography* 26.1 (2003): 1–23.

Squier, Susan Merrill. *Babies in Bottles: Twentieth Century Visions of Reproductive Technology*. New Brunswick, NJ: Rutgers University Press, 1994. Print.

Stephens, John. *Language and Ideology in Children's Fiction*. London and New York: Longman, 1992.

——. "Constructions of Female Selves in Adolescent Fiction: Makeovers as Metonym". *Papers: Explorations into Children's Literature*. 9.1 (1999): 5–13.

——. "Agency". Rudd, David (ed). *Routledge Companion to Children's Literature*. Abingdon and New York: Routledge, 2010: 141–42. Print.

Stephens, John and Sylvie Geerts. "Mishmash, Conceptual Blending and Adaptation in Contemporary Children's Literature Written in Dutch and English". Van den Bossche, Sara and Sylvie Geerts (eds). *Never-Ending Stories: Adaptation, Canonisation and Ideology in Children's Literature*. Ghent: Academia Press, 2014: 193–214.

Stephens, John and Robyn McCallum. *Retelling Stories, Framing Culture: Traditional Story and Metanarratives in Children's Literature*. London and New York: Routledge, 1998.

Stiles, Anne. "Cerebral Automatism, the Brain, and the Soul in Bram Stoker's *Dracula*". *Journal of the History of the Neurosciences* 15 (2006): 131–52.

Subrahmanyam, Kaveri and Patricia Greenfield. "Online Communication and Adolescent Relationships". *The Future of Children* 18.1 (2008): 119–66.

Symonds, J.A. *Renaissance in Italy, Part 2: Italian Literature*. London: Smith, Elder and Co., 1898.

Tapscott, Don. *Growing Up Digital: The Rise of the Net Generation*. New York: McGraw-Hill, 1998. Print.

Thrift, Nigel. *Non-Representational Theory: Space/Politics/Affect*. New York: Routledge, 2008. Print.

Toffoletti, Kim. *Cyborgs and Barbie Dolls: Feminism, Popular Culture and the Posthuman Body*. London and New York: I.B.Tauris, 2007. Print.

Trites, Roberta Seelinger. *Disturbing the Universe: Power and Repression in Adolescent Literature*. Iowa: University of Iowa Press, 2000. Print.

Turkle, Sherry. *The Second Self: Computers and the Human Spirit*. New York: Simon and Schuster, 1984. Print.

Turner, John S. "Collapsing the Interior/Exterior Distinction: Surveillance, Spectacle and Suspense in Popular Cinema". *Wide Angle* 20.4 (1998): 93–123.

van den Hengel, Louis. "Zoegraphy: Per/forming Posthuman Lives". *Biography* 35.1 (2012): 1–20.

Vint, Sherryl. *Bodies of Tomorrow: Technology, Subjectivity and Science Fiction.* Toronto: University of Toronto Press, 2007. Print.

Wezner, Kelley. " 'Perhaps I am Watching You Now': Panem's Panopticons". Pharr, Mary F. and Leisa A. Clark (eds). *Of Bread, Blood and the Hunger Games: Critical Essays on the Suzanne Collins Trilogy.* Jefferson, North Carolina: McFarland and Company, 2012: 148–57.

Wolfe, Cary. *What Is Posthumanism?* Minneapolis, MN: University of Minnesota Press, 2010.

Index

adolescence, 72
Adoration of Jenna Fox, The (Mary E. Pearson), 9, 17–18, 29, 36, 39, 104, 107, 108, 113–20, 123–7
agency, 3, 5, 14, 17, 20, 21, 22, 54, 66, 82, 87, 92, 95, 97, 106, 107, 109, 112, 117, 119, 121, 129, 137, 142, 149–51, 155, 177, 187, 188
see also subjectivity
A.I. (Artificial Intelligence), 27
Anda's Game, (Cory Doctorow), 22, 39, 74, 81, 85–8, 91–2, 96–8, 104, 107, 108, 113, 116–19, 126–7
Anderson, M.T: *Feed*, 29, 37, 130–6, 149, 151–2, 154, 161
Andrejevic, Mark, 135–6, 152–3
anti-humanism, 18, 20
Applebaum, Noga, 3, 6, 25–6, 28, 31–5, 37, 84, 128, 159, 161–2
ASCII art, 174–5
avatars, 97–8, 118, 150

Bakhtin, Mikhail, 107, 119
Balsamo, Anne, 105
Basu, Balaka, Katherine R. Broad and Carrie Hintz, 29, 84
Baudrillard, Jean, 26, 156
Beckett, Bernard, 4
Genesis, 36, 42, 55–9, 69
Being Emily (Rachel Gold), 36, 161, 163, 177–9, 181
Bhabha, Jacqueline, 71, 78
blogging, 130, 133–6, 152–3, 155, 156, 159, 161, 163–7, 179–84
body, 100, 109, 113, 115–16, 118, 120, 151, 177
and feminine subjectivity, 63, 64, 101, 105–27, 188

and race, 139–41
and subjectivity, 22, 30, 60, 62, 100, 104, 178
technological modification of, 16–17, 18, 23, 105, 112, 115, 116
see also Cartesian dualism; embodiment
Bostrom, Nick, 16, 18
see also transhumanism
Bradford, Clare, 26
Bradford and Baccolini, 133
Bradford, Mallan, Stephens and McCallum, 27–9, 30, 40–3, 84, 103–4
Branwyn, Gareth, 183
Brooks, Karen, 158
Bukatman, Scott, 129

Card, Orson Scott: *Ender's Game*, 8, 73–4, 78–82, 90–3, 98
Cartesian dualism, 57, 81, 100, 104–7, 111, 114, 115, 151
chat rooms, 155, 161, 163, 164
Cinder (Marissa Meyer), 18, 41–2, 60–6, 69, 187
citizenship, 71, 73, 75, 77–9, 87, 88, 91–6, 98, 99
see also civil rights; digital citizenship
civil rights, 75, 85, 91, 94–5
see also citizenship; digital citizenship
Clark, Dorothy, 159
Clark, Roger, 129
class, 88, 90, 113, 119, 137, 142
Cline, Ernest, 4, 21, 72–3, 98
Ready Player One, 85–90, 187
clones, 25–6

cognition, 57
  see also embodied cognition
Collins, Suzanne: *The Hunger Games*,
  36, 39, 84, 130–2, 137–8, 141–5,
  149, 150–1
computers, 73, 88, 94, 95, 98, 102,
  117, 128, 156, 173, 178, 185,
  186, 190
Cosi Fan Tutte, 167, 175
critical posthumanism, 19–20
Cusick, John M, 4
  Girl Parts, 42, 60–1, 63–9
cyber bullying, 158
cybernetics theory, 101
cyberpunk, 81, 102
cyberspace, 4, 70, 77, 81–5, 89, 90,
  104, 163–4, 170–1, 180–4
  as arena for digital activism, 76
  and femininity, 172
  and narrative form, 159–71
  origin of term, 162–3
  as place, 156–7
  post-cyberspace generation,
    3–4, 35
  sexuality, 179–84
  see also internet; virtual reality
cyborgs, 18, 20, 21, 26, 41–2, 51,
  52, 60, 61, 63, 104–6, 108, 111,
  116, 117, 120–3, 125–6,
  187, 189

dataveillance, 129
Davies, Tony, 13, 187–8
Day, Susie, 4
  *serafina67 *urgently requires life**,
    36, 130–6, 149, 151–4, 180
Declaration of Independence,
  94, 96
democracy, 76, 87, 94–6
Descartes, Rene, 57, 115
  see also Cartesian dualism
Didur, Jill, 19–20, 27
digital activism, 76, 85
digital citizenship, 8, 71, 77, 85
  see also citizenship
digital divide, 88

discrimination, 86, 117, 121,
  145, 147
Dobrowolsky, Alexandra and Jane
  Jenson, 94
Doctorow, Cory, 4, 21, 72–3, 77,
  81, 98
  Anda's Game, 22, 39, 74, 81, 85–8,
    91–2, 96–8, 104, 107, 108,
    113, 116–19, 126–7
  Homeland, 74–8, 81–5, 90, 91,
    98, 187
  Little Brother, 8, 22, 36, 74–8, 81–5,
    91, 94–6, 98, 130–2, 136–7,
    141, 145–51, 153, 187
Dresang, Eliza, 159–61
Dusk (Susan Gates), 17
dystopia, 2, 17, 41, 42, 59, 71, 84,
  97, 98

Eager (Helen Fox), 27, 40–1
embodied cognition, 100
embodiment, 100–8, 123, 125, 127,
  177, 179
Ender's Game (Orson Scott Card), 8,
  73–4, 78–82, 90–3, 98
*Entr@pment: A High School Comedy in
  Chat* (Michael Spooner), 36,
  161, 162, 164–72, 175, 184–5
Eyeleash: A Blog Novel (Jess C. Scott),
  161, 162, 175–7, 179–84

Facebook, 171–2
Farmer, Nancy: *The House of the
  Scorpion*, 17, 29
Feed (M.T. Anderson), 29, 37, 130–6,
  151–2, 154, 161
femininity, *see* subjectivity
feminism, 36, 106
Ferren and the Angel (Richard
  Harland), 40–1, 103–4
focalisation, 59–60
Foucault, Michel, 18, 19, 129, 137
Fox, Helen: *Eager*, 27, 40–1
Frankenstein, 121–2
Fukuyama, Francis, 23–4

Gates, Susan: *Dusk*, 17
Gender, 104, 110, 116, 153, 177
  see also body; subjectivity
Genesis (Bernard Beckett), 36, 42,
  55–9, 69
Gilmore, Leigh, 50, 123
Girl Parts (John M. Cusick), 42, 60–1,
  63–9
globalisation, 71, 79–82, 86–9
Gold, Rachel, 4
  Being Emily, 36, 161, 163,
  177–9, 181
Goldman, E. M: *The Night Room*, 161
Gooding, Richard, 30–1
Graham, Elaine, 35, 39, 189–90
Grosz, Elizabeth, 18, 101, 120
Gutierrez, Anna Katrina, 79

hacking, 77, 96, 131, 138, 148
Haddix, Margaret Peterson:
  Turnabout, 25
Haggerty, Kevin, 129–30
Haraway, Donna, 26, 102, 104,
  105, 113
Harfield, Timothy D, 11
Harland, Richard: *Ferren and the
  Angel*, 40–1, 103–4
Harpham, Geoffrey, 1
Hately, Erica, 159
Hayles, N. Katherine, 4–5, 6, 21, 26,
  27, 48–9, 50, 54–5, 67, 100–3,
  105, 129, 155, 156, 163, 176
Homeland (Cory Doctorow), 74–8,
  81–5, 90, 91, 98, 187
Honeyman, Susan, 113–14
House of the Scorpion, The (Nancy
  Farmer), 17, 29
Howarth, Lesley: *Ultraviolet*, 161
humanism, 11–13, 19, 22, 64, 102,
  103, 114, 127, 187–8
Hunger Games, The (Suzanne
  Collins), 36, 39, 84, 130–2,
  137–8, 141–5, 149, 150–1

internet, 70, 72, 77, 85, 86, 128, 135,
  148, 157, 176, 181

access, 3, 157–9
  risks for children, 158, 184
  see also cyberspace
intersubjectivity, 172
intertextuality, 46–8, 56, 61, 62,
  161, 175

Jansson, Tove, 175

Kidd, Dorothy, 72
King and I, The (Rodgers and
  Hammerstein), 165–6

Lee, Tanith: *The Silver Metal Lover*, 8,
  41, 42–54
  Metallic Love, 8, 36, 41–57, 69
Lévy, Pierre, 172–3
Leydet, Dominique, 78, 79, 91
Little Brother (Cory Doctorow), 8, 22,
  36, 74–8, 81–5, 91, 94–6, 98,
  130–2, 136–7, 141, 145–51,
  153, 187
Livingstone, Sonia and Magdalena
  Bober, 157–8
Lyon, David, 129, 131, 133–4, 137,
  138, 140, 144, 146–7, 154

Madden, Mary, Amanda Lenhart,
  Maeve Duggan, Sandra Cortesi
  and Urs Gasser, 157
Mallan, Kerry, 26, 30, 94–5, 104
Mark, Jan: *Useful Idiots*, 130–2,
  137–41, 149, 151
Martin, James, 98
McCallum, Robyn, 26
McDuffie, Kristi, 82–3
McGrath, John, 138
McNeil, Laurie, 161, 171–2
Mendlesohn, Farah, 6–7, 32–5, 37,
  128, 159
Metallic Love (Tanith Lee), 8, 36,
  41–57, 69
Meyer, Marissa, 4
  Cinder, 18, 41–2, 60–6, 69, 187
Montgomery, Kathryn and Barbara
  Gottlieb-Robles, 70

Moravec, Hans, 102, 113
Morrissey, Thomas, 29–30
Mortimore-Smith, Shannon, 143–4
Mossberger, Karen, Caroline J.
    Tolbert and Ramona S. McNeal,
    85–6
Myracle, Lauren, 4, 21
    ttyl, 161, 162, 164, 171, 184–5

Nakano, Hitori: *Train Man*, 161, 162,
    164, 168–76, 185
narration, 45–6, 50
Nayar, Pramod, 14, 19, 20, 57–8, 60,
    81, 82, 100, 102–3
Newcombe, Erin, 29, 30
Night Room, The (E.M.
    Goldman), 161
Nineteen Eighty Four (George Orwell),
    96, 130
non-representational theory, 124
Nunes, Mark, 156–7

O'Hara, Kieron and Nigel Shadbolt,
    135, 147
Ostry, Elaine, 23–4, 28, 133

pain, 122–3
Paton Walsh, Jill: *A School for
    Lovers*, 167
Pearson, Mary E, 4
    The Adoration of Jenna Fox, 9,
    17–18, 29, 36, 39, 104, 107,
    108, 113–20, 123–7
point of view, 27
polyphony, 164–71
Poster, Mark, 134
privacy, 128, 138, 140, 146–7,
    158, 180
Putname, Robert, 85

quest narratives, 22

race, 137, 138, 153
racism, 66
Ready Player One (Ernest Cline),
    85–90, 187

reality television, 130, 132,
    143, 144
Robins, Kevin, 176
Robinson, Wendy, 53
Rogers, Richard, 134, 135
Rose, Jacqueline, 33
Ryan, Marie-Laure, 175

School for Lovers, A (Jill Paton
    Walsh), 167
Scott, Jess C, 4, 21
    Eyeleash: A Blog Novel, 161, 162,
    175–7, 179–84
Seaman, Myra, 105
*serafina67 *urgently requires life**
    (Susie Day), 36, 130–6, 149,
    151–4, 180
sexuality, 61, 67, 117, 118, 179–84
Silver Metal Lover, The (Tanith Lee), 8,
    42–54
Simon, Bart, 36
Skinned (Robin Wasserman), 18, 36,
    104, 107, 113–15, 117,
    120–3, 127
Sorapure, Madeleine, 161
soul, the, 53, 57, 100
Spooner, Michael, 4
    *Entr@pment: A High School Comedy
    in Chat*, 36, 161, 162, 164–72,
    184–5
Stephens, John, 17, 26, 162
Stephens and Geerts, 46
subjectivity, 5, 13, 18, 20, 21, 37, 58,
    115, 138–9, 141, 170–2, 176,
    183, 185
    cyborgian, 106
    feminine, 96, 101, 105–27,
    154, 176
    posthuman, 48–9, 53, 55, 67, 71,
    104, 105, 125, 149, 179, 187
    and surveillance, 149–54
    see also agency
Subrahmanyam, Kaveri and Patricia
    Greenfield, 158–9, 163–4

surveillance, 76, 96, 128–54, 176, 189, 190
    lateral, 134–6, 153
    participatory, 128, 134, 135
    social sorting, 131–2, 137, 138, 141
    spectatorship, 131, 132, 143, 145, 150
    see also dataveillance
Symonds, J. A, 12

Tapscott, Don, 70
technophobia, 32, 34, 48, 74
technorealism, 155
terrorism, 75, 85, 138, 145
Thrift, Nigel, 124
Toffoletti, Kim, 102, 127, 149, 151
Train Man (Hitori Nakano), 161, 162, 164, 168–76, 185
transgender, 177
transhumanism, 15–17, 102, 103
Trites, Roberta Seelinger, 179
ttyl (Lauren Myracle), 161, 162, 164, 171, 184–5

Turnabout (Margaret Peterson Haddix), 25
Turner, John, 143

Uglies (Scott Westerfeld), 8, 39, 84, 104, 107, 108–12
Ultraviolet (Lesley Howarth), 161
Useful Idiots (Jan Mark), 130–2, 137–41, 151

video games, 71, 89, 96–7, 107, 117, 177
Vint, Sherryl, 67, 81, 101, 102, 106, 108–9, 112, 190–1
virtual reality, 28, 71, 87, 97, 99, 116–19, 133, 134, 136, 153, 155–6, 176, 183, 188
    see also cyberspace; internet

Wasserman, Robin, 4
    Skinned, 18, 36, 104, 107, 113–15, 117, 120–3, 127
Westerfeld, Scott, 4
    Uglies, 8, 39, 84, 104, 107, 108–12
Wezner, Kelly, 142
witches, 113, 121–2
Wolfe, Cary, 11, 14–15, 102

Printed by Printforce, United Kingdom